New York

Ellis Island

ARTURO'S ROUTE

Jacksonville

ATLANTIC
OCEAN

La Habana

CARIBBEAN
SEA

THE MANGO ORCHARD

Robin Bayley

The Mango Orchard

Travelling Back to the Secret Heart of Mexico

BE
9/14

KN
10115

preface
publishing

Published by Preface 2010

10 9 8 7 6 5 4 3 2 1

First published in Great Britain in 2010 by Preface Publishing
20 Vauxhall Bridge Road
London SW1V 2SA

An imprint of The Random House Group Limited

www.rbooks.co.uk
www.prefacepublishing.co.uk

Addresses for companies within The Random House Group Limited
can be found at www.randomhouse.co.uk

The Random House Group Limited Reg. No. 954009

A CIP catalogue record for this book is available from the British Library

Hardback ISBN 978 1 84809 223 5
Trade Paperback ISBN 978 1 84809 240 2

Mixed Sources
Product group from well-managed
forests and other controlled sources
www.fsc.org Cert no. TT-COC-2139
© 1996 Forest Stewardship Council

The Random House Group Limited supports The Forest Stewardship Council (FSC),
the leading international forest certification organisation. All our titles that are
printed on Greenpeace approved FSC certified paper carry the FSC logo.
Our paper procurement policy can be found at
www.rbooks.co.uk/environment

Typeset by Palimpsest Book Production Limited,
Grangemouth, Stirlingshire

Printed and bound in Great Britain by Clays Ltd, St Ives plc

Contents

One mango is delicious, a bowlful of mangoes is a blessing,
but a mango orchard is riches indeed . . .

Michael McCarthy, *Independent*,
Thursday, 2 January 2003

For Grandma

Prologue

I REMEMBER THE first time I had the feeling that somewhere, something was waiting for me, in a land I didn't yet know. I had just fallen off my bike on the gravel drive of my grandmother's home. She brought me inside, sat me at the kitchen table, where she was kneading bread dough, and gave me a Ribena to take my mind off my bloodied knee. I had just begun to make circles in the flour with my glass when she said to me, 'Are you ready for a story?' She smiled as she dusted her hands on her apron. She knew I was always ready for one of her stories.

A long time ago, there was a bandit in the jagged-peaked mountains of the Sierra Madre. He was known as El Jefe, *the Chief. It was said that no one who had seen his face lived to tell the tale.*

But my father, your great-grandfather Arturo, knew this wasn't true. He had met him.

Arturo worked at the cotton mill but when he had any free time he would ride through the cactus forest and wade across the river to the mango orchard — his favourite place in Mexico. It was sheltered from the wind and shaded from the sun. Arturo loved the dancing colour of the butterflies that came there, the songbirds and the gentle ripple of the river. The ground was carpeted with long thick grass, which cushioned the ripe mangoes that fell from the trees.

One day when Arturo was there he heard a noise and looked up to see El Jefe standing in front of him. He had two bullet belts strung across his black shirt, wore alligator-skin boots and a black sombrero tilted forward so his eyes were hidden.

'Times are hard, Don Arturo,' he said, in his deep and boomy voice. 'We need to clothe and feed our people. Would you be willing to help us?'

Arturo nodded. He didn't mind being asked for money because he felt sympathy for El Jefe's people. He remembered what it was like to be poor. 'I'll leave a bag of silver in the fork of this tree,' he replied.

The next day Arturo set out from his house with the bag of silver. This time he didn't watch the butterflies or listen to the river flow. When he was sure no one was looking, he left the bag in the fork of the tree and quickly climbed back on his horse. The next day the bag was gone.

Arturo didn't see El Jefe for many months. There was a rumour he had been killed in a duel. There was another that he had died leading the revolution against the army. But one day, when Arturo was writing a letter in the mango orchard, he heard footsteps and the snap of dry twigs. Then he heard someone stumble and fall. He got up to see El Jefe limping towards him. His shirt was ripped and there was a trickle of blood running down his face.

'Don Arturo,' he said, his voice hoarse and barely louder than a whisper.

'Can I help you?' Arturo asked. 'Would you like some water?'

El Jefe shook his head. 'You've been good to us, Don Arturo.

For that reason, I have come to tell you to leave. An attack is being planned. Today. If you do not go, you will be killed.'

Mexico had been your great-grandfather's home for many years. His job, his two houses and all his friends were there. But he had to make a choice.

He rode out of town that afternoon, never to return.

'Is it true, Grandma?' I asked her.

She replied as she always did: 'There are three versions to every story: my version, your version and the truth.'

I walked through to Grandma's sitting room to look at the two black and white photographs that hung side by side above the fireplace. In one, a man dressed in a high-buttoned suit sat in a straight-backed chair. He held a silver-topped cane and had a wedding band on his finger. His forehead was broad, hair swept back, moustache wide with waxed tips. His eyes were clear, his expression serious, his look one of austere respectability. This was Arthur, my great-grandfather, as Grandma remembered him.

The other picture was of a man on horseback. He wore long-spiked spurs and a sombrero and carried a lasso, sword and pistol. This was the picture I loved. I imagined the man cutting swathes through jungles, hunting tigers, riding with *El Jefe's* men through cactus forests, the army in pursuit. A heavy cloth bag was slung over the horse's back, his contribution to the rebels' cause and the price of his freedom. On his finger there was no wedding band, on his face there was just the hint of a smile. This was Arturo, the great-grandfather Grandma told me about in her stories.

Two names, one man. Two versions and a missing truth.

*   *   *

ARTHUR GREENHALGH was born on 9 October 1875 in Tottington, the Lancashire village where his father, Henry, ran a cotton mill. It was through Henry that Arthur met Don Domingo, a Spanish businessman whose family owned a cotton business in Mexico. When Don Domingo left England to join the family firm, he asked Arthur to organise shipments of machinery to Mexico for them. Arthur was still a teenager when his widowed father went bankrupt and died, leaving him without work and penniless. He later told Grandma he had been plagued with the fear he would wake up old one day having never gone anywhere or done anything with his life. However, Don Domingo, impressed with Arthur's organisation of the shipments, came to his rescue by offering him a job. One September morning in 1898, Arthur kissed his sweetheart Mariah goodbye and set off on his Mexican adventures.

Over a hundred years later I too was plagued by the same fear about life passing me by. I'd gone to college, then to live in London. I had much that many would envy: interesting loyal friends, my own flat, a good job. But something felt missing, unresolved. There was something about Grandma's stories of her father that haunted me. I had always admired the way he had headed off, alone, into the unknown. And I had always been fascinated, almost horrified, by the way he'd had to leave Mexico in such a hurry and never returned. Why would he have been killed if he had stayed? What, I wondered, had he left behind?

ONE DAY Grandma called me. She had been looking through some stuff in her garage and found something she thought I might like to have.

'What is it?' I asked, but she wouldn't say, only telling me I wouldn't be disappointed.

The following weekend I went to stay at her Sheffield home. She led me to the dining room, and there, on the table on which her father had written the letters to 'the friends he had left behind', was the brown leather suitcase he had used when he first set out for Mexico. I ran my hand over the top of the case – smooth to the touch, virtually no scuff marks. It was engraved A.G., there was a US customs sticker not quite detached from its side and an address tag fastened to the handle with red ribbon.

'Is it locked?' I asked Grandma.

'Open it.'

I pushed the clasps. They sprang back with a sharp *clunk*, as if the contents were desperate to get out. I lifted the lid. There was a faint smell of hymn books. The white cotton lining was spotted with rust marks. A book and two envelopes lay in the bottom of the case. I picked up the smaller of the two envelopes. In handwriting not unlike my own it was addressed to Mariah Nuttall in Tottington, Lancashire.

'My mother,' said Grandma. 'It's a letter my father wrote to her on his way to Mexico.'

'I didn't know this existed,' I said, holding it carefully with slightly shaking hands.

'I'd forgotten all about it until I found it last week.'

I peeked inside the envelope. The sheets were folded twice; the blue-black ink had bled through the thin paper. I put it to one side, wanting to read it later and savour every word. I reached for the other, fatter envelope. There were about twenty photographs inside. Unlike those on Grandma's wall, they were postcard-sized and curled round each other. The first was of a man in baggy white trousers carrying a barrel in front of him and a churn behind his back, both suspended from straps stretched across his bowed head. On the reverse of the photo was a lengthy note written in pencil. *'Here in Zacatecas, water has to be bought, like milk, by the "litro" (about the same as a quart) . . . The colour of the poor people is quite deadly, owing to the metals in the river water.'*

'He was always very concerned for the poor,' said Grandma, taking the photo from me and looking at it.

There were other photos: of a family making tortillas on flat stones by a river, hat salesmen, donkeys laden high with ceramic jugs and wicker baskets, a woman paddling a log raft, field workers gathering palm leaves – *'these men live up in the mountains and hunt with bow and arrow'*, a mine in Guanajuato, a man in a jacket and tie standing with his hands on his hips, towering over loincloth-clad Indians. There were several pictures of the town of Chapala, one of a junk-like sailing boat, another of a strange obelisk called the Tower of Hope. Arturo didn't appear in any of the photos, but each one had a detailed handwritten description on the back.

Then I came to one of a beautiful young Mexican woman in a shawl, holding a round-backed guitar. On the back was just one word: *'María'*.

'Who's this?' I asked.

'Pretty, isn't she?' Grandma paused as she studied the photo. 'I don't know who she is, love.'

I tipped the envelope upside down to see if there were any more photos or anything about María. A ring fell onto the table.

Grandma gasped and raised her hand to her mouth.

I picked it up and turned it round in my fingers. It was a simple silver ring set with a small amber-coloured stone.

She took it from me. 'It's the Truth Stone.'

'Truth Stone?' I'd never heard of such a thing.

'My father found it on a mountain path near the mango orchard. The local Indians told him the stone would change colour according to how close you were to the truth.' She put it on her finger. 'If you are telling or living an untruth, the ring turns dark brown or red. If you are telling the truth, it goes green or blue.' We both watched the stone. At first nothing happened, then it turned darker, into a purple-maroon colour, before becoming sky-blue. Grandma smiled at me. 'See?'

I was fairly sure it was just a mood stone that changed colour with the heat from her finger, but I nodded and turned my attention to the remaining item in the bottom of the case. 'What's the book?'

'The guidebook my father used.' Grandma passed it to me. It was an 1893 Baedeker guide to the United States and Mexico. Like the photos, the guidebook was full of my great-grandfather's notes. I flicked through the book and it fell open at a section he had underlined several times: 'Mexico affords a survey of so novel and picturesque a civilisation as amply to repay the time and trouble.'

In that instant I knew I had to go to Mexico.

GRANDMA LET me take the guidebook, letter and photos back to London. She kept the Truth Stone, promising to tell me its colour every time we spoke.

At work a few weeks later a reorganisation was announced. I saw my opportunity and took the offer of voluntary redundancy. I called Grandma with my news and told her of my plan to follow her father's path to Mexico. She wasn't as excited as I thought she'd be.

'You have a good job,' she said. 'Don't give it up. I remember what it's like to be poor. When my father came back from Mexico we had nothing.'

'But I have a pay-off. It's enough for me not to worry about working for six months or more.'

'It's so uncertain.'

'Like it was when your father left.'

'I just don't want you to go all that way for nothing.'

'It won't be.'

'How do you know?'

'I have a feeling there'll be something.' I knew it was the right thing to do but didn't want to go without her blessing. How could I win her round? Then I had an idea. 'Grandma, what does the Truth Stone say?'

She was silent for a moment. 'Just come back safely.'

Throw Your Shit Away and Start Living

SS *Cephalonia*

20th September 1898

My Dear Mariah,

Nothing could have prepared me for today. I can scarcely believe that it was only this morning that we waited together by Uncle John's shop for the dairy cart to take me to Bury. As I sit here, looking out of my porthole, I am haunted by what you said – that it is harder for the one who stays behind. I pray it is not true. This journey I have to think of as a matter of necessity, something I have to do, as a soldier ordered away on duty.

Let me tell you about the voyage so far, so when you make the trip yourself, it will be more familiar to you.

Once I had placed my case on my bunk, I watched fourth and fifth class board farther down the ship. Entire families struggling with their lives' possessions, each carrying luggage according to their size and weight: rolled up mattresses, canvas sheets packed full and tied tight with twine, mangles, frying pans, kettles and enamel irons. I saw women with their skirt hems stiffened with mud, and their husbands and sons with no collars and only short scarves tucked into their waistcoats. Judging

from their clothing, some must have spent their last
pennies on their passage to America. I only hope they
find something when they get there.

The gong sounded. All non-passengers were to leave
the ship. Henshaw, a chap from my cabin, was embracing
his wife, sobbing. I turned away. The engines began to
throb and the water to churn, as the mighty propellers
began to thrash. The Cunard stewards circulated the
decks, distributing paper streamers, red, blue, yellow and
green. A woman in steerage held on to a ball of wool.
Her mother, on the dock, held on to the other end,
hoping that America did not lie further away than the wool
would stretch. Flowers were thrown from the promenade
deck. There was a rattle and roar as the anchor chain was
upped. The ship eased away from the quayside. The
streamers stretched, pulled tight and snapped. The ball of
wool unravelled and trailed in the water. The shouts from
the shore became distant. I could no longer make out the
faces of those left on the pier.

Part of me felt torn, like the streamers draped down
the ship's side, but I was glad that the moment of parting
had finally come. We had already said goodbye. I was
already on my own, waiting for our new life to begin.

It had once been the golden door through which Arturo, like
millions of others, had passed in search of his fortune. Now,
CUNARD was just legible in rust-coloured letters in the arch above
the gate, and the pier was a deserted strip of pockmarked tarmac
that stretched out into the middle of the Hudson River. The
water was choppy, tombstone grey and looked freezing cold. The
type of place where the Mafia might come to dispose of a body.

My eyes watered from the bitter wind as I walked the length of the old jetty and sat down on a solitary bench facing the water. I had hoped the fresh air would clear my head, which was still throbbing from the champagne on the flight the day before. Seagulls cartwheeled and wailed above me, their cries making my headache worse. By my feet were a pile of stubbed-out cigarettes and three nearly empty bottles of Boca Chica rum.

In front of the bench was a concrete barrier covered in graffiti. Although much of it was less than polite and suggested things that were anatomically impossible, for some people the end of the pier had obviously proved inspirational. '*Imagine if we all wanted less and not more,*' read one message in green pen. Another, in chalk, read like a personal message, telling me to leave my materialistic London life behind. '*Throw your shit away and start living.*'

From the end of the pier I could see the Empire State Building disappearing into low cloud and hear the distant buzz of fast-moving traffic on 11th Avenue. In Arturo's day there had been a saying, 'In America all roads lead not to Rome, but to New York. And in New York all roads lead to the Battery.' The waterfront was no longer the centre of the city, but the city was still the centre of the world.

I took Arturo's letter out of my pocket, my numb fingers fumbling in the cold.

We arrived at Six o'c, too late to disembark, but early enough to enjoy the magnificent sights of New York coming into view. A flotilla of craft followed in our wake. The captain sounded the fog horn and it echoed around the bay. The flotilla replied with whistles and toots.

The sight everyone was waiting for was the Statue of

Liberty. It passed us on the port side. So many people rushed over to the rails to get a good look, I thought we might capsize. I heard more than one person say, 'Oh look, there's Columbus!' I can't think that Mr Columbus would have been happy with the confusion, as the statue is most decidedly, as one of the other passengers described, 'A big lady.'

Once he arrived in New York, Arturo still had another three weeks of travel to get to where Don Domingo's job was waiting for him. First he took the train to New Orleans, then caught a steamer across the Gulf of Mexico to the port of Veracruz. From there he journeyed up to Mexico City and on to Guadalajara, and travelled by stagecoach for the last leg of the journey.

Arturo had promised to send for Mariah as soon as he could afford to buy a house for them. He worked in the foundry of Don Domingo's mill without a day's holiday for two and a half years, inviting her to come and join him in early 1901. The story of their reunion was another of my grandma's favourites.

The day the envelope arrived, my mother, Mariah, ran to her sister Noria, yelling, 'I'm going to Mexico! I'm going to Mexico!'

She read Noria Arturo's letter about the home he had bought. It was on the smartest avenue in the centre of town and had its own stables. It had a big oak door and blue shutters and there were ten-foot-tall sunflowers growing in the garden. When Noria saw the ticket Arturo had sent, her jaw dropped. It was for a first-class cabin on a Cunard steamer to New York. 'First class!' said Noria. 'Only lords and ladies travel first class!'

Mariah felt she was in a fairy tale. Her wish had been

granted and her Prince Charming was about to whisk her away.

But when she told her father, he was less impressed. 'He hasn't asked me!' he roared. 'And you're not going to New York on your own as an unmarried woman.'

Mariah was heartbroken. She wrote to Arturo to tell him the bad news. Arturo sent a letter to her father straight away. He apologised for not asking his permission and begged him to allow her to go. He promised they would get married as soon as she arrived in Mexico.

But this was not good enough for Mariah's father. 'I'm not having my unmarried daughter travelling across the Atlantic alone,' he said.

Mariah, more distraught than ever, wrote to Arturo again. He immediately sent a telegram to her father. 'Will get married before sundown on day she arrives in New York.'

At last, Mariah's father consented.

The day she left to catch the boat from Liverpool, the whole village lined the streets to wave her off. The mill workers left their looms and cheered as her carriage passed.

Mariah had never stayed in a hotel before, let alone travelled in a first-class stateroom with velvet curtains and mahogany furniture. She loved every moment of the journey, but most of all she was excited at the prospect of seeing Arturo again.

She cried when she saw him at the quayside, dressed in a new suit, holding a giant sunflower, waiting for the only girl he'd ever loved, the girl who'd crossed an ocean to marry him.

A man wearing Rupert the Bear checked trousers walked in through the Cunard gate. A white terrier in a padded jacket trotted ahead of him on a long lead, panting steamy breath. The dog cocked its leg against the fence at the edge of the pier, probably the exact spot where Arturo would have paced up and down, the dried sunflower in his hand, waiting for Mariah to walk down the gangplank.

I had always imagined my great-grandparents walking from the boat with their suitcases straight into a church. But now I was on the pier, looking at the warehouses of the Meatpacking District, I saw how unlikely that was. The Baedeker guide had two pages of small type, listing hundreds of places of worship in Manhattan. There were no pencil marks next to any of them.

For some reason it felt important for me to find the actual place my great-grandparents had married. Perhaps because of all the stories, it was the one I was most confident was true. But for me to find the church, I would need their marriage certificate. To find their marriage certificate, I had to get the exact date Mariah had arrived. For that, I needed to go to Ellis Island.

I walked back along the pier and onto 11th Avenue to look for a cab. My headache had gone and the clouds around the top of the Empire State Building had begun to clear.

I HAD wanted to cross the harbour to Ellis Island alone on deck, imagining being ferried from the Cunard pier after a two-week voyage from Europe. Instead, I spent the journey crushed against the deck rails, trying to ignore the prerecorded commentary, piped music and smell of hot dogs.

The main Ellis Island building with its huge arched windows and 150-foot atrium was more like a Victorian palace than an immigration centre. It would have cowed even the most self-assured arrival. On entering the great hall, the immigrants were tagged, then the men separated from the women and children, and herded, cattle-like, into metal pens towards the dreaded medical inspections. Immigrants had to prove they were not 'deformed or crippled', and to swear they were not afflicted with 'a loathsome or dangerous contagious disease'. Each then had to endure a 'mental test' to show he or she wasn't 'an idiot, or imbecile, or a feeble-minded person'.

It was heartbreaking to read about the people who had travelled halfway across the world and had even got to see the Manhattan skyline, only to fail the medical or mental test and be put on the next steamer home. But being on the island also allowed me to understand America for what it really was, a pioneer nation built on hope. America promised a new start. The immigrants were, as Arturo had put it, 'waiting for their new life to begin'.

I found my way to the library on the third floor and within a quarter of an hour located the record of Arturo's arrival in New York in 1898. Finding Mariah's date of arrival didn't take much longer. She arrived on the RMS *Etruria* on 24 February 1901. I had been looking for Nuttall, her maiden name, but when I found her on the manifest, she was listed as Mrs Greenhalgh despite the fact that she wasn't yet married.

I went to the reception desk to pay for the copies. 'So my great-grandparents passed through this building?' I asked the man at the desk, the word RANGER embroidered on the shoulder of his olive-green sweater.

'The main chamber would have held up to 5,000 immigrants at any one time, carrying their possessions with them.' He spoke in a dreary, detached voice, his gaze a yard above my head, as if he were addressing a large tour group. Then he stopped and looked at me as though suddenly snapping out of automatic pilot. 'This your great-grandma?' he said, picking up the manifest.

I nodded. 'But I don't understand why she called herself Mrs Greenhalgh when she wasn't yet married.'

'Less questions.'

'I'm sorry?'

'If you said you were married, it raised less questions.'

'So when she came through here she just said she was married, even if she wasn't?'

'She didn't come through here,' he said.

I pointed at the name on the manifest. 'But it says here –'

'She was travelling first class. Immigration officers would see the first-class passengers in their staterooms and would only ask the most cursory of questions and invite them to leave the ship at their leisure. You pay first class, you get a first-class service. You pay steerage, you get Ellis Island.'

THE FOLLOWING morning, armed with the date on which Mariah had arrived, I set out to find my great-grandparents' marriage certificate. The ranger at Ellis Island had directed me to the City Records Office, near the grand New York City Hall building.

All the windows in Room 103 were closed and it had the smell of a school classroom at the end of a long day. On the tables were large notices: NO COATS, BAGS, BRIEFCASES AT THIS TABLE! Although there was no indication of where one might leave them.

I made my way to the reception desk. Every archive is different and I needed to know which reference cards would lead me to which indexes, filing cabinets and microfilms. Before I had the chance to open my mouth, a man at the desk barked, 'Have you registered?' He was tall, bald but with long sideburns, his glasses greasy with fingerprints.

'I didn't realise I needed to register.'

'You do,' he said and turned round to busy himself with some papers.

When I'd filled in the form, I asked him, 'Could you possibly help me find the marriage certificate for –'

'Five dollars,' he said. His arms were folded across his chest, faded tattoos on both forearms.

'For what?'

'Any certificate. Five dollars. You godda pay.' He slid another form across the desk in my direction and added, 'Fill it in.'

I sighed, pulled a pen from my pocket and began to work through the form.

'Pencil!' he roared. 'Can't you read?' He pointed at a notice saying that only pencils were to be used.

I didn't have a pencil.

'Here,' said one of his colleagues giving me a don't-mind-him roll of the eyes. She helped me find three batches of microfilms: Manhattan Grooms 1897–1902 DE–KN, All Grooms 1899–1901 FA–GR, and All Grooms 1901–03 GR–LO, before leading me to a reading machine. She then took my scarf and coat and hung them up for me.

I worked my way through the first one and a half piles of microfilms. I found Greenbergs, Greenhoots, Greenhalls and even a Greenhut, but no Greenhalgh. Mariah had arrived on 24 February and I'd already reached the end of the month and not discovered anything. I couldn't understand why it wasn't there. The only reason I could think of was that Arturo had waited a couple of days to register the marriage. I got to the end of March, and the second batch, and still I hadn't found it. Perhaps he had waited until after the honeymoon? Into April, mid-April. Still nothing. Maybe he'd decided not to register the marriage at all.

As I scrolled towards the end of the penultimate reel, I began to convince myself that I didn't really need to find the marriage certificate. I knew they had married in New York; I didn't need a piece of paper to prove it. Yet, if I couldn't find a marriage certificate in the ordered archive of the New York City Records Office, what hope did I have of tracking down a mango orchard somewhere in Mexico?

Then, there it was. Marriage No. 6603, 17 April 1901. Groom, Arthur Greenhalgh. Bride, Mariah Nuttall. All the details were there: their ages, the names of the bride's and groom's fathers, the minister, Dr Mark Darwood, and the two witnesses, Jorge A. Canalizo and Justo Aceredo.

Archives are generally quiet places, the only noise coming from the shuffling of paper and the rattle of microfilm readers. But every now and then, this calm is interrupted by people dancing celebratory jigs or punching the air in triumph. I greeted my eureka moment with a clenched fist and a quietly hissed, *'Yes!'*

I studied the certificate on the screen in front of me. Who could these witnesses be? Their names were Spanish, but I had never heard of them. Were they just two people off the street or friends who had accompanied Arturo from Mexico? And if so what had they been doing since Arturo met Mariah off the boat?

Then it hit me. My great-grandparents hadn't got married 'before sundown on the day she arrived'. They hadn't married the same week or even month. They had waited almost two months. This had been their little secret. Until now. For the first time Arturo and Mariah had found themselves on their own, free from the constraints of convention and parental intervention, and they had behaved like two young lovers having fun. I was proud of them.

The address on the certificate was in West 18th Street. If the church was still there, I could walk down the aisle as they had done.

A couple of subway rides later I found the street, lined with spindly, leafless trees. I could see no church. A brown-uniformed UPS delivery man carrying a bubble-wrapped package was ahead of me. He stopped and checked his clipboard outside an apartment block with a maroon canopy over the entrance. I looked at the certificate. It was the exact address: 350 West 18th Street. The UPS man pressed a bell and disappeared inside. For a moment I thought about following him in but stopped myself. What would I say? 'Hello, I'm looking for the church which used to be where your apartment is now. Have you seen it?'

I SPENT a few more days in archives and libraries but soon realised I was just scratching the surface of my great-grandfather's journey. The real discoveries were going to be in Mexico.

New York

Atlantic
Ocean

GULF OF
MEXICO

Antigua
Guatemala

Juanita

I N THE early hours of the morning the only people in Antigua's central plaza were a family sleeping on a strip of cardboard between the pillars of the municipal building and a security guard, dozing outside a bank, a pump-action shotgun cradled in his arms.

Once the taxi had driven off, the silence was complete apart from the whirr of an air-conditioning unit on the bank. The stillness was scented by orange blossom and an early-morning mist hung lightly over colonial arches, hiding the tips of the church towers and obliterating the cone-like volcano that presides over the town.

I had come to Antigua, Guatemala, as it was reputed to be the best place in Latin America to study Spanish. I planned to do a one-month intensive course before heading on to Mexico. If what I could see from the central plaza was anything to go by, I was going to like my time there. Brightly painted one-storey houses lined narrow cobbled streets. Flowers tumbled over garden walls and poked through the cracks of colonial ruins. There was the smell of wood-burning stoves and freshly baked bread.

I picked up my bags, hoping to find a café where I could while away the hour before the schools opened. A group of squat Indian women dressed in brightly woven *huipile* traditional tunics chatted as they walked in twos and threes ahead of me. On their heads they balanced wicker baskets piled high with produce to be sold at market. I followed them under an archway with an antiquated clock set into it, past street vendors arranging their displays of jade, silver and polished coconut husks on small strips of velvet, just like the traders I had seen in Arturo's postcard photographs.

I found no café, but followed the baking smell to a *panadería*, then returned to the central plaza with my bag of *pan dulce*. I was just about to start looking for a Spanish school when a boy with a straight-legged limp, dressed in a vest and patched track-suit bottoms, thrust a leaflet at me. 'You school?' he asked.

I nodded, my mouth still full of bread.

'I take you.'

He led me through a couple of streets, past high whitewashed walls with twists of razor wire along the top, to a shaded court-yard with giant pineapple plants growing in the middle. On the wall by a desk was a poster of a short-skirted woman dancing and the words CLASES DE SALSA. WHAT FUN!!! The boy pointed to a chair by the desk. 'You sit.' He then disappeared through a doorway and returned a few minutes later with a man of about fifty. His face was clean-shaven, jowly and pockmarked, and he wore a faded khaki baseball cap.

'I'm Eugenio, the school director,' he said, shaking my hand warmly. 'You're American?' His English was perfect.

'From England, actually.'

He smiled. 'The original version. Even better! I've dedicated my life to the study of English. I studied in the States, but my dream was to attend Cambridge or Oxford, to wear a boater and go bunting. Is that the right word?'

'Punting, I think.'

'Ah, thank you,' he said, and wrote the word down in his notebook. 'Now, you want to learn Spanish?'

'*Ya hablo bastante pero tengo oxidado*,' I said. I already speak a reasonable amount but I'm rusty. I had spent several summers in Spain when I was younger.

'Perfect.' He nodded, ignoring my attempts to speak his language. 'How long do you have?'

'*Un mes.*' One month.

Again in English, he said, 'You've come to the best school in Antigua. In one month we'll have you speaking like a native.'

A native of where? I wondered to myself.

'We offer a total Spanish immersion programme. Four hours of classes in the morning, activities in the afternoon,' he said, pointing to the salsa poster. 'And a room with one of the best families,' slapping the table to emphasise his point. He looked at his watch. 'What are you doing now?'

I had no plans, although speaking some Spanish might be nice.

'Good. Come on. I'll take you to your new family.'

Ten minutes later I was being led round a single-storey house that had, according to Eugenio, been a cardinal's palace and had recently been used in a TV ad. The maid who showed us round told us the owner, a judge, was in, but was '*ocupado*'.

'Does the judge live here alone?' I asked.

'*La señora* works in the mayor's office and travels a lot,' said the maid. 'Their daughter, Ana, goes to boarding school in Guatemala City.'

She showed me my room. It had an armchair, Frida Kahlo prints on the wall, and an en-suite bathroom with a bidet. The maid said she would make my bed with fresh sheets every morning, do my laundry and cook me breakfast, lunch and dinner.

She led us to a marble-topped table in the courtyard and brought us glasses of fresh papaya juice. Eugenio smiled as he told me the price for studying at his school and staying in the judge's home. It was very reasonable.

'Come back to the school and we can do the paperwork,' said Eugenio, still smiling.

There was no logical reason for me not to follow him. I had come to Antigua to find a language school and a family to live with and had found both, but my intuition was telling me to walk away. I searched for a logical explanation for the feeling but couldn't find one. It just didn't feel right.

'I'll let you know,' I said to Eugenio as we stepped out into the street.

The smile slipped from his face and veins stood out in his temples. 'I thought we had a deal. An Englishman's word is his bond. Isn't that what they say?' He wanted to use me for English tuition even when he was angry.

'I didn't give you my word. But I can promise you I'll come back and tell you when I have made up my mind.'

Eugenio waved his hand dismissively. 'If you don't come back, you will have made your intentions perfectly clear.' He turned and walked in the opposite direction.

By MID-AFTERNOON I had visited eight schools. They were all in beautiful colonial buildings, their directors were all English-speaking and charming, but none of them seemed right. It was the hottest part of the day and as I dragged my bags around, mouth dry and head aching from the high altitude, looking for a ninth school to visit, I began to question whether I had been right not to accept Eugenio's offer. Perhaps I would have been assigned a brilliant teacher. Maybe the judge would have been a jovial evening companion.

A bus trundled down the road in front of me. A man leaned out of the open door shouting, *'La frontera, la frontera!'*

I wondered if I should jump on, go to the Mexican border and forget all about Antigua's famed language schools. I might well have done just that had I not, at that moment, seen a sign for the Cervantes language school. It didn't look promising, positioned between a tyre repair shop and a grassless football field, but I decided to give it a go. If it was no good, I would go straight to Mexico.

Cervantes was run by Josefina, a plump lady with curly hair and purple eyeliner. Unlike Eugenio, she spoke no English and seemed more interested in finding out what I wanted to learn rather than show off what she knew.

I told her I wanted to sharpen up my Spanish to help me in my search for my great-grandfather's footsteps.

She clapped her hands together. 'You're an investigator like me! I've been drawing up my family tree since my uncle told me we have Italian blood. I've traced as far back as my great-great-grandmother, who was a maid for a nobleman in Verona in the late 1700s.'

'Have you been there?'

She laughed. I realised the naivety of my question considering what she probably earned, but she saved my embarrassment. 'Perhaps one day,' she said. 'Where are you staying?'

I told her I hadn't found anywhere yet.

She tutted. 'That's no good. Would you like me to send you to a really nice family?' I noticed she used the word *genial* – nice or kind – rather than *buena* – good.

I nodded. I felt a sudden profound yearning for a *genial* family. I felt homesick for a home I didn't yet know.

'The lady's name is Olga,' she said, writing down the address and handing it to me. 'The house is round the corner. Just say I sent you. Classes start at eight tomorrow morning.'

A DIMINUTIVE woman with salt-and-pepper hair answered my knock on the door. She wore a neat bright-blue pinafore over a baggy white T-shirt. Behind her was chaos. Two boys, who she introduced as her sons Luis and Eduardo, were both wearing Argentinian football shirts with a '10' on the back. They were chasing a deflated ball between the turkeys, chickens, dogs, macaws and parrots that also occupied the backyard. '*Niños, niños!*' she said, picking up a parrot on a broom handle and returning it to its perch. She steered me towards the kitchen, where her daughters, Lili and Pati, were fighting over a sheet of tracing paper. School books were spread all over the table and scattered on the floor.

An elderly woman came in from another room and waved her walking stick at the boys outside. 'You'll have to be quieter than this with the change of regime.'

I had been in Latin America less than a day and there was already a revolution?

'It's too noisy, too noisy,' she continued, speaking in strange staccato Spanish with a heavy German accent.

'This is Doña Margarita,' said Olga, introducing us.

She ignored the hand I held out to her. 'There's a coup in the works,' she said, switching into English, but with the same disjointed delivery. 'I have it on good authority that half the cabinet are ready to leave their desks and put on a bullet belt.' She made her way to the door, but then suddenly stopped, turned round to look at me and said, 'I suggest you become a cowboy!'

'I'll bear that in mind,' I said.

She slammed the door behind her.

Olga laughed. '*Lo siento*,' she said. I'm sorry. 'That's our neighbour. Doña Margarita always thinks there's about to be a revolution.'

She showed me upstairs and I stopped on the balcony before going into my room. A riot of orange, yellow and purple flowers grew from hanging baskets and earth-filled oil cans. I looked up at the silhouette of a smooth and treeless volcano. 'Does it ever erupt?' I asked.

Olga shook her head. 'It's like a sleeping angel, watching over us. But Fuego is a bit more lively.' She pointed into the distance to two more volcanoes, one of which glowed red, spitting lava into the early-evening sky.

I smiled to myself as I unpacked my bags. There were no Frida Kahlo prints on the wall. I had no bidet, but I felt more at home than I ever could have done in the judge's house.

Soon Eduardo, the older of the two boys, came to tell me that supper was ready. The kitchen table still had school textbooks piled at one end, next to a clay pot of refried beans, a saucepan of boiled plantains, slices of avocado and cheese, bowls of salsa and a basket full of tortillas wrapped in a checked napkin.

Olga stood at the end of the table handing out plates. 'Take a seat and help yourself.' Though the household was chaotic and noisy, Olga had unquestioned authority. She had brought up the family single-handed since her husband had gone to work in Miami nine years before. He'd not yet come back.

A slim young woman in a gold sleeveless polo-neck sweater was sitting next to Lili, a black velvet jacket folded over the back of her chair.

'This is Juanita,' said Lili. Her jet-black hair brushed her shoulders and framed her amber eyes, which seemed to glow like the lava I had just been watching from the balcony. From the first time I saw her, I was bewitched.

Lili caught me smiling. 'Do you think Juanita is *bonita*?'

'*Es hermosa*,' I said, before I could stop myself. She's beautiful. I felt myself blush. Olga's children cheered and blew kisses.

'How many girlfriends have you had?' asked Lili.

I kicked her under the table.

'Who kicked me?' she asked, looking at me wide-eyed and grinning.

'Yes, how many girlfriends do you have?' said Juanita. 'You've got *patas de gallo* – rooster's feet – round the eyes; you've obviously had some adventures.'

'Are you going to marry Juanita now?' asked Luis, who was nine.

I felt myself redden again and saw Juanita kick him under the table.

Olga came to my rescue. 'Josefina told me you're going to Mexico soon.'

'My great-grandfather once lived there. I'm going to see what he left behind.'

Juanita looked at me thoughtfully. 'He left in a bit of a hurry.'

I stared at her, unable to respond with more than a nod.

'Juanita's a *brujita*,' explained Lili. A little witch. 'She can read your eyes and tell you your future, and past.'

Juanita smiled, neither encouraging nor discouraging her friend.

'Have you done your homework?' said Olga to Luis and Eduardo. The boys scraped their chairs as they reluctantly got up to leave. 'Pati?'

Pati got up too, carrying her plate to the stone sink outside. 'Go on,' said Lili.

Juanita was not going to be hurried. 'What's that spot in your eye?'

'I burned it with hydrogen peroxide when I was younger, trying to dye my hair. What does that say about my future?'

She smiled. 'That you won't have blonde hair.'

'How do you do it, then?' I asked Juanita.

'Just look at me.'

I looked at her and was held by her eyes, yet I felt myself falling, as if tumbling through a kaleidoscope. I sensed myself age, then become young, as though my life were being stretched from one world to another. Throughout it all I was faintly aware of someone humming. She touched my hand and the humming stopped.

'Welcome back,' she said.

I blinked. Back from where? 'What did you see?'

'You are going forward to go back. It's a circular journey.'

'Anything else?'

Her smooth forehead knotted momentarily, then there was the brief hint of a smile. 'And . . .' She hesitated.

'What?'

'I'll tell you another time.'

WHEN SHE got up to leave, I noticed she had a silver-headed black cane. Even her walking stick looked like a fashion accessory. I accompanied her to the door and whispered, 'Can I take you out tomorrow night?'

'We'll see,' she said, and slipped out of the door.

'Be careful with Juanita. She's suffered enough,' said Olga when I walked back into the kitchen.

'Why does she have a walking stick?'

'A year ago she was in a car crash. She was on her way to a party in Chimaltenango, a town near here. Her mother – she's a *brujita* too – had seen it in her coffee grains and forbade Juanita to go, but she went anyway. The car she was in hit another head on. The girl sitting on Juanita's knee was decapitated and several others were also killed.'

I had a sudden horrific mental image of blood and twisted metal.

Olga began to clear away the dinner plates. 'She was in hospital for six months. Broke her leg, pelvis, shoulder, arm, hand and jaw. It's a miracle she's alive.'

I helped her take the rest of the plates through to the sink in silence. Then, smiling, Olga said, 'So where are you going to take her tomorrow?'

IN THE morning I hurried to see Josefina to ask if I could delay the start of my classes by an hour, then followed Olga's directions to Juanita's house behind the old well.

Her mother came to the door. Juanita wasn't there, she said. She looked me over and suggested kindly, 'You might want to have a shave.'

I was only a few weeks into my journey. Had I already forgotten how to look respectable?

I called back again, showered and shaved and wearing a fresh shirt. She still wasn't there.

'Juanita likes flowers,' her mother said with a smile.

It would have to wait until lunchtime, as I had to get back to school. Josefina was looking at her watch when I arrived.

'You've been here only one day and you're already *Latino*,' she said with a smile. We went upstairs and sat at the only desk in a classroom with scuffed lino tiles. There was a whiteboard, '*Subjuntivo*' written on it in magic marker.

'*Como se llama?*' she asked. What's her name?

I could tell there would be no room for secrets in Antigua. 'Juanita.'

'Lives by the old well with her mother and sisters?'

I nodded.

She smiled. 'She's pretty.'

I nodded again.

'Okay, how will you ask her out?'

I hadn't thought that far.

She pointed to the whiteboard. Subjunctive. 'It doesn't exist in English, but if you want somebody to do something, or you're expressing a desire, you have to use the subjunctive. Believe me, you don't want to get this wrong.'

We spent the rest of the morning practising asking Juanita out, and then I went straight to the flower market. I chose what I hoped would be appropriate – pink roses. Red roses seemed presumptuous. I had a notion that white signified death. I just hoped that in Guatemala the pink rose didn't symbolise infidelity or devil worship.

Again, her mother came to the door. A gentle nod when she saw the flowers seemed to indicate that she approved, but still Juanita wasn't there.

'I'll send her over to Olga's when she gets in.'

I went back to the house and waited. I tried reading but

couldn't concentrate. Later in the afternoon I chatted in the kitchen with Olga as she soaked beans, cut up plantain and warmed tortillas for the evening meal. When she'd finished and Juanita still hadn't arrived, I went up to my room. Ten minutes later there was a knock at my door. I jumped off the bed. It was Eduardo.

He had been sent up to summon me for supper. I tried to hide my disappointment and made my way downstairs, taking the pink roses with me just in case Juanita arrived during the meal.

'Any news?' I asked Olga.

'*No te preocupes,*' she said as I sat down at one of the two spare places at the table. Don't worry. 'She'll be here soon.' The whole family was looking at me with smirks on their faces.

'*Qué?*'

There was a tap on my shoulder, and there she was. Having chased round after her in circles all day (was this what she had meant by a circular journey?), seeing Juanita was like slipping back into a heavenly dream.

I handed her the flowers and we sat down at the table without breaking eye contact. She had her hair tied up and tucked into a cashmere baker boy cap and she wore a high-collared black shirt. More chic than *brujita.*

She didn't explain her absence. I wondered if she knew that I had called at her house three times or waited in most of the afternoon. Surrounded by Olga's family I couldn't ask. Private conversation was limited to sneaked glances and stolen smiles.

'What did you learn in your Spanish class today?' she asked me. It was as if she knew exactly what I had been rehearsing.

'Subjunctive.'

'Give us an example. What would you like Juanita to do?' Luis asked, grinning through a mouth full of tortilla.

'*Quiero que Juanita te pegue.*' I want Juanita to hit you.

'Bravo!' said Juanita, leaning across the table and playfully swatting Luis across the back of the head. She smiled at me and gave me a wink. I caught her looking at me on several occasions, and each time she passed something to me our hands brushed against each other.

When Olga began to clear the table, I walked Juanita home. We reached her front door and stood facing each other like a couple of awkward teenagers.

'It's great to see you,' I said.

'Thank you for the flowers,' she said, fingering a balled-up paper tissue.

'You're welcome.'

She looked at me and the whole world seemed to stop. I saw only her beautiful face, lighting my life before me. I leaned forward to kiss her.

After a second she pulled back and said quietly, 'What do you think you're doing?'

'Trying to kiss you . . .'

'*Buenas noches,*' she said and went inside.

'Can I see you tomorrow?' I called, but she'd gone.

I hardly slept all night. As dawn broke, I was still turning it all over and over in my head.

On my way to school I slipped a note under her door, apologising for being so forward. Latin courtship was proving to be more subtle than I thought. In Guatemala you see love and romance everywhere. The men dress to woo; the women dress to be wooed. Sex is everywhere – in the way they dance, the rhythmic and seductive patterns to their speech and the plunging necklines and short dresses, revealing tantalising expanses of smooth brown skin. How could this be the case and yet it be so difficult to get past first base? Or even to get in the ball-park?

In the note I had asked Juanita to come round in the evening, which she did. During the meal she didn't offer to read my eyes. She didn't wink at me or brush her hand against mine, but at least we were talking.

I walked her home again after the evening meal and asked her out for coffee the next day.

'No, I can't, I have a fiesta to go to.'

My heart sank.

'But you can come too, if you like.'

THE FIESTA was a *quinceañera* – a fifteenth birthday – which she attended out of a sense of family obligation rather than for her own enjoyment. Her cousin, whose birthday it was, wore a white wedding-like dress while aunties clucked around her.

'*Ay mi hija, mira! Que vestido!*' Look at you! What a dress!

'You look like your *mamá* when she married.'

'*Que guapa, que guapa!*'

'*Los chicos* are going to die for you!'

'Doesn't she look beautiful?'

Juanita and I sat on plastic seats at the edge of her aunt's patio, holding paper plates weighed down with *torta* and sipping poly-styrene cups of Coca-Cola. We were there an hour until Juanita felt we'd been there long enough to leave.

We walked up to the gardens of an old convent, which had been tumbled and rebuilt and tumbled again by a series of earth-quakes. We sat on a fragment of what had once been an outer wall. She told me more about her life, about how she had been born when her parents were in the throes of divorce. Even before she could crawl she was being passed from relative to relative.

'My first memories are from my aunt's village when I was two years old. I remember guerrilla fighters passing through it. Many of them were just kids. There was one known as *El Águila*, because he had a curved nose like an eagle's beak. My aunt took quite a shine to him, cooked him *pollo picante*. One day the army came through, wanting to know who had been helping the rebels. They held a gun to my aunt's head, but she just denied it. She was a strong character.'

'They would have shot her for giving a kid some chilli chicken?'

She shrugged. 'That was just how it was.'

'How long did you stay there?' I asked.

'My aunt died when I was nine.' Juanita paused and took a deep breath. 'She survived the guerrillas and the soldiers, and was hit by a truck when crossing the road. She'd gone out to buy me an ice cream.' She wiped her nose and forced a smile, *'Así es la vida.'* That's life.

I put my hand on hers. I had only meant it as a comforting gesture, but the touch of her hand felt intensely intimate. She wound her little finger round mine, but then pulled away to brush a strand of hair from her face.

'What did you do then?' I asked.

'I went to stay with a cousin and then with another aunt for a couple of years. When I was twelve, I was sent to Guatemala City to stay with my uncle, a politician. He lived in a two-storey house in the best district of the city.'

'It must have been a bit different from living in *el pueblo*,' I said.

'*Sí*. I'd never even had a hot shower before and suddenly I was going clothes shopping in a chauffeur-driven car.' She giggled. 'That's where I learned how to be *elegante*.'

'Sounds like a good life.'

'It was, but then my uncle and aunt separated. That was three years ago, when I was eighteen. That's when I came to live in Antigua.'

I looked at her beautiful, lineless face. It was difficult to believe such a life could have been lived without leaving a trace. It made me reflect on my cosseted and privileged upbringing. 'What happened to your father? Is he still alive?'

'He lives with his second family. He calls round every week or so.'

I was about to ask her how she felt about this arrangement, but she changed the subject.

'Tell me about your great-grandfather.'

'He died before I was born but I always felt I knew him; Grandma told me so many stories about him.'

She paused then asked me carefully, 'Did he have any children in Mexico?'

'My Great-Aunt Sophia. She was born in a convent there and baptised in the local cathedral. But when she was two she became ill. They were afraid they might lose her, so he and his wife took her back to Lancashire. Arturo, my great-grandfather, then came back to Mexico alone. Grandma was born shortly after he left. He didn't go back to England until the outbreak of the Mexican Revolution.'

'When was that?'

'November 20, 1910.'

Juanita looked impressed. 'Someone paid attention in history class.'

'I know that because Grandma celebrated it every year. It was the date Arturo came back from Mexico, the day she first met him.'

Juanita nodded. 'She was her Daddy's girl.'

'She adored him.'

Juanita pulled a blade of grass from the ground and began to nibble the end of it. 'Did he sing?'

I laughed. 'How on earth do you know?'

'Something in your eyes yesterday.'

'Apparently, before he went to Mexico, Arturo was a good singer. He was the lead tenor in the chapel choir. He sang in Mexico too, but when he returned to England he was told he could no longer sing in the choir.'

'Why not?'

'They said he sang in the "Mexican way".'

'What does that mean?'

'I don't know, but he never sang again.'

Juanita nodded, as if it was what she had suspected. 'I saw a lot of sadness there.'

'Was that what you were going to tell me about what you saw in my eyes?'

She shook her head. 'It was something else.'

'What?'

Juanita stood up, brushing the back of her skirt with her hand. 'I have to go. I'll tell you tomorrow.'

AFTER SCHOOL the following lunchtime I walked up to the plaza, where I had arranged to meet Juanita. As I waited I watched a four-piece marimba band playing outside the bank. A fifth member patrolled the sidewalk, holding out a cut-open maraca. The band had been through their entire repertoire and I had heard some of their songs several times by the time Juanita turned up. We went to a café, where she ordered an *Americano* coffee in a tall glass, which she drank through a straw. I was dying to know what she had seen in my eyes, but when I asked her she simply smiled and wouldn't be drawn.

We began to meet every day after my classes had finished. She was almost always more than an hour late but would offer no apology or explanation about where she'd been. She didn't own a watch and seemed to regard time as a concept that simply didn't apply to her. Her mood also appeared to be governed by unseen forces. Some days she was chatty and flirtatious, on others she was distracted and indifferent. It both charmed and enraged me.

After I had been in Antigua for nearly a month Juanita's mother gave me permission to take her out for the evening, as long as I brought her home by ten thirty. I took her to a jazz club. In reality it was little different to any of the other bars around town in that it played *merenge* and *salsa*, but with occasional songs by Santana, UB40 or Sting thrown in.

Juanita was being more elusive than ever. Every conversational avenue I explored led to a cul-de-sac.

'I have to go to Guatemala City to pick up my post. I'm expecting a letter from my grandmother,' I said.

'Okay.'

She was frustrating the hell out of me, but I was determined not to show it. 'When I'm there I can extend my visa, otherwise I'll have to leave the country.'

She shrugged.

As I walked her home, she paused and looked up at the star-filled sky. I followed her gaze and together we saw a shooting star, like the tail of a fluorescent kite.

She gasped. 'Wow! This is a very good sign. It means we will have good luck!'

We will have good luck? She spoke as if it was the message she had been waiting for and reached for my hands.

'I don't know what you want,' I said to her in English. 'I wish I did but I don't.'

'*Te quiero,*' she whispered. She pulled me towards her and kissed me.

Sheffield

13 December

Hello love,

Thank you very much for the letter from New York. It's extraordinary about my parents waiting two months to get married. I can't think why they didn't say.

I'm afraid my horizons are now very limited and the news from me is much more prosaic. My ankle is much better now, thank you. I suppose I should know better than to run for the bus at my age.

I can't believe you'll soon be in Mexico. My father put a lot of energy and affection into his life there and I'm sure he'd be very pleased that you feel motivated enough by the stories I told you to go and find out more.

You asked me an awful lot of questions in your letter. I don't know if I'll be able to answer them all, but I'll do as best I can.

The name of Don Domingo's company was 'the House of Egery' – I think that's how you spell it. One of the other people out there was Arthur Ecroyd, the 'flash Harry from Oswaldtwistle' whom I have told you about. He was a drinker and gambler who stayed behind in Mexico when my father left, and was murdered soon afterwards.

The factory was a cotton mill, which would have needed a water supply. It wasn't too far from the port of San Blas, where my father went with a mule train to collect raw materials and machinery for the mill.

As well as working at the mill, my father also helped

improve the village's water supply and helped build a church so the people didn't have to travel so far on a Sunday.

I'm afraid that in spite of all this, I still can't remember the name of the place where he lived. I know he had two houses – one next to the factory in the small village and one in the small town, somewhere near Guadalajara. He was there on his own for a few years until he was joined by my mother, and then again, after bringing Sophia home. He stayed until the revolution, when he sailed back on the *Lusitania*.

I wish I could remember more, love. I don't suppose you'll find anything after all this time. Things change, and people will have died – and I don't want you to waste your time on a wild goose chase. But who knows, perhaps there'll be a chance meeting.

Well if I'm to get this to you, I had better run to the Post Office. Don't worry, it's just a figure of speech. I promise I won't run; I will walk carefully!

Mind how you go. Lots of love,

Grandma

When I got back from the capital, I went straight round to see Juanita. I showed her the letter from Grandma and the one-month extension to my visa. But she didn't seem to share my excitement.

'That's not very long. You should have asked for two months, or maybe three.'

'One month was all they would give me.'

'It will go very quickly.'

*   *   *

ONE MONTH did go very quickly. I went to Josefina's classes every day, knowing that I needed my Spanish to improve, but my mind was increasingly distracted, thinking about my next meeting with Juanita.

We spent as much time together as possible, but our moments of intimacy were few and far between. I was ever aware of the watchful eye of her family – and Olga – as well as the painted metal plaque above her front door, *SOMOS CATÓLICOS* – We are Catholics.

One night, as I walked her home from Olga's house, she said to me, 'I have to make an important phone call in the morning. Come by and remind me at ten o'clock, would you?'

The next morning I knocked on her door. It opened almost immediately.

'*Pasa, rápido!*' Juanita hissed, sticking her head out of the door to check that no one had seen me go in. She leaned against the door to shut it. 'There's no one here.'

'And the phone call you had to make?'

'I'm afraid that was a little lie.'

'Your family?' I asked, looking about me as she began to unbutton my shirt.

'They're not here.'

'Are you sure no one will come back?'

'Quite sure.'

'What would happen,' I asked as nonchalantly as possible, 'if by chance your father did come back and find me here with you?'

'He'd shoot you,' she said casually.

I greeted this news with a certain amount of alarm, but what-ever arguments I could think of for running out the door, there were other more irresistible arguments getting ever more naked in front of me.

She led me on and on, further into the heart of the house.

We stopped outside a flimsy wooden door with a HELLO KITTY sticker on it. 'Wait a moment,' she said.

'What?'

She retraced our steps to the living room, picking up our discarded clothing. 'Just in case.'

She pushed open the door and I followed her inside.

It was a single bed with a black metal frame and a sagging mattress. On the wall was a small picture of the Virgin Mary with the words DIOS ES AMOR.

'Feel this,' Juanita said, tracing my finger down the scar that ran the length of her right thigh.

'Does it hurt?'

She shook her head, then laughed. 'It tickles. Feel this.' And she ran my finger down her left thigh. There was no scar.

'Does that tickle?'

'In a different way.' She giggled again. Suddenly, Juanita froze.

'What?'

She held her finger to my lips. I heard the front door lock clicking open, then the heavy wooden door slamming shut. Footsteps made their way across the stone floor of the living room, pausing to drop keys on the coffee table. The footsteps got closer. Juanita and I were on rather than in her bed, but we had no other choice than to lie still, naked and exposed. The slightest movement would make the bed creak, which would be audible to the person who had stopped walking and was now standing outside the bedroom. I could see the shaft of light beneath the door interrupted by the shadows of two feet. We both held our breath.

Whoever it was seemed uncertain why they were there. The feet scuffed the floor and went past Juanita's bedroom towards the kitchen at the far end of the house. Then they started to make their way back. Again, the footsteps paused outside Juanita's door. The door knob moved slightly.

'*Oh dios,*' Juanita whispered, her grip on my arm tightening. I watched the rapid beat of the pulse on her neck.

The knob moved again and the footsteps moved more purposefully away from us. We heard keys being snatched from the coffee table and, seconds later, the front door brass knocker clattered against the door as it swung shut.

'*Dios mío. Que susto!*' My God, what a fright! said Juanita, who had let go of me and was now staring up at the ceiling, the back of her hand resting on her forehead. We both lay there for several minutes, not saying anything. Then she said, 'Well they've gone now. There's no point in you going too.'

'*No me iba a ningún lado.*' I wasn't going anywhere.

My Spanish was improving rapidly, yet though I had no problem communicating with Juanita, I felt underprepared to negotiate my way around Mexican archives and interview historians and experts in the Mexican textile industry. Josefina was teaching me vocabulary she felt would be useful to me in my investigations: the words for birth certificate, records office, archive, index system, weaving and spinning machines, cotton mill and mango orchard.

'Where are you going to start?' Josefina asked me one morning.

'I'll start where my great-grandfather first arrived, in Veracruz on the Gulf Coast, then follow the route he took to Mexico City and Guadalajara and on to Chapala, which might be the place where he lived.'

'What makes you think that?' she asked.

'My grandmother told me he had two homes, one in a small town near Guadalajara, the other next to the mill he worked in, in a nearby village. There are plenty of villages around Chapala, plus it's on the shore of the biggest lake in Mexico, and the mill would have needed a good water supply. My great-grandfather took photos of it.'

Josefina twisted her mouth pensively. 'It's not much to go on.'

I didn't need reminding.

'Who owned the factory your great-grandfather worked in?'

'A Spanish family.'

'Good. I have a friend who could help you.' She picked up her handbag and flicked through her diary. 'Here he is: Gastón. He was doing a doctorate at the same time as I did my degree. He wrote his thesis on foreign-owned businesses during the *Porfiriato*.'

'The what?'

'The reign of the Mexican president, some say dictator, Porfirio Díaz. He led the country for thirty years until he was ousted in the Revolution. Gastón would be able to tell you where the foreign-owned cotton mills were.'

'Can I meet him?'

Josefina looked pensive again. 'Do you have to go straight to Mexico, or can you take a little detour?'

'Where does he live, on the coast?' I said, joking.

'Bogotá, Colombia.'

'DIDN'T I tell you?' said Doña Margarita, Olga's eccentric neighbour, who came to supper one evening.

'What?'

'The country is in chaos.'

Olga had described Doña Margarita as a conspiracy theorist who was correct just often enough to keep people listening. Born in Germany to English parents before the First World War, she had escaped the Nazis by going to England in the 1930s, but

44

when the Second World War broke out, she discovered England was not a good place to have a German accent and moved to Latin America. She was paranoid with good reason. Both her husbands had been kidnapped – the first by government forces, the second by guerrillas – and neither was seen again.

What she said about the country being in chaos was true. Strikes and demonstrations were now daily occurrences, the participants in masks to hide their identity. There was talk of young men disappearing from rural areas and being press-ganged into the army or rebel groups. For a couple of days even the buses stopped running. Few people had cars, so the country ground to a halt. There were scare stories about *gringos* kidnapping Guatemalan children for adoption or even for organ transplants.

A few weeks before, an American woman had stopped for lunch in the nearby town of Cobán. She paused to take pictures of a little *campesino* girl by a fountain. The girl's mother screamed that the *gringa* was trying to abduct her daughter. The mother's hysterical shouting drew a crowd, which turned into a furious mob. They beat the American woman to death.

'Mark my words,' said Doña Margarita, 'there'll be bombs in Guatemala City this week. A general strike is about to be called. I'm going to get some emergency supplies.' She stomped off, slamming the door behind her. The bombs never came. The general strike began a few days later.

THE POLITICAL unrest was no great worry to Juanita or me, however. Our most pressing and depressing concern was the looming deadline of my departure. Although I had always wanted to go to Colombia, and going to meet Josefina's friend Gastón provided the perfect opportunity, I could see no further than

Juanita and my pending separation. I had booked a flight (the cheapest available, via the island of San Andrés, to Cartagena). It was non-changeable, non-refundable, with a fixed date. Juanita likened our last days to being with someone with only a short time to live.

It felt as though we were concentrating a whole life together into one month. I thought about staying and setting up home in Antigua. It was a tempting thought, but I knew I couldn't, not at that moment. The same sense of intuition that had guided me to Juanita was now urging me to move on. Arturo called.

On our last night Juanita and I went to a poetry evening at a café-bar where world music played softly in the background and the smell of joss sticks scented the air.

A moustachioed American, his ample paunch straining at a silver Harley-Davidson belt buckle, leaned towards me as discreetly as his bulky frame would allow. 'Do you have any drugs on you?'

Before I could work out whether he wanted to buy or sell, he said, 'Cos if you have, ditch 'em right now. We're about to get busted.'

Poetry gave way to panic. A squad of policemen appeared at the café entrance, machine guns slung across their chests. Some wielded riot batons, others shone flashlights in people's eyes. Chairs scraped and clattered, people screamed. Neither Juanita nor I were carrying any ID and, for that alone, we could be thrown into a police cell. Juanita took my hand and led me to the far side of the courtyard into a darkened room before the police had had a chance to fan out. I collided with a table, knocking it over. A metal plate crashed to the floor.

'Shit!' I froze, like a thief caught in the act. Just a few feet away policemen were shouting, telling everyone to stand against a wall and produce their *documentos.*

'*Vamos!*' Juanita yanked me through the darkness until we came to a door. She pushed. It was locked.

'Shit!' I said again as she slid back the bolts and pushed. The door opened and we fell out into the street.

'*Vámonos!*'

We ran. Juanita, who couldn't even sit up unaided a year before and had still been walking with a stick until a few weeks ago, was *running*.

We came to a stop by the stone fountain where women from the surrounding hills came to do their washing. We leaned into each other as we caught our breath. I began to laugh with exhilaration. 'You know your way out of a tight spot, eh?'

She buried her head in my chest and I continued to laugh until I realised that her shoulders were not heaving with laughter.

'*Tranquila, chica,*' I said. '*No pasa nada.* We're okay. We escaped.'

'It's not that, *tonto.* It's you.' She looked at me with tear-stung eyes. 'You're going, leaving me here. You have no idea what it's going to do to me. Remember, it's much harder for the person who stays behind.'

On my last morning in Antigua I woke early, my mind and heart in clear confusion. My departure made no sense to Juanita or me, but I knew that it was what I needed to do. I had fallen in love and that seemed to be part of my destiny, but now was not the moment to stand still and let myself take root. It wasn't that I wanted freedom; I wanted to find my place. But no matter how much I tried to convince myself that it was here and now, in my heart I knew that it wasn't. Juanita knew it too.

On a patch of wasteland on the way to the bus station I stopped and looked into her eyes. 'Tell me what you see,' I said.

She looked away as if she were scared to know the truth, then turned back and gazed into my eyes with a distant look on her face. I heard humming and felt myself floating, tumbling, falling until she brought me back with a squeeze of the hand.

'Beware of a bald devil with a mouth full of gold.'

It sounded preposterous and I laughed, but she remained stony-faced.

'What else?'

'I don't recognise where it is and I can't tell you when,' she said, 'but if you follow the right road, I will see you again.'

A round-faced boy of about sixteen wearing a green football shirt and chewing a plastic straw walked a few yards ahead of a bus as it crawled out of the station. He called out, like a rag-and-bone man with a stutter trying to rustle up passengers, *'Ch-ch-chimal-chimal-chimal-chimaltenango!'*

Chimaltenango was twenty kilometres away, and it was from there I was to catch a bus to Guatemala City Airport. I could have caught one directly from Antigua, but Juanita had some business to attend to at a lawyer's office there and this way we got another precious couple of hours together.

I slung my bags onto the moving bus and we jumped aboard. Once we were seated, she rested her head on my shoulder and fell asleep as I smoothed her hair. After half an hour, we passed four crosses beside the road. Juanita suddenly woke up and I realised it was where she'd had the accident. Maybe she felt the lingering presence of the souls of those who had died, but she said nothing. I kissed the top of her head and she nestled back into my shoulder.

*   *   *

ON THE main route from Guatemala City to the Mexican border, Chimaltenango was a town visited only out of necessity.

While Juanita saw the lawyer, I waited in the main square in front of the police station, an oppressive grey stone fort that looked like it had been custom built for human rights abuses.

A school procession slowly circled the plaza. Girls dressed like beauty queens with crowns and sashes sat on car bonnets, blowing kisses and throwing sweets to passers-by. Boys, in stiff-shouldered suits, threw firecrackers. On any other day I would have clapped and waved as the children passed, but now all I could think about was Juanita.

Juanita crept up behind me and put her hands on my eyes. 'Guess who?'

I kissed her fingers. 'Hungry?'

'Not really, but let's go anyway.'

We headed for Pollo Campero, Country Chicken, which looked to be the best eatery Chimaltenango had to offer. A self-styled Guatemalan KFC, with *combo comidas*, piped music and bright orange decor, it felt more like a school canteen. We ordered a couple of drinks and a serving of *papas fritas a la francesa* at the worn Formica counter and sat at a table in the corner, under a speaker blaring out the Chicago song 'If You Leave Me Now'. I reached across the table to take her hand as tears began to run down her cheeks.

I had assumed that I'd know how to say goodbye. But the words remained unspoken and the grease from our uneaten French fries had soaked through the cardboard cup.

'*Eres el amor de mi vida,*' I said. You are the love of my life.

'*Tu también.*' You too.

'It's been the most incredible adventure.'

She blanched and I realised I had said something wrong. I had used the word *aventura*, which also means 'affair'.

'It was so much more than that . . .' she said.

I tried to explain but she shook her head, understanding it was not what I had wanted to say.

Juanita and I walked outside, the world rippling only very slightly in our swell. We clung to each other. One last kiss. One last *Te quiero*. Then I turned and walked away.

Pablo

One day, soon after Arturo arrived in Mexico, Don Domingo went out of town for a meeting. He left Ecroyd in charge and told him to make sure they finished a job for their biggest client, who had demanded it be delivered to them by the end of the day.

'No problem,' said Ecroyd, who immediately walked round the factory to shout at everyone, telling them to work harder.

Don Domingo had been gone less than half an hour when there was a loud BANG! And smoke started to pour out of the biggest loom.

'Send for the engineer!' called Ecroyd, and immediately the chief engineer arrived with his two assistants, carrying his heavy bags of tools. They stripped the machine. They replaced the warp beam and greased the heddle rods. They oiled the chains and checked the treadles. The machine still didn't work.

'Hurry up!' shouted Ecroyd, looking at his pocket watch.

The chief engineer and his two assistants tried everything they could think of. They adjusted the harnesses and tested the pedals. They rebalanced the breast beam and repositioned the thread board. Still the machine didn't work.

Ecroyd was now pacing up and down, mopping his forehead with his handkerchief. 'What can we do?' he muttered to himself. Then he had an idea. He went to another mill nearby and asked them if their engineer could have a look. The engineer came back with him and checked and tested, greased and oiled. And still the machine didn't work.

Ecroyd didn't know what to do. The order would not be completed, the client would be angry, and he would be for the high jump.

Arturo had been working in the foundry all morning and hadn't seen the kerfuffle with the loom. When he came out to get some lunch he saw the two chief engineers and their assistants rushing about, and Ecroyd sitting by the loom with his head in his hands, scarlet with rage.

'What's going on?' he asked.

'We can't get the loom to work,' said Ecroyd.

'Let me have a look,' said Arturo.

The engineers looked at Arturo and sniffed. 'He'll never be able to do anything if we can't.'

But Ecroyd was desperate. 'Have a look and tell us what you think.'

Arturo took off his jacket and climbed on top of the machine, then he crawled underneath. He saw that a piston had come out of its shaft. 'Get me some ice,' he said.

'Ice?' said the chief engineer. His two assistants laughed. 'This is no time for fun and games.'

'Get him some ice,' said Ecroyd.

*Arturo packed the ice round the piston, and held it in place
with pieces of torn-up cloth.*

'What do we do now?' asked the chief engineer.

'We wait,' said Arturo.

The chief engineer's assistants began to laugh again.

'We don't have long,' said Ecroyd, checking his watch.

Arturo smiled. 'Ten minutes should do it.'

*After ten minutes Arturo unwrapped the cloth and removed
the ice. He manoeuvred the piston to the lip of the shaft and
it slotted into place. Arturo picked up his jacket and went to
get some lunch, whistling to himself, leaving the chief engineer
looking at the piston and scratching his head.*

Seven hours and thirty-five minutes after I'd said goodbye to
Juanita, I arrived at Cartagena airport. I took a taxi to Getsemaní,
the old artisan quarter of the city. It stopped outside a liquor
store with bars on the windows.

'The hotel is down there,' said the taxi driver, making a popping
noise with his chewing gum. He pointed down an unlit street
beyond a food stand selling *arepas* and a group of men sitting on
beer crates, drinking rum and spitting through gaps in their teeth.

I pressed the bell at the hotel entrance and was buzzed in. At
the reception desk a gaunt woman in a shapeless lacy dress was
arguing with a large man in a pork-pie hat.

'*Hombre*, you say you're a big businessman, but you just sit
on your fat *trasero* all day!'

'*Callate!* Shut up, woman. You don't know what you're talking
about.'

'You're fat, lazy and you've got no *cojones*. That's your trouble.
No balls!'

I wondered if this couple had ever been in love and how they got to despise each other so thoroughly.

It was late. It had been a long day and I needed a room. 'Do you have any vacancies?' I asked.

They both looked at me, then at each other. The woman sighed and snatched a key from a hook. 'Follow me,' she said.

The room she showed me was windowless and dank. There was no ceiling fan, no hot water, the walls were smeared with the contents of someone's nose and the sheets were stained with blood.

'Fine,' I said, too tired to look for anywhere else.

She threw the key on the bed and walked back towards reception and started yelling again. 'My father has more energy and initiative than you. And he's been dead twenty years!'

I wrapped myself in a tatty brown bedspread and read the letter Juanita had given me as we parted. Despite the mustiness of the bedspread, I could still smell Juanita on my clothing, still find strands of her hair on the shoulder of my jacket. Until that moment I had managed to remain positive, grateful for having found her. Now, holding her letter and staring at her photo, I felt the full force of my loss and sobbed.

I must have slept for a few hours as I woke with a start, the sheets a knot at the foot of the bed. The room was hot and airless and there was a strong smell of marijuana. I tripped over the sheets and fell head first into the door, which came open, letting in the painfully bright Caribbean sun.

'Hey la!' said a voice coming from the same direction as the smell of marijuana. 'Tree?'

As my eyes adjusted to the light, I saw a giant palm tree, its leaves scratching the roof. Then I noticed a man with shoulder-length dreadlocks, sitting under it, his legs up on a table, grinning through a cloud of smoke, holding a joint towards me.

'It's a little early, isn't it?' I asked.

'It's never too early for the Tree of Knowledge.' He cackled with laughter and held out his hand, an embroidered JAH LIVES! bracelet on his wrist. 'I'm CB, from Kingston, Jamaica. CB stands for Sea Breeze.'

I smiled. 'Nice to meet you. I got in last night from Guatemala.'

'I heard you, mon. You nah sound so happy.'

I felt no embarrassment at him having heard me cry. 'I left a girl behind there.'

CB nodded solemnly, his dreadlock beads knocking together. 'You gotta keep movin', mon,' he said, taking a final drag from the joint and flicking it over the garden wall. 'Never let your feet grow slow. Never get married. But if you do, invite me to your wedding and watch my Rasta-style dreadlock dress suit.'

I laughed, enjoying the joyful rhythm of his speech and his uncomplicated view of life. 'I wasn't planning on getting married just yet.'

'Good idea, mon. You know the word for wives in Spanish is the same as for handcuffs?'

'*Esposas*, yes,' I said, laughing again.

'I've been handcuffed, mon. It ain't no fun.' CB grinned at me. 'So tell me, why did you leave?'

'I'm on my way to Bogotá, looking for a guy who might be able to tell me where my great-grandfather worked in Mexico.' I looked up at the sun directly above us and suddenly panicked. 'What time is it?'

CB shrugged. 'Why?'

'I need to get a bus.'

'Before breakfast? Come on, Mr Mention, put your flip-flops

on, we'll have a *jugo de maracuyá*. Then I'll give you a present. Then you can go.'

I HAD been on the bus from Cartagena all afternoon and half the night when it braked hard and stopped. A rush of warm humid air filled the cabin, followed by the silhouettes of three well-built men carrying sub-machine guns. They shone torches in the passengers' faces, then one of them called to the driver to switch on the lights.

'*Señoras y señores*,' said the man who seemed to be in charge. 'Excuse the interruption to your journey. We require a few minutes of your time.' He spoke in a clear and commanding voice and, like his two colleagues, was dressed in khaki combat fatigues and webbing, from which hung pistols and hand grenades. His face was smeared with camouflage paint. An Alsatian held on a short chain leash wrapped around the man's fist sniffed at the floor.

I was the only *gringo* on the bus. Nowhere to run, nowhere to hide.

'Please take your identification documents and go and stand outside with your bags. Two lines, men by the front, women at the back.'

Were women and children to be set free, and men to be taken as hostages and marched into the jungle? It was difficult to read the expressions on the other passengers' faces as they rubbed sleep from their eyes and began to make their way off the bus. No one said anything apart from a woman comforting a crying baby. I stood up and found my passport.

When I got off I saw there was a small clearing next to the road lit by burning oil cans. Beyond, I could just make out the outline of orderly rows of coffee plants. There were another six armed men waiting for us. One of them stood behind a stack of sandbags, on which he rested a machine gun.

I looked around and whispered to the man standing next to me, 'Who are these guys?' I was praying they weren't left-wing FARC guerrillas or the right-wing *Paramilitares.*

'Did you see their boots?' he said, in a voice much louder than seemed prudent.

'*Qué?*'

'It's the army. They have laces.'

We went to stand in line at the front of the bus.

'Pablo Gutiérrez,' he said, offering his hand. 'At your service.' In the light from the bus window, he looked about forty, wore a patterned jumper and baggy trousers and had the broad grin of an eternal optimist. 'Where are you from?'

'I'm English.'

'*Ah! Qué bien! Los Beatles. El Lancaster bomber.*'

People usually mentioned Lady Di, Bobby Moore or Sherlock Holmes. Pablo, as I was to discover, wasn't like most people.

'What is the army looking for?' I asked him, nodding towards the soldier with the dog.

'Drugs and guns.'

I was suddenly very cold. My heart pounded hard against my chest. The Cartagena carrot! The six-inch spliff made from the highest-grade Colombian grass that CB had insisted on giving me as a present before I left the hotel. I had stuffed it into a side pocket and not thought any more about it.

The soldier unclipped the dog's leash and it started sniffing passengers and bags. I watched, terrified, as the dog got closer and closer to my luggage. It disappeared from view for a minute, re-materialised with its snout pushed into the side pocket of my bag. I could actually hear my heart beating. I thought blood was going to start pulsing out of my ears at any moment.

The soldier shone his flashlight in my face. '*Identificación, pasaporte, por favor.*'

I handed him my passport, sweat gathering on my brow.

He flicked through it and inspected the Colombian entry stamp. 'Where are you staying?'

I didn't have anywhere to stay and had planned to look for a hotel once I got to Bogotá.

Before I had the chance to speak, Pablo stepped forward. 'He's a friend of mine. He's staying with me.'

The soldier looked at him evenly. 'And you are?'

'My name is Pablo Gutiérrez, *señor*. I'm on my way back from an engineering conference at the university in Medellín.' He handed him his ID card and a creased piece of paper that looked like a conference invitation.

I held my breath as I watched the soldier struggle to read Pablo's documents in the poor light. The soldier's dog began to whine. I coughed and scuffed at the ground with my feet to make some noise in the hope that the soldier wouldn't hear the dog.

'*Bien,*' he said, kicking the dog away from my bag and thrusting the papers back at Pablo. 'Get on the bus.'

I had been advised against accepting drink and hospitality from strangers on buses, especially in Colombia. I had heard many horror stories in which travellers had lost all their possessions, been kidnapped or killed. There was even a story I had heard in Antigua about a bus passenger who had passed out after accepting a spiked drink. He woke up in a bath full of ice with a kidney missing.

Something told me I would be all right with Pablo, though.

Within a few minutes of climbing back aboard the bus, I had accepted a drink of *agua de canela* from his flask and agreed to stay with him when we arrived at his town on the outskirts of Bogotá in the morning.

'Are you heading down south?' he asked me.

'I'm going to Bogotá to meet someone, then I fly north to Mexico. My great-grandfather lived there.'

'And you are retracing his footsteps?'

'Yes.'

I must have looked surprised because he said, 'I have done that too. If I want to get close to someone who's gone, I go to where they've been. I used to go to places my mother loved when she was alive, but I don't do it any more.'

'Too painful?' I asked, as a juggernaut passed, its headlights dazzling us through the bus window.

'No, she comes to find me.'

'How?'

Pablo smiled. 'She was special, my mother. She was a doctor, but she was also a *bruja* – a witch.' Another one. 'She could communicate with her friends all over the country, just like anyone else, I suppose, except she didn't have to use a telephone. She was telepathic.'

'How does she . . . get in touch?'

'She sends her friends to talk to me. They find me and warn me of something if I'm in any danger, or if I'm going down the wrong path.'

I wanted to tell him I could do with that kind of help, bearing in mind I didn't know where my great-grandfather had lived. As if he had his mother's telepathic powers, he said, 'Something will guide you when the time is right.'

I didn't question what he said. I had to believe that I'd get a helping hand from someone, or something, if I was going to find anything in Mexico.

'WAIT HERE a minute,' said Pablo when we arrived at his house the following morning. 'I'll just have a word with my wife.'

He disappeared inside. I could soon hear an urgently whispered argument. I heard a woman saying 'No' quite clearly, several times.

I wondered if it might be simpler to disappear and catch a bus on to Bogotá, but something kept me rooted to the spot. The argument seemed to reach its conclusion with the woman screaming, *'No, en absoluto, no!'*

Pablo opened the door. 'Let me introduce Daisy, my wife.'

The morning sun caught her honey-coloured eyes. Her long light-brown hair was tossed over one shoulder, her arms were folded across her chest and her lips gathered into a pout.

'Mucho gusto,' I said hopefully, holding out my hand.

She was younger than I thought she would be. And more beautiful. Her pout melted into a smile. *'Encantada,'* she said. 'Pablo was just saying you are going to stay with us.'

'I really don't want to put you out,' I said.

'Don't be silly. Come in. It would be an honour. Let me get you a drink. Pablo, get his bags. Put them in our room. We can sleep with the boys.'

Pablo winked at me and I followed him to their bedroom. The room was very much of two halves. On one side of the bed was a dressing table draped in silk scarves and ribbons and covered in creams, powders and perfumes. A pink and white teddy bear was balanced on top of the mirror. On the other side of the bed was a guitar covered in Castrol Oil stickers, leaning against the wall, and Airfix models of Spitfires and

Lancaster bombers hanging on black thread from nails driven into the ceiling.

A little boy came in. He was wearing a red skateboarding helmet. 'Where are you from?' he asked.

'Hey,' said Pablo. 'Introduce yourself properly.'

The boy stuck out his hand, 'José Gutiérrez. At your service.'

I shook his hand and told him I lived in London.

'*Otro planeta!*'

'Not quite, but it is a long way away.'

'I saw the sea once.'

Pablo patted José's helmet fondly and said to me, 'Come on, I'll show you my workshop.'

He led me out of the back door into what he called his 'cave of creation'. Five men were hard at work. The workshop flashed with the white light of soldering irons and whirred with the sound of lathes and drills. 'This is what we're working on at the moment,' he said, smoothing the side of a metal box the size of a telephone kiosk, wires and circuit boards spilling from the back. The display panel at the front was full of twitching needles and blinking lights. 'It's a circuit testing device. I have to deliver this to the engineering department of Bogotá University by the weekend. *Bonito, eh?*'

In the far corner was a woman sitting in front of a typewriter. 'That's Mariela, my secretary,' said Pablo, 'Daisy's sister.'

She waved hello and carried on typing.

We walked outside into the yard, which was piled high with rusted metal skeletons that had once been 1940s Citroëns and 1960s Austins and Fords.

'This one is a real beauty,' he said, stroking the bonnet of what had been a 1970s Dodge. 'Look at her contours.' The car, now propped up on blocks, was as big as a fishing trawler and looked as though it had been left to rot in dry dock.

I didn't like to say anything, but to me it was scrap metal. To Pablo it just needed a bit of loving attention.

'This is the car we are taking on holiday,' he said.

'Where are you going?'

'To Santa Marta to see my father.'

Santa Marta was on the Caribbean, just up the coast from Cartagena. 'That's a thousand kilometres. How long will it take you?'

'Two or three days.'

'Pablo,' I said, 'it doesn't have any seats or doors. Or wheels.' He smiled brilliantly. 'It will.'

PABLO AND Daisy went to bed early, leaving me time to prepare for my interview with Gastón, whom I planned to go and find the following morning. It was a long way to go for one meeting but, as Josefina had said, one hour with Gastón could save me weeks of traipsing around Mexico. There were, after all, several dozen or several hundred small towns near Guadalajara, depending on your definition of near.

I took a VW van *colectivo* into Bogotá. Josefina had given me two addresses for Gastón, one at the university, the other at his apartment, which he shared with his sister in La Zona Rosa, a fashionable district in the north of the city. In the fax he'd sent back to Josefina he had said that he worked from home most of the time, so I decided to try his apartment first. I found it easily enough, on a residential street off a small park. I pressed the buzzer and a female voice answered almost immediately.

'*Sí?*'

'I'm looking for Gastón. I'm a friend of Josefina.'

I heard sandals slapping on concrete, several locks being unbolted and finally the door opened.

'Ah,' said a woman of about forty-five. She wore purple-framed glasses and had short unnaturally light auburn hair. 'You're here to see Gastón?'

'Yes.'

'Have you come far?'

'Guatemala.'

'Ah,' she said again. 'You had better come in.'

I followed her into a room with bookshelves from floor to ceiling and a leather-topped desk against the far wall. She disappeared for a moment, I presumed to fetch her brother, so I dug out my notebook in which I'd written the questions I had prepared. She returned carrying a bottle of orange-flavoured Postobón, a straw rising and falling with the bubbles. 'Are you in Colombia for long?' she asked.

'No. As soon as I've seen Gastón I'll fly to Mexico. I'm doing an investigation there.' I wanted to sound as businesslike as possible.

'You came to Colombia just to see my brother?'

'Yes.'

'Ah.' She took off her glasses and rubbed her eyes. 'He's not here.'

'Is he at the university?'

'He's at the University of Alberta.'

'In Canada?' I asked, horrified.

She nodded sadly. 'He went there last week. He was awarded a visiting professorship.'

'When does he return?'

'Six months.'

I HAD intended to buy a plane ticket to Mexico while I was in Bogotá, but the siesta had just begun and I couldn't face waiting for two hours for the travel agencies and airline offices to reopen and so returned to Pablo's house. When I got there I found Pablo in the backyard, eating his lunch, perched on the back bumper of a 2CV chassis. 'No luck?' he asked, taking a swig of water from a jam jar.

'All this fucking way for nothing.' I sighed.

Pablo smiled. 'A journey without problems is not worth a bag of cold rice.'

I couldn't imagine Pablo's optimism being dented by anything. 'I'll try to remember that,' I said, sitting down next to him.

'What are you going to do now?' he asked.

'I'll go to Bogotá tomorrow and try to get a flight to Mexico.'

'Why?'

'To look for evidence of the life my great –'

'I know that, but why Bogotá? Why not get a flight from Caracas?'

I laughed at the ridiculousness of the suggestion. 'Why would I travel all the way to Venezuela when I'm half an hour from Bogotá?'

Pablo tutted as he shook his head. 'No, no. Don't go to Bogotá. Caracas is much better. There are more flights and it's much cheaper.'

'But how would I get to Caracas?'

'We'll take you on the way back from Santa Marta,' he said, wiping his mouth with the back of his hand and taking another drink from the jam jar.

'You'll take me all the way to Caracas?'

'To the border. It's just a bus ride from there.'

Quite a long one. 'It seems such a long way to go.'

'You said you came all this way for nothing. Here's the reason: a short holiday. You think your great-grandfather didn't take a break every now and then?'

'I guess he must have at least travelled around Mexico to have taken all those photos.'

'*Bien!*' said Pablo, slapping me on the back. 'We set off early tomorrow morning.'

I WAS up by seven. At ten the Dodge was still in pieces on the workshop floor. At midday Mariela, Daisy's sister, turned up with her daughter Erika, a pretty sixteen-year-old in a Metallica T-shirt. I hadn't realised they were coming with us too.

During the course of the day Pablo found a bench seat for the back of the car and doors of differing colours. He then fitted a new gearbox, four mismatched tyres and poured in enough petrol to get to the nearest *gasolinera.*

By mid-afternoon the car was assembled and ready to go, but like a master chef who refuses to be hurried by the hunger of his diners, Pablo decided that the car had to have a complete respray. When it was finished he stood back, beaming at his now yellow car with pride. 'Okay,' he said. '*Vamos!*'

Pablo sat in the front with Mariela and José. In the back, Erika sat with baby Dany, Daisy in the middle. She patted the seat next to her. 'Sit here,' she said to me.

Pablo began to reverse out of the yard, but suddenly stopped. '*El baño!*'

There was a turquoise toilet on a pile of rubble, next to the shell of the 2CV. 'I promised this to my father.' With my help he strapped it to the roof of the car and, finally, with the light beginning to go, we set off.

'May God, the saints and spirits bless us all on this journey and protect us until we are home again,' said Pablo, crossing himself and kissing his fingers as we drove out of town.

An hour and a half into the journey the car spluttered to a

halt on a blind corner on a steep hill. It was pitch black outside. All the lights had gone and the engine had simply stopped.

'Shall we go back?' I asked.

Everyone roared with laughter.

'Ay, you're so funny!' said Daisy, poking my leg coquettishly.

I pretended I had meant it as a joke and got out of the car to offer support to Pablo. He emerged from beneath the bonnet, a torch between his teeth. 'Could you hold this please?' He passed me the torch and slid under the car. A truck thundered by, missing Pablo's extended feet by a matter of inches.

'Pablo, that truck nearly got you!' I shouted.

'Don't worry, they can see me. But I can't see a thing. Come down here with that torch, will you?'

I pulled myself under the car from the other direction, away from the passing traffic, and shone the torch on the underside of the engine. Pablo was humming happily to himself.

Eventually, he managed to get the sidelights working and first and third gear just about operational. It would have to do. We limped on until one in the morning, when we arrived at the mountain town of Moniquira, where we slept at a hotel on the square.

PABLO WOKE at dawn with a flash of inspiration about how he could fix the gearbox. He borrowed some welding equipment from a local garage and shortly before midday drove the car in front of the hotel, the turquoise toilet still strapped to the roof. Mariela, Daisy and Erika all cheered.

'Look at this,' he said proudly, indicating where the gear stick had once been. It had been replaced with what looked like two rusty riding stirrups. 'This one is for first and reverse, the other for second and third. Fourth would have taken too long to figure out.'

'How does it work?' I asked, thinking about how impressed my great-grandfather would have been with Pablo's ingenuity.

'Easy. You press in the clutch and push this lever for first gear. To change up, you put the first lever into neutral and push the other forward. For third, you pull it back again, making sure you don't touch the first lever, of course. That would break the engine.'

Having had several more hours sleep than Pablo, I offered to take a spell at the wheel. It was the first time I had driven a car in Latin America. Apart from getting used to a twenty-foot car on the wrong side of the road, I had to accustom myself to the Frankenstein monster that Pablo had created. It was baffling enough to watch him drive it, quite another to drive the thing myself. The steering wheel acted merely as a vague influence on the direction of the car. The accelerator was a steel pin which tended to slip between big toe and second toe and a great deal of care had to be taken with the makeshift gear sticks, which heated up with the engine and had already burnt Pablo's leg. I managed to keep the car moving and on the road long enough for Pablo to grab half an hour's sleep. When we had a puncture, I gratefully relinquished the driver's seat.

But there were advantages to travelling in Pablo's car. First of all there was no danger of missing anything because we passed it too quickly. Secondly, unlike the air-conditioned SUVs or hermetically sealed long-distance buses that passed us so frequently, we could feel the changes in temperature and the aromas from farmland to jungle, from mountain air to salty sea breeze. I liked this, but I had no choice anyway, as the windows wouldn't shut.

On the third morning after leaving Bogotá the smell of fried fish and plantain began to waft through the car.

'You smell that?' called Pablo. 'That means we're nearly there.

Who wants to go for a swim before we go to see *abuelo*?' He parked on the Santa Marta seafront, next to an electronic display board which flashed three messages in turn: the time (1.35 p.m.), the temperature (35°C) and, oddly, the altitude (1 metre above sea level).

Erika, suddenly playing the teenager, said she didn't want to go swimming and stayed in the car to look after baby Dany. The others raced down the beach to be first in the water, leaving a trail of discarded clothes behind them. I left them to it and went to call Juanita and Grandma to tell them about my change of plans.

It was the first time I had spoken to Juanita since we parted, and she cried as soon as she heard my voice. When she recovered she said, 'Be careful, remember what I said about the bald devil with the mouth full of gold.'

The line to England was crackly and Grandma's voice faint, but she was able to hear that I was okay, and I that she wasn't surprised at the time I was taking to get to Mexico. 'My father took his time too. He sailed to Veracruz when it would have been much quicker to take the train over land. When do you get to Guadalajara, love?' she asked. 'I sent you a letter there about something I found in the loft.'

'What is it?'

'Sorry?'

'What did you find in the loft?'

'Sorry, love. I can't hear you. Write to me from Mexico. Mind how you go.'

WE DROVE out of Santa Marta up to Pablo's father's *finca* in the lower reaches of the Sierra Nevada, a mountain range that plunges from 16,000 feet straight into the Caribbean Sea. As we turned off the main road and onto the sand track to his father's home Pablo told me the region was famed for its spirituality. It was where ancient tribes still lived, near the site of the Lost City, and the real-life location for Gabriel García Márquez's mythical Macondo. It was also, he said, the only place on the planet apart from the North Pole where compasses don't work. I was listening to what he was saying but kept wondering what it was that Grandma had found in the loft. Maybe I wouldn't miss Gastón's advice after all.

Pablo's father, Don Pablo, was wearing an ironed checked shirt and tracksuit bottoms. Plastic slippers dangled from his feet as he sat swinging in a hammock. It was his wife, who appeared in the garden carrying some drinks, who noticed us. '*Ay mira, el baño!*' she screamed, laughing at the turquoise toilet strapped to the roof of the car.

By the look on Don Pablo's face, he'd completely forgotten his son was going to visit, and only seemed to remember when he saw the toilet.

Don Pablo had become a widower fifteen years before and had remarried the previous year. His new wife was Gloria, a good-looking business-minded woman twenty-five years his junior. Despite not remembering Pablo was coming, and never having known that Pablo might turn up with all his family, his wife's family and a *gringo*, Don Pablo found a bed for all of us and Gloria organised lunch. 'You're all very welcome,' said Don Pablo, '*Mi casa es su casa.*'

THAT EVENING Pablo, Daisy and I walked down the sandy track to the *empanada* stands in the village. The sound of the crickets' monotone song followed us down the hill and fireflies blazed around us, leaving trails of fluorescent green light in the air.

'The local tribes used to catch fireflies to scare the Spanish *conquistadores*,' said Pablo. 'They smeared the flies over their bodies until they glowed in the dark, then jumped out at the Spanish, who'd shit themselves, thinking they'd seen a ghost.'

'Is it just tribespeople who live up there?' I asked Pablo, pointing at the mountains silhouetted beyond Don Pablo's house.

He looked awkward for a moment. 'The soil here is some of the most fertile in the world. It's where they grow *la coca*, which sometimes means trouble. A few years ago there was a major battle here between FARC, the *Paramilitares* and the army.'

'Because of *la coca*?' I asked, swatting at a mosquito.

He nodded. 'It was chaos. There were rocket launchers, helicopter gunships, troops all over. My father had to leave for a few weeks, and when he got back there were bodies everywhere and bullet holes in the walls of his house you could fit your fist through, and all his possessions gone.'

'How come?'

'Before the *Paramilitares* resumed control, there was no one here to keep order, and all the houses were looted. He managed to track down his TV though. An old man called to say he had it and wanted to trade it for a horse.'

In the village the three food stands were lit by a couple of bare light bulbs suspended from nearby trees. *Vallenato* music from a small transistor radio competed with the meatier sounds from a billiards bar close by. Men chatted in small groups, drinking bottles of Águila beer. One or two looked up as we approached but no one said anything.

'Give me a minute, will you?' said Pablo. He went to join a small circle of men at the edge of the clearing.

'*Vamos*,' said Daisy, hooking her arm in mine. 'Let's go to the bar, and I'll let you buy me a drink.'

I ordered a beer and a bottle of Postobón for Daisy and followed her to a table in the corner. I was thinking we should take our drinks and go back to where Pablo was, but she seemed in no hurry. She pulled her chair close so our knees touched and started to peel the label from the bottle.

'Are all English people like you?' she asked, resting her hand on my thigh.

I said I didn't think I was anything special.

'You know, you are the first foreigner I've ever met.'

'You've never met anyone from outside Colombia?'

'Maybe, but not from *lejos*.' Far away. 'I'm sure I'll meet others,' she said, squeezing my leg, 'but you'll always be the first.'

'You're the first Colombian I've met called Daisy,' I said. I was trying to keep the conversation on the straight and narrow. I was thinking of Juanita, and Pablo was just outside.

She smiled and took a sip from her drink, leaving a slight trace of lipstick on the bottle, and looked at me through the strands of hair that had fallen across her face.

'Come on,' I said, coming to my senses. 'Let's go and see where Pablo has got to.'

'If you say so.' Daisy pouted and slapped my bottom as I walked in front of her to open the door.

We walked back to the clearing, where Pablo was still with the same group. He was talking to a tall imposing man who wore a baseball cap with gold embroidery on the peak, like an admiral's cap. All eyes in the group were permanently turned towards him. He had a bushy black moustache. When he talked, they listened. When he laughed, they all laughed.

We were too far away to hear what they were saying but I noticed Pablo didn't look comfortable. His body language was excessively polite and respectful. I saw the man with the baseball cap nod in my direction. *I* didn't feel comfortable. Had they seen Daisy and me through the window?

Their conversation continued a few moments more, then Pablo walked towards us, putting his finger to his lips as he got close. 'Come with me,' he said.

Silently, we followed him back up the hill towards the house.

When we were out of earshot, he said, 'That was *El Jefe* of the *Paramilitares* in the area. He is the boss round here. He and his people have killed thousands over the years.'

I felt the back of my throat go very dry.

Daisy suddenly went pale. 'He killed Don Pablo's neighbours last year, didn't he?'

'I don't know, I wasn't here,' said Pablo, looking like he wanted to change the subject.

'Pablo,' I asked quietly, 'why was he pointing at me?'

'He wanted to know what you were doing here.'

'Why did he want to know?'

'He likes to know what's going on in his *barrio*. Not many *gringos* come here. He wanted to be sure you weren't with the CIA.'

I laughed.

'You don't want to know what they do to CIA agents.'

I stopped laughing. 'What did you tell him?'

'That you were a friend of the family.'

'He knows your family?'

'When my father moved here, the *Paramilitares* visited him. They asked him for a contribution. They return every now and then. It doesn't cost much, maybe thirty dollars each time, but it can be worth it. He asked if you'd had any trouble, and said if you had, he'd sort it out personally.'

Little seemed to have changed in Latin America in a century. But unlike Arturo I'd not had to leave a bag of silver in a mango tree for the bandits to offer me their protection. Don Pablo had done it for me, but it felt as though my great-grandfather was keeping a watchful eye on me, making sure I was safe in a lawless land.

THE FOLLOWING day I found myself in trouble that even the *jefe* of the *Paramilitares* couldn't sort out. My visa had expired. I'd only been given a week when I entered the country as I didn't have an onward ticket and I'd completely forgotten about renewing it on the journey to the coast. I would have to miss a day on the beach with the others, and go to the Departamento Administrativo de Seguridad immigration office to get it renewed.

The immigration office was a white-walled colonial building on the outskirts of town. The officer on duty sucked on his teeth as he looked through my passport, shaking his head as if he were a plumber assessing a broken boiler. '*Tenemos problemas.*' We have problems.

'I was unable to come earlier, *señor.* I had an upset stomach,' I lied.

'Your doctor's note?'

'I just took Pepto-Bismol for a few days and now I'm okay, but at the time my visa expired I couldn't get out of bed.' I realised how pathetic this sounded. Like saying the dog ate my homework.

The officer shook his head, a look of disappointment on his face. 'Please come this way.' He led me down the corridor to a door marked DIRECTOR. He knocked on the frosted glass and waited.

'*Pase,*' called a voice from within. The room was bright, clutter-free. A Colombian flag leaned against the wall in the corner. Behind a desk in the centre of the room was a small man in a neatly pressed white shirt with tidy greying hair and trimmed moustache. He listened attentively as his colleague explained my situation. His elbows rested on the desk with his hands in prayer position, fingertips nestling into his moustache. When the officer finished his account of my case, the director removed a fountain pen from the breast pocket and took out a blank pad of paper from the top drawer of his desk.

'You have two choices,' he said. 'You can pay a . . .' he paused slightly '. . . *fine* of 120,000 *pesos,'* – about $150 – 'or you can be deported.'

It didn't sound like a great choice.

His pen hovered over the blank paper.

How easy would it be to go through Mexico and the USA with '*Deportado de Colombia*' stamped in my passport? I could always 'lose' my documents, but that might well cost more.

As I was thinking, the director and his colleague were still looking at me, waiting for an answer. If I opted for deportation, I'd get a free ride to the Venezuelan border, which would save me money. My funds were running low and I was buggered if I was going to pay $150 for overstaying my visa by a few days. On the other hand, if I got deported I might have to spend a night in a Colombian prison, in which case I might very well be buggered.

Then I realised I didn't have the money. I had lent Pablo most of my cash so he could pay for car repairs. I couldn't pay a bribe in traveller's cheques or with a credit card. I would have to buy some time.

'I don't have any money with me,' I said.

The director looked slightly surprised. 'You have one hour. If you're not back in that time, we will send someone to arrest you, and you will be deported immediately.'

I had one hour to find Pablo.

I ran into the street and tried to flag down a taxi. Three sped by. The fourth stopped. He already had another passenger, a sailor on his way back to his ship.

'*Pagaré doble.*' I said. I'll pay double.

'Okay,' said the driver.

The sailor shrugged and moved over for me to get in. He was obviously not in too much of a hurry to get back to his ship.

'*Rápido!*' I said to the driver.

He pressed his foot to the floor, his hand permanently against the horn. Weaving in and out of traffic, he mounted the grass verge, shouting at street-side vendors to get out of the way, drove on the wrong side of the road and straight over a roundabout. The sailor was holding on to his hat, looking like he regretted his decision.

We turned into the sand track leading up to Don Pablo's house and skidded to a halt in a cloud of dust in front of Pablo, who was loading the car for the day at the beach. It had taken me half an hour to get to the immigration office that morning. The journey back to the house took twelve minutes. If I had arrived thirty seconds later, I would have missed them.

'Oh good, you're coming to the beach,' said José from the back of the car, where he was sitting with Erika and Daisy.

When I explained my predicament to Pablo he was momentarily at a loss for what to do. Then with a bright smile he said, 'Hop in.'

'*No te preocupes,*' said Daisy, patting my leg as I got in. 'Don't worry, we'll sort it out.'

We drove to the clothes store Don Pablo's wife ran in the town centre. When Pablo told his stepmother what had happened, Gloria got in the car and directed us to the town hall, where she said she *knew* someone. From the look on Pablo's face, I wondered if this someone was an ex-lover of hers.

Whoever he was, he wasn't there.

'*No importa*,' said Pablo as we drove on. 'Plan B.' He didn't say what this was, although the rest of the family seemed to guess instinctively.

He parked the battered yellow car down the street from the immigration office and Gloria, Daisy, Erika and Mariela went to work, shortening their skirts, lowering their necklines and applying dabs of make-up. They then slunk into the foreign nationals' section, leaving Pablo and me to look after baby Dany and explain to José why we weren't on our way to build sand-castles.

Fifteen minutes later they walked out of the immigration office, shimmying like a line of chorus girls. Daisy was flushed with excitement. 'We told the director that only a powerful yet compassionate man like him could forgive your slight, careless, foolish contravention of a teeny-weeny rule.'

'He couldn't keep his eyes off your legs!' Mariela said to her. 'Or your breasts!'

Until they came out of the office I hadn't realised how nervous I'd been. It had been like waiting to hear a judge's verdict. I had been found not guilty and I hugged them all.

Pablo drove us past the port and up a winding, cliff-top road. We stopped to buy fish, bottles of beer and Postobón, and drove on to a beach which we shared only with a pair of pelicans. Daisy and Mariela lit a fire and began to cook the fish, Erika played with the boys and Pablo and I talked.

'What would have happened if I had turned up at your house after you'd gone to the beach?' I asked him.

'You didn't.'

'But what would have happened if I had?'

'Some things are meant to be. You don't question it; you just accept it. One of my mother's friends came to find me the other day and told me that my mother has been reincarnated as the daughter of my eldest sister, Blanca.'

'You believe that?'

'It makes sense. My mother and Blanca were always fighting. They were too similar, you see. According to my mother's friend,' he said, pointing to the heavens, '*el Señor* sent my mother back and will continue to do so until she and my sister resolve their differences.'

I nodded.

'Did you ever wonder why you feel *obligado* to go to Mexico?'

'I've always felt there would be something there for me to find. I don't know what. It's just a feeling.'

'Maybe you are your ancestor reincarnated. Maybe there was something he didn't resolve in his lifetime.'

I shrugged. 'Perhaps.'

'Some people are called and don't follow the path that has been preordained for them. To do that is to deny destiny. But you are following your path. You may find nothing, but you are responding to the call.'

PABLO HAD originally said we would be at his father's for a few days only. A few days became a week, and one week, two. I didn't complain. Every day we drove to a different beach or inland lagoon. We would swim, play frisbee, ride driftwood into the sea, build *castillos* in the sand. I'd play tag with José and Daisy and Erika. Pablo would talk with me about his mother and the spirits, or with Mariela about work. Every day we'd drink beer and eat barbecued fish until the mosquitoes came out and then make our way back in the dark, forgetting we had no headlights.

The night before we were due to leave for the Venezuelan border Pablo had another idea: to go to Cabo de la Vela on the Guajira peninsula. 'It's on the way to the border,' he said, then added *'mas o menos.'* More or less.

WE SET off two hours before sunrise. Neither Don Pablo nor Gloria was up to wave us off. Pablo deliberately hadn't told them when we were going. That way, he avoided saying goodbye.

'The Guajira people are *especial*,' said Pablo as we drove off. The rest of the family were sleeping. Daisy's head was against my shoulder. 'They're tribal, desert traders who protect their own fiercely. A few months ago several Guajira men were arrested in Riohacha. A group of their friends went to the police to demand their release. When the police refused, the group threw rocks at the jail wall until it collapsed, and all the prisoners walked free.' Pablo looked at me in the rear-view mirror and chuckled. 'We do things differently here in Colombia.'

'One of the things the Guajira are famous for,' continued Pablo, 'is their memory. There are stories about people who have killed someone returning twenty or thirty years after the event and being gunned down in the street immediately. They never forget a face. I've heard some of the Indians in Mexico are the same. Maybe that's why your great-grandfather never went back.' Pablo laughed. 'Maybe he did something *malo!*'

We stopped in Riohacha, the last town of any note on the road east, and bought bottles of water, mangos and a pineapple. The landscape became more arid and scrubby, the heat more intense, the road less passable. When we arrived in a small settlement of mud shacks in the late afternoon, the track simply ceased to exist.

'*Ay caray!*' said Pablo. He clunked the car into reverse and stopped by a rusted water pump. 'There must be someone we can ask for directions.'

We looked around but could see no one. Tumbleweed rolled in between the wattle huts and wind began to whistle through the car.

'This place is creepy,' said Erika.

Pablo turned the car round. The sun was creeping closer and closer to the horizon and I was beginning to prepare myself for sleeping in a wind-buffeted car on the edge of the Guajira desert.

'Over there!' said Erika, pointing at three willowy figures dressed in dark brown robes. They wore hoods to protect themselves from the sandstorm blowing around them.

'*Son brujas,*' said José. They're witches.

They started walking slowly towards us.

'*Vámonos!*' screamed Erika.

Pablo drove slowly towards them.

'Pablo,' pleaded Erika, 'let's get out of here.' Although I could tell from her tone she didn't expect him to.

He stopped the car a couple of yards from the robed figures. Only their eyes were immediately visible, but they soon let their hoods drop to reveal gentle smiles and a slight inclination of the head to suggest a greeting. When we asked if they wanted a lift, they climbed in the car, their sackcloth robes rustling as they fitted themselves in between Daisy and Erika. They didn't speak any Spanish but directed us by pointing with their rough hands. After fifteen minutes, we let them out at a fork in the track.

The road they guided us to would barely constitute a bridleway in England, but after the hard-packed, rutted mud tracks we had been travelling on for the previous few hours it seemed as smooth and wide as an autobahn. It did indeed feel like we had found civilisation: three cars passed us in the first five minutes. A fourth, a jeep full of men holding on to a metal rail in the back, sped towards us. It flashed its lights and the driver gave us a thumbs up. We waved and smiled back. As it passed, there was an explosion and our windscreen shattered. Glass caved in all over Dany, who was on Mariela's lap in the front seat. The rubber seal flailed in the wind, sending the remaining fragments of glass flying in every direction.

'Pablo, stop!' yelled Erika, but he carried on driving.

I shut my eyes and ducked down to protect myself from flying glass. After about a minute I felt the car slow down and come to a halt.

'I didn't stop,' said Pablo, 'because they were going to rob us. If they'd seen us slowing down, they would have realised we'd been hit. They would have turned round, caught up with us and *bam*! He fired an imaginary pistol.

Erika still seemed upset. 'They wouldn't have realised we were slowing down. The brake lights don't work.'

We quickly removed the rubber seal and swept the shards out of the car. It was almost dark now and we were in the middle of nowhere, without a windscreen. I lent Pablo my sunglasses. Although they protected his eyes from the dust, they also screened out all the remaining light from the sun, but Pablo felt this was the lesser of two evils. With the rest of us covered with blankets, we continued slowly, arriving in Cabo de la Vela at 8 p.m., an hour and a half after darkness had set in.

I WAS woken around dawn by a morning chorus of cockerels, dogs, the piercing yelps of children playing and the retching and spitting of the hotel owner. This symphony of noises ceased as soon as I was fully awake and could sleep no longer. Then silence.

Cabo de la Vela means 'end of the candle' and at first light it became fairly obvious how it had got its name. There was nothing there apart from walls painted with political slogans or Coca-Cola advertising, a few bare concrete buildings and a strong smell of fish. We stayed in a breeze-block building that had 'hoTeL' written on the underside of what looked like a cinema seat leaning against its wall. It was the first place we'd been where Pablo had been able to park his car without fear of bringing down the tone of the neighbourhood.

Tired from the journey, I was not feeling well disposed to Cabo de la Vela. I couldn't believe we'd spent sixteen hours on a hazardous journey to arrive at a place where the dogs outnumbered the people and the day's entertainment appeared to be turning on the generator to light a shop that sold a few tubes of toothpaste and tins of what looked like spam.

It was only when I had walked round the back of the hotel that I saw that, as well as being on the edge of a bleak dry desert, the town was also on the edge of the Caribbean Sea. The water lapped gently against a white powder beach. I kicked off my sandals and waded in, crunching the occasional mussel shell underfoot. Tiny fish tickled my ankles as they nibbled at weeping mosquito bites. Up to my waist now, I looked up at a pelican circling noiselessly above me, then back at the beach, where a couple of men were righting an upturned fishing boat. Once it was the right way up, they fitted an outboard motor and threw in some nets and eased it into the water. I floated on my back, buffeted gently by waves bobbling over me, until the trill of the boat's motor cut through the ocean's silence and I waded my way back to the beach.

Pablo soon joined me, looking well rested and re-imbued with enthusiasm. '*Buenos días*. Are you ready for a trip to the end of the world?'

I found it difficult to believe that there was any place more desolate and remote than Cabo de la Vela, but apparently there was. Just one.

El fin del mundo – or Punta Gallinas – is the most northerly point of South America. To get there, you have to cross a desert.

'Pablo, there are no roads,' said Daisy.

'Exactly!' he said as we set off, with the accelerator pressed to the floor to avoid the car sinking into the sand. The car took off on several occasions, producing metal-twisting groans each time it hit the ground. I wondered how long Pablo's long-suffering vehicle would last. The answer was, not long. He accelerated down a hill and up another. We took off and landed heavily one time too many, and despite the revving engine, the car came to a halt and filled with sand and dust.

'Oh shet!' said Pablo, who'd still not quite got the hang of the expletive I'd tried to teach him. We looked under the bonnet. The fan belt had snapped. Even I knew this was more serious than normal, especially considering we were hidden behind a dune in the middle of a desert.

Pablo rooted around in the boot and came back smiling. He had two new fan belts in his hand. The only problem was that they were made for a completely different engine: the belts were three inches too long.

Daisy looked annoyed. She had thought – as we all had – that trying to cross the desert was lunacy but had – again like all of us – been browbeaten by Pablo's enthusiasm.

'Penknife please,' he called from the front of the car. It was the only tool we had with us. He opened each blade and considered the options. His optimism never ceased to amaze me. For him a mechanical disaster was a puzzle to be solved. After a bit of experimenting, he discovered that the bottle-opener blade fitted the nuts that held the transmission in place. He explained what he intended to do in the way Hercule Poirot might summarise the motives of the principal murder suspects in an Agatha Christie novel. He unfastened four nuts and turned the casing upside down so the wheel that drove the fan belt was three inches higher and pulled tight against the belt that had been too long. The whole operation took only ten minutes.

Pablo stood back and looked at it for a second, then asked Daisy to turn the engine over. The third time she tried, it caught, and we held our breath as we watched the new fan belt – probably designed for the tank Pablo believed his car to be – drive the wheel that turned another wheel that drove the fan.

We continued, at a slightly slower pace, and after another half-hour arrived at a hook-shaped spit of jagged rock. And beyond it there was just blue. The Caribbean Sea joined the sky imperceptibly at the horizon to form a perfect vignette of every shade from turquoise to sapphire. There was nothing else. No shops, no dogs, no litter, no buildings; no sign that humans had ever walked the earth.

We climbed the rocks and took photographs. It felt like a significant moment. Here I was at the edge of the continent, staring north into the blue abyss. It seemed to stretch into infinity, offering endless possibilities. Somewhere beyond that blue was the place I was heading for. Mexico. In a few days I'd finally be there. It was time to move on.

THAT NIGHT was our last before they dropped me at the border. We made a bonfire on the beach at the back of the hotel with an Argentinian couple who had ridden a motorbike all the way from Tierra del Fuego. It had taken them three months to get from the most southerly tip of the continent, and they had arrived in

Punta Gallinas a few hours after us. They were now sitting round the fire, celebrating, swapping stories and passing bottles of rum and *aguardiente.*

After a good few swigs of rum, Pablo began to speak to me in pidgin English. 'Somethin' I tell you.'

'Yes?'

'I in love with woman who no is my wife.' He looked at me, his expression a mixture of bashfulness and pride.

'Let's go for a walk,' I said.

As I helped him up he said, 'And you know her.'

I couldn't think of anyone I knew with whom Pablo could be in love. The only people he had introduced me to were members of his and Daisy's families.

'It's Mariela,' he said sheepishly. He looked at me, his eyes bloodshot and sad. '*Qué hago?*' he asked, switching into Spanish. What shall I do?

I asked him how it had happened and how far it had progressed. It turned out to be little more than a crush, but he felt burdened with guilt for having feelings for his sister-in-law. 'I spend more waking hours with Mariela than I do with Daisy. She understands my work and takes an interest in what I do.'

'She's your secretary.'

'But I can talk to her about anything. Daisy never has the time. Mariela looks after me, makes sure I have something to eat when I'm working late at night.'

'Mariela doesn't have two young children to care for.'

'No,' he said sadly.

'Do you really want to leave Daisy?'

Pablo didn't answer but looked at me with a steely seriousness I hadn't yet seen. 'I know Daisy is attracted to you.'

I fought the urge to swallow, said nothing and held eye contact with him, suddenly conscious of my heart beating loudly in my chest. Nothing had gone on, but I didn't want to give him any cause to suspect that it had.

'It was a great risk to introduce you into the family. My dad's friends thought I was *loco* to let my young wife spend so much time alone with you. She is beautiful, isn't she?'

I nodded, hoping that admitting to Daisy's beauty would not be seen as an admission of guilt. But where was this going? Our eyes were still locked, my heart still pounding.

'You had nothing and I had everything to lose.' A moment passed, as if he were waiting for something to be confirmed. 'But I trusted my instincts, which told me you would be a loyal friend and could be trusted.'

He slapped me on the back and we walked back to the bonfire. I needed a drink.

The following morning, as we packed up ready to leave, Pablo called to me, 'Last night I thought a lot about what we discussed.' And then in English added, 'I love my wife!'

AT THE first town we came to on our way towards the Venezuelan border, we stopped to buy a windscreen, a fan belt and a new back tyre, which had finally worn through and exploded a few minutes before. We were now like a pit-stop crew. Everybody knew what they had to do.

I jacked up the car, and once I had removed the wheel, José handed me the hammer. The brake discs had jammed and Pablo had taught me how to release them by hitting them until they sprang back into position, and then spray them with Daisy's coconut moisturising lotion.

Having finished that, I was seconded to help Daisy look for wire, which was needed to unblock a tube in the depths of the

the Mersey, surrounded by tugs pushing and pulling it towards its berth. As it got closer, I could see the decks were full of passengers waving at their families on the quayside. My mother suddenly starting waving frantically. 'Look, look! There he is!' I looked but couldn't make out who she was pointing at as I didn't know what my father looked like.

Slowly, the Lusitania *came towards the quay. The four funnels were bigger than any factory chimney and the sides of the ship soared high up into the sky, like the walls of a fortress.*

We waited and we waited. Express men started to load luggage onto carts and passengers began to come through the customs hall. My mother was trying to occupy us by getting us to count the flags stretched between the masts. We seemed to have been waiting for hours when a man walked towards us carrying a brown suitcase. 'Hello, hello!' he said. My mother hugged him and began to cry. Then the man bent down and hugged my sister and me. 'I'm your father,' he said. His face was darkened by the sun, he had big light-green eyes, a wide moustache, and I remember thinking he was handsome and that he smelled of cigars and coffee. I gave him the bunch of flowers I had picked for him. 'Thank you, preciosa,*' he said, 'and I have something for you.' He took a card from his coat pocket and handed it to me. It was a menu from the* Lusitania, *printed in gold leaf and signed by the captain.*

In most towns in most countries in Latin America there are hotels that charge by the hour and are known affectionately as *hoteles del amor.* They are usually cosy places for husbands and wives to escape the extended family and enjoy a little privacy or, perhaps more often, to escape each other and enjoy a little privacy with someone else.

This was not one of those places. The walls of the hotel entrance were covered in wood-patterned Formica and lined with plant pots containing plastic ferns and orchids. Next to the reception desk was a tawdry drawing room in which four women in leather miniskirts sat on pink fluffy cushions smoking cigarettes. They were watching *telenovelas* on an old TV whose tube had nearly gone, turning all the flickering images garish shades of green.

The receptionist had a small gold crucifix round her neck which stuck to her skin as she leaned forward.

I asked her if I could have a room.

She glanced at my shirt and shorts, soiled by baby Dany. '*Sí, mi amor.* Are you on your own? Would you like some . . . company?'

I longed for some company. I missed Juanita. 'No, thank you.'

She led me to a concrete courtyard at the back of the building, through a sliding door, to what looked like a long garden shed. It was sectioned off into ten rooms and covered with a corrugated-iron roof. I wondered how often hotel guests checked in without the added 'room extra' of a prostitute. I wondered too how many guests arrived covered in baby poo.

As I held my soiled clothing under a tap, I felt my first pang of real loneliness since watching Pablo's yellow car weave out of town. I changed and went out to get something to eat. The restaurant had bright strip lights and no menu. I asked what there was to eat. *Pescado* or *carne.* I ordered the fish, which had the taste and consistency of carpet. As I ate, I wondered what Arturo might have recognised of my surroundings. Would the inns he stayed in have offered room extras? And if they did, would he have been tempted?

When I got back to the hotel, a party was taking place next door. The loud music, drunken singing and laughter from the other side of the wall competed with whores' gasps and screams from the adjacent rooms. As if to confirm my solitude, everyone within ten yards of me was drinking or having sex. At that moment I understood why men resort to prostitution: a quick fix for loneliness. But the one working girl still sitting in reception when I came in hardly constituted a temptation. She looked as if she had got drunk before she put her make-up on and then got lost on the way to the bingo.

I shoved earplugs into my ears as far as they would go and lay down on my bed. I tried to imagine where Pablo and Daisy would be. I looked at my watch. It was eleven. By now they'd be somewhere in the highlands, still with no headlights. I pictured Pablo driving as the others slept, coaxing the yellow car up mountain passes with two gear sticks and three gears. Maybe he'd be humming *Los Beatles* to himself. I drifted off and began to dream. Pablo's yellow car became the Yellow Submarine being pursued by the Blue Meanies, led by the paramilitary chief. Pablo (or was it Ringo?) lost control of the submarine and it knocked into the sides of the ocean. Bang, bang, bang, then CRACK!

Gunfire. I sat bolt upright in bed, dazed but fully awake. I pulled out my earplugs but could still hear my heart beating and feel blood pulsing in the roof of my mouth. Another volley of shots snapped and ricocheted. There was a scream, then the music stopped. There was another shot, immediately followed by a crashing thud as a deadweight landed on the metal roof over my head. I listened in the dark to the scraping of tables and chairs, urgent whispers, footsteps, a door slam. And then silence.

I was afraid to move in case the bed creaked and attracted attention. I imagined a heavy boot kicking open my door and a pistol being levelled at my head. After an hour my door remained closed and I had heard nothing more than dogs barking. Tiredness took hold and once again I slept.

*   *   *

When I woke up the following morning, two urgent thoughts competed for my attention. Firstly, I was in a brothel with a body on my roof. Secondly, I couldn't move. My back, which had been giving me the odd twinge, had completely seized up. The muscles were in spasm and even the smallest movement sent a jolt of pain down my spine. I tried to roll onto my side. Agony. I tried sitting up. Worse.

While I was lying there, unable to move, I remembered Arturo had a reputation for being able to ease aches and pains. According to Grandma, he used Golden Ointment to cure everything from bruises to rheumatism. In the absence of that, what would he have recommended? Gingerly, I reached under the bed, feeling for my medical bag. I found painkillers, anti-inflammatory pills and some Deep Heat cream. I swallowed the pills, rubbed in the cream and waited. Partly out of necessity and partly to distract myself, I read what my guidebook said about the nearby border town of Maicao. It made grim reading. It cautioned against using the crossing if at all possible, and at all costs after dusk.

An hour and a half later, just before checkout time, I was on my feet, even if not quite upright. I slowly made my way out of the hotel and caught a taxi to the bus station.

Maicao didn't so much come into view as appear by degrees to confirm my fears. The town was every bit as seedy as the guidebook had described. It looked like all its colour had been bleached out by the sun. The streets were unpaved and the shops had no windows. Scrawny dogs nosed lazily through piles of refuse. Men stood on street corners, chewing slowly, waiting impassively behind black sunglasses.

There were no people left on the bus by the time we arrived at Maicao. Not even the bus driver wanted to be there. He had no passengers for the return journey, but he didn't seem to care.

As soon as he had fished out my bags from the hold, he jumped behind the wheel, beeped his horn for the razor-wire-topped gates to be opened, and he was off.

There was hardly anyone to ask about buses to the border, but the elderly man I found, wearing a vest and flip-flops, told me to look for a hardware store from where cars left for the Venezuelan city of Maracaibo.

I walked out of the station to look for the store. Dogs, they say, only bite people who show their fear. I tried to walk with a self-assured swagger, but with the pain in my back it was probably more of an old man's shuffle.

A spotty boy with a smudge of a moustache asked me what I was looking for. He wasn't asking to be friendly.

'I want a car to go to the border,' I said flatly.

'*No hay*. All the cars have left for the day.'

I thought he might say this. No cars might mean a *gringo* would pay a high price to get one. I continued walking.

He called after me. 'Maybe I can find one, *jefe*.'

I turned round to look at him. I had no strength or patience to play games. 'Listen,' I said, 'I want to be in the next car to the border and I want to change 300,000 Colombian pesos.' I had nowhere near 300,000 pesos, but I hoped that by saying I did he would lead me to someone who controlled cars as well as the money changing.

'This way.' He took me the last half-block to the hardware store. Coils of electrical cable, metal chains and blue nylon rope hung from a beam above the door. Filling every inch of the door frame was a towering man flicking through a wad of banknotes. The spotty boy spoke to him with machine-gun rapidity, too fast for me to catch. The only word I understood was *plata*, meaning silver. Slang for cash.

The big man – he was a good head taller than me – stepped down onto the street. 'You have some money to change,' he growled. It was a statement rather than a question.

A red Buick pulled up. Two men in dark glasses wearing chunky gold rings, watches and medallions walked past me and climbed in. They looked like caricature pimps, but I decided I would take my chances with them rather than risk a night in Maicao. 'Are you going to the border?' I asked.

'*Vamos a Maracaibo,*' one said.

'How much?' I asked, turning to the big man. He gave me what sounded like a fair price and I handed him the cash.

'And the money you wanted to change?' he said, flicking through the banknotes again. 'My friend said you had 300,000 pesos to change. I'll give you a good price.'

'Your friend got it wrong. I have thirty dollars.' I handed him a ten- and twenty-dollar bill.

He snatched them from my hand and shot an angry look at the boy. He thrust the notes into his pocket, threw a fistful of Venezuelan *bolivares* at me. '*Vete!*' Go!

The driver slammed the Buick into gear and in ten minutes we had reached the border. The Colombian exit post was a brick hut with blacked-out windows. I could hear salsa playing on a transistor radio inside but couldn't see anyone. A hand reached out from under the window and took my passport, stamped it and pointed at the Venezuelan border post across a rutted, baked mud track.

A Venezuelan customs officer strutted towards us, waving a stick at the car. 'Open it.'

The driver got out and opened the boot with a screwdriver.

The customs official pointed at my bags. 'Take those into the office.'

As I lifted them out, a shock of pain shot through my back and I let out an involuntary cry. 'Aagghh!'

The customs man pointed and said again, '*La oficina*.'

I dragged my bags and heaved them onto the table.

'Open,' he said.

I unzipped and unclipped my bags. He poked at my clothes with his stick and pulled a T-shirt out. A cassette fell onto the desk. I suddenly remembered I still had CB's Cartagena carrot. Fuck, fuck, fuck.

The customs man picked up the cassette. 'Ah bien, *Los Beatles!*' He smiled and wished me a good journey.

AFTER TWO hours of scrub and arid landscape punctuated only by occasional bamboo-and-plastic-sheeting settlements, Maracaibo shone like a neon-scarred American city. It was criss-crossed with an intricate lattice of ring roads, flyovers and underpasses, and dotted with pizza parlours, furniture shops and floodlit car lots. As soon as we hit the urban sprawl, it was obvious that Venezuela was quite distinct from Colombia, its neighbour to the west. There was an atmosphere of decaying extravagance in Venezuela, not from the colonial era but from the oil booms of the 1970s and 80s. Most of the cars were big American luxury models that would have been the pride of any home twenty years before. Now they were rusting hulks, often with rags where the petrol cap had been, that pumped out thick black smoke like rural taxis.

AFTER ANOTHER day's travel, I stopped for a couple of nights in the town of Coro, which is halfway to Caracas. Although pretty enough, there was nothing about Coro that particularly enticed me to stay, but my back was hurting and it was getting no better being bounced around in buses. I decided a day's rest would help. It was something to look forward to: I would lie on my bed and do some writing.

The sound of a pneumatic drill on the balcony outside my room early in the morning put paid to that idea. The hotel was being refurbished and I was going to have to find somewhere else to spend my day.

I found a bench in Plaza Bolivar, a small wooded park in front of the cathedral. Only a few minutes after I got there an unkempt figure in grubby jeans and soldiers' boots popped up from behind some shrubs.

'I've got a son in New York,' he said in English, 'and I've got a horse and a wife, and I prefer the horse.' He began to scratch himself all over, then said, 'Yes sir!' and ambled off.

A few minutes later a toothless man in a frayed straw hat tried to sell me lottery tickets.

'But these are out of date,' I said. 'They're from last year.'

'Ah, but you never know your luck.'

Another man tried to get me to buy an old egg whisk, and others offered me pornographic playing cards, a cage of budgerigars and an Action Man, complete with parachute. Others merely came by to say hello and tell me about their day. I had no idea Venezuelans were so friendly.

I was beginning to wonder whether writing to the accompaniment of a pneumatic drill might be preferable to constantly fending off the inquisitive and the unhinged when I was approached by a kind-faced man whose daytime occupation seemed to be selling coffee off the back of a supermarket trolley.

'*Buenos días,*' he said, as he sat down next to me, '*Quien es su salvador?*' Who is your saviour?

I didn't get a chance to reply because, apparently, he had the only saviour there was and was keen to tell me all about Him. The coffee salesman wore a navy-blue baseball cap and had a sun-baked hairless face apart from some sparse stubble on his chin. A few people, including some who had previously come to talk to me, gathered to observe us, watching my reaction.

His rhetoric was reaching its crescendo when a drop of sweat mixed with sun cream dripped into my eye. 'Aagghh!' I shouted. It stung like hell. Tears rolled down my cheek.

The coffee salesman put a fatherly hand on my shoulder. 'You will see, my friend.'

'It's okay, I can see.'

'*Milagro!*' yelled someone from the crowd. 'It's a miracle!'

'He can see!'

'It was just sun cream,' I insisted, but I couldn't convince anyone that the coffee salesman hadn't just got himself a conversion.

When my vision had cleared enough for me to leave, I turned back at the park gate to see a posse gathered round the coffee salesman, who was holding his hands to his eyes and reenacting the whole encounter. He looked very pleased with himself.

BOTH IN Coro and on the onward journey to the capital people warned me that Caracas bus station was thick with thieves. 'They take anything and take it quickly, take it without you noticing.'

I stepped down from the bus, and could only have been on Caracas soil for ten seconds when I felt someone going through my pockets. I spun round and was met by a sea of blank stares from innocent-looking faces.

It was past midnight and, keen to get out of the station as soon as possible, I jumped in the first taxi I saw and threw my bags onto the back seat, which was as wide as a three-seater sofa and covered with a leopardskin print.

'*Chicas?*' the driver asked me. I could only see the grey stubble on his thick neck and the deep shadows under his eyes in the rear-view mirror.

'Just a hotel, thanks.' I gave him the name of a hotel my guide-book recommended.

'*Hotel con chicas?*'

'No, really. Just a hotel.' He shrugged and drove at speed, weaving in and out of the traffic. Caracas shone more brightly than any city I had been in since New York. I looked out at the skyscrapers and shopping malls, illuminated logos for Coca-Cola, Pizza Hut and Levis.

When we arrived at the hotel, I paid the driver and asked him to wait while I checked it out. Fearing he wouldn't, I took my bags with me. Sure enough, when I returned to be taken to another hotel, he had disappeared. I waited for another taxi for ten minutes before a car with dragster wheels and flames painted down the side screeched to a halt across the street. Fairy lights in the back window had been fashioned into the shape of a Christmas tree. They flashed in time with the heavy bass beat of salsa music, loud enough to register on the Richter scale.

'Hey man!' the young driver shouted in English. His eyes were giddy with drink. 'What you doin'?'

I was looking for a taxi to take me to another hotel, but I decided not to tell him, fearing he would offer to take me there himself. I had no desire to get into a car the size of a whale driven by a drunken teenager.

'I'm going in here,' I said, pointing to the hotel I had just walked out of in disgust.

'Come on, man. Let's go party!'

I heard a chorus of whooping voices from the back of the car and realised I needed to get away before I became a party accessory.

The car was beginning to cross to my side of the road. Trying to look purposeful, I bent down to pick up my bags. A spasm shot down my back and into my legs. Attempting to ignore the pain and still hunched forward, I dragged my bags back up the stairs to the hotel reception.

'I've decided I'll take the room after all.'

Cigarette smoke shot out from the manager's nostrils like a cartoon bull. 'You pay in advance.'

I paid and he slid the room key across to me with a look of supreme indifference.

It was the most awful hotel room I had ever seen. The dimly lit corridor leading to it had a foul odour. There was no window and the only light came from a forty-watt ceiling bulb that had been partially painted blue. Ash from several mosquito coils dusted the bedside table. There was a used condom in the bed and included in the numerous pieces of graffiti written in black marker on the headboard of the plastic bed frame was '*Anda y jode tu madre.*' Go and fuck your mother.

I lay down on the edge of the bed, reached into my bag and pulled out all the bits of paper I had on Arturo. I wanted to double-check that I really had seen all the clues, so I looked through the records I had found in New York. His first arrival in 1898, Mariah's arrival three years later, Arturo's second voyage out in 1905, and in 1910 the final trip home on the *Lusitania*.

Then I noticed something.

I had misread the manifest. On 11 November 1910 Arturo was not returning to Liverpool from New York. He was arriving in New York from Liverpool, en route to Mexico.

Why would he be going to Mexico just before the outbreak of the Mexican Revolution? And when had he finally returned home?

I stared up at the mosquitoes circling the painted light bulb. What was it that had drawn Arturo and now me to Mexico? I thought back to the comfortable life I had left behind in London. There had been times when I had harangued staff in five-star hotels over the lack of a complimentary bathrobe or a less-than-perfect trouser press. I wondered what my former colleagues would have made of my present lodgings. As the saying goes, you don't know what you've got until you lose it. In my case, I had to lose what I had in order to find what I wanted, even if I still didn't really know what that was. *'Throw your shit away and start living,'* as the graffiti had said on the pier in New York. The next day I would fly north to Mexico. I was one step closer to finding what I was looking for. One step closer to home.

THE NEXT morning I made my way to the airline offices. I had my bags with me, hoping to go directly to Simón Bolívar International Airport. The first office quoted me prices for flights from Caracas that were three times the price they had been in Colombia. The next three were even more expensive.

The final office I came to was that of a Colombian airline. A girl in a yellow bikini smiled from a giant VISIT COLOMBIA poster stuck to the window.

'I'm trying to get to Mexico,' I told the woman at the sales desk.

She seemed to recognise that I hadn't had a great morning. 'Sit down. I'll see what I can do.' She was pretty, in her thirties and had her hair pulled into a bun held in place with a Bic biro. She handed me a cup of ice-cold water and began tapping into her computer.

After a few minutes she wrote a flight number and a very low price on a piece of paper. 'There's just one thing,' she said, wincing. 'It doesn't leave from Caracas.'

Two days later, after forty-eight hours of solid travel, I boarded my flight to Mexico from Cartagena in Colombia.

Absolute Morality and Moderate Prices

Did I tell you about Arturo's first night in Mexico, when he stayed at the Imperial, the grandest hotel in the country?

At the entrance was a notice: NO COMEDIANS. NO BULL-FIGHTERS. Uniformed men in white gloves helped him down from the back of the taxi cart and carried his suitcase to his room, which had an electric ceiling fan and a four-poster bed carved with the family crest of a Spanish nobleman who had once stayed there. From his balcony he could smell the orange and lemon blossom and hear the guitar band that played by the fountain in the evening when families gathered in the plaza. The men wore suits and palm-leaf sombreros; the women wore long skirts and shawls.

Arturo went for a walk and was immediately surrounded by men selling the most outlandish fruit. Prickly pears the size of a small child and the aptly named dragon's eyeball. Some were small and star-shaped, others long and spiky. The fruit that most fascinated him was yellow, sausage-shaped and sold in bunches. He had never seen bananas before.

Veracruz was where your great-grandfather fell in love with the romance of Mexico. He loved the whitewashed, flat-roofed houses and the patios full of birdsong and pointy-leaved tropical trees. He saw young men waiting for hours outside their sweethearts' homes. Sometimes they sang or recited poetry but usually they just waited until they caught a glimpse of their beloved. And then they returned, satisfied, to their homes.

Leafing through the in-flight magazine on the late-night flight from Cartagena, I found an article about the hotel where Arturo spent his first night in Mexico. According to the piece, the Imperial had been celebrities' hotel of choice in the late nineteenth and early twentieth centuries. Past guests included three Mexican presidents. Their advertising at the time promised, as well as luxury, 'Absolute Morality and Moderate Prices!' There was a picture of the hotel as Arturo would have seen it. The facade was white, the hotel name painted evenly on the guttering, and CANTINA – CAFE – HOTEL – RESTAURANT – BAÑOS printed above the entrance. Obviously guests were expected to be clean.

Two flights and one taxi ride later I stood in the main square of Veracruz, staring at the same hotel. I took a swig of warm water from the bottle I had been unable to drink from during the lurching potholed drive into town and looked around the square. The fountain was well shaded by high palm trees, their trunks painted white. On a stone bench two old men, their string vests visible through their shirts, were playing draughts. The board was a ripped box lid with checks drawn in green pen, the pieces beer-bottle tops.

The hotel now looked smarter than in its supposed heyday. Mexican, US and Spanish flags hung above the doorway and black iron balcony railings gleamed in the morning sun. Its elegant exterior was demeaned only by the PVC banner promoting *tipico* breakfasts for just forty-nine pesos – about £2.50.

I had hoped Veracruz was going to be like Cartagena, a colonial jewel on the shores of a tropical sea, but although it had a laid-back Caribbean feel, its tattiness made me wonder if this was rather the Gulf Coast's Scunthorpe. For every gem like the Hotel Imperial, there were many more decaying buildings with peeling paint and walls blackened by damp. Though it wasn't high season, I was surprised by the lack of tourists. There seemed to be many more Hawaiian-shirted men selling boxes of cigars and counterfeit watches wrapped round their fists than there were tourists to sell them to.

A Hotel Imperial doorman welcomed me to the stained-glass-roofed lobby, but when I saw their 'moderate prices' I contented myself with a forty-nine-peso breakfast. At least I would get to eat in the same restaurant as Arturo.

I piled my plate high with mango, pineapple, papaya, yogurt and honey, and was beginning to work my way through it when a woman in oversized white-rimmed sunglasses and a pink sun visor sat down next to me, the smell of her sun cream at odds with the smell of fresh bread from the kitchen.

'Are you American?' she asked.

'English,' I said, wondering what this woman wanted.

'Joan, from Colorado,' she said, shaking my hand. 'I just shacked up with the local oyster man.' She spoke with the enthu-siasm of a teenager who'd found love for the first time, but her hands were loose-skinned and sun-damaged and I could see grey roots to her blonde hair through the top of her sun visor. 'I have some friends coming in a few days. I'm road-testing all the joints I might send them to.'

'You'll send them here?' I said, pointing to the hotel.

'They can't stay with me. My oyster man and I . . .' She smiled wistfully. 'It's by the water. We can hear the waves at night, and the moonlight shines through the holes in the walls, but my friends want air con and cable TV.' She noticed my bags by the table. 'You not checked in yet?'

'I really wanted to stay here because this is where my great-grandfather stayed when he first arrived in Mexico but I can't afford it.'

'When was he here?'

'1898.'

She whistled. 'A long time ago, baby. It was basic. There was just an open sewer down the middle of the road.'

'You've been here a while, eh?'

Her mouth twitched as if she thought I was asking whether she was old enough to have smelled the open sewers herself.

'I mean, you obviously know your local history,' I added quickly.

'There's a lot of it. The Spanish *conquistadores* first landed here, and it's been invaded four times since. And there have been countless outbreaks of yellow fever and an affliction charmingly called *vomito negro*. Veracruz is like a cockroach: it could survive anything.'

'How come you're here?' I asked.

'After my kids left home I started a Spanish degree and came here to get some practice and, well, I stayed.' She smiled, and waved at a waiter. '*Más café, por favor.*'

The waiter refilled her cup and she removed her sun visor and glasses. Her eyes were dark and bloodshot and I suddenly had an image of Joan and her oyster man on wild, rum-fuelled nights, trying to reclaim their lost youth.

She wrapped her freckled hands around the cup, seeming to draw strength from every sip. 'Tell me more about this great-grand-father of yours. What was he doing here?'

'He arrived in Veracruz on a boat from New Orleans, on his way from England to somewhere near Guadalajara. From here he took the train up to Mexico City. I don't suppose it runs any more, does it?'

She shook her head. 'Just goods trains.'

'I don't know exactly where he ended up, but I thought that if I started my Mexican journey in the same spot, I might get some clues.'

'Intergenerational memory.'

'Sorry?'

'I studied it years ago. Something that's passed from one gener-ation to another without either generation being aware of it: a gap in the unconscious. In the 60s, we all tried to convince ourselves our ancestors had wanted us to chill out, drop out and smoke doobies.' She laughed. 'Probably a load of hogwash. I'm sure my ancestors really wanted me to be a subservient house-wife.'

It struck me that when Joan talked about communicating with ancestors she saw it as part of an outdated hippy ideal. Yet when talking with Pablo or Juanita such ideas seemed perfectly natural. For them the supernatural and physical were not worlds apart. Whether it was flower power or *brujería*, I liked the idea that I might have inherited a memory, emotion or unresolved dilemma from Arturo. Maybe that was why I had always believed there was something to find and that I would recognise it when I found it.

Joan stood up. 'Come on, let's find you a hotel. Then we'll see what clues he left for you.'

We walked to a blue-walled *pensión* where Joan had stayed when she first arrived in the city. I left my bags and then she accompanied me to the city archive, where she knew a historian. But after spending the morning with him, I realised that in Veracruz at least, Arturo had left me nothing.

'You know that in Spanish they have the same word – *historia* – for history and story?' said Joan as we left the archive.

I nodded.

'That's why I love the history of this place so much: it's full of good stories. I love the one about the Spanish *conquistador* Hernando Cortés. He landed a few miles up the coast and founded Veracruz. Once they had set up camp, Cortés ordered his men to burn the boats that had brought them across the Atlantic, to discourage them from thinking about returning home.'

'A bit drastic,' I said.

'Maybe, but it worked. Cortés only had a few hundred men and yet they conquered Mexico and the whole of Central America. It was brutal but impressive.'

Had Arturo, I wondered, 'burnt his boats' when he arrived in Veracruz?

The Fast and the Furious

Arturo's train from Veracruz climbed up, up, up through the tropics, into the rainforest and high into the jungle. Monkeys were howling and parrots and toucans – their feathers every colour of the rainbow – screeched as they flew over the train. There were trumpet-shaped flowers taller than telegraph poles, jungle grass matted with multicoloured blooms and orchids strung like garlands from tree to tree. He saw hummingbirds – there were hundreds of them – and butterflies with wings like pages of a brightly painted newspaper. He saw huts cut out of the undergrowth, walls of bamboo, and palm-leaf roofs. Arturo didn't want to blink – he didn't want to miss a thing.

Hour after hour the train panted uphill, under waterfalls, past jagged rock poking through pine forest and mountain oak. They crossed trestle bridges so slender and ravines so deep the train seemed to be suspended in mid-air.

High in the mountains the train stopped at a station and immediately Indian women wearing ponchos and with long braided black hair appeared at the carriage window, offering food of every description. Baskets of pineapple, mango and pomegranate, pyramids of rice and beans on banana leaves, squares of fudge and tin tubes of ice cream, kept cool on slabs of ice six inches thick, wrapped in straw.

At this station he left the train because he wanted to explore a chasm, said to be so deep it reached the edges of hell. He wanted to hire a horse but was told it was too steep and too deep, so instead he was carried in a sedan chair. At the top of the gorge eagles and vultures circled endlessly, waiting for man or animal to fall. When they reached the bottom, they had to light a lantern to see and Arturo saw a snake slither over his foot.

The bus's hazard lights were flashing, the door shut, its engine silent. Already thirty minutes late leaving Veracruz and there was no ticket man, no baggage handler, no other passengers and no driver. I sat on the platform and waited. Someone was bound to turn up before too long.

Twenty minutes later a man in a white vest and crumpled trousers came through the metal door marked AUTOBUSES FLECHA AMARILLA: ADMINISTRACIÓN. He rubbed his hand first over his face then through his closely cropped grey hair and wandered into the ticket office. I supposed he would put on a fresh shirt, march over to the bus and drive to Mexico City. Instead, he yawned, stretched and sat down, resting his head on the countertop. I wondered if *Flecha Amarilla* had ever heard of the word timetable.

Another twenty minutes later the man in the crumpled trousers was in exactly the same position. I was beginning to doubt I was ever going to leave Veracruz when there was a pneumatic hiss from behind me and the door swung open. A man in his forties in a *Flecha Amarilla* company shirt stepped down from the decommissioned Greyhound, followed by a plump girl of around eighteen in tight pink leather trousers – both of them bathed in a post-coital glow.

'*Amigo*, what's the time?' he asked me.

I showed him my watch.

'*Ay caray!*' He grimaced, then winked at me and walked into the ticket office. He woke the man in the crumpled trousers and said something which made them both roar with laughter. He then stood in front of the bus a few minutes more to see if any passengers would turn up other than me and the girl in the pink trousers. They didn't, and finally we set off.

The price of Arturo's train fare to Mexico City, according to his Baedeker guide, was $14, almost $400 in today's prices. My bus ticket cost significantly less, but I doubt Arturo had to wait while one of his fellow passengers received the special attentions of the train driver.

The bus, like all second-class buses, went slowly, stopped everywhere and was ventilated by narrow windows wedged open as wide as they would go. As long as I wasn't in a hurry, I generally preferred them. Often the only difference between them and their more glamorous *primera clase* cousins was that first-class buses had air conditioning. Although this might normally be considered a benefit, either the air con tended to be so efficient that the passengers half froze to death, or within minutes of leaving the terminal the driver would switch it off. Only then would you discover that the windows were bolted shut.

Second-class buses stopped in obscure villages for inexplicably long periods of time. I could watch wizened old men walking beside mules weighed down with plantains or loosely bundled clumps of corn while I washed down *torta con panela y jalapeños* with an ice-cold Coke.

Although it was empty on leaving Veracruz bus station, the bus seemed to stop at every corner on its way through town. Within ten minutes it was full, and people were standing in the aisle. It still had a notice written in English above the driver's head: *THIS COACH IS FITTED WITH A RESTROOM FOR THE COMFORT AND CONVENIENCE OF OUR PASSENGERS.* I looked at where it had been ripped out. Why have a toilet when you can have two extra seats and five more passengers? It was several hours before we stopped for a break.

A boy of about thirteen climbed in at a traffic light, carrying an armful of newspapers. He shouted his review of the papers in his newly broken voice. 'Oaxaca mayor has been fired!'

A man standing at the back of the bus cheered.

The boy looked at him. 'A copy for you, *señor?*'

'*Sí,*' the man shouted.

While the passengers passed the paper to the man at the back, the boy carried on with his review: 'Murder in the capital. Great pictures!' He held up a page of photos of a bloodied corpse lying on a pavement. 'Read about Garcia's wonder goal against Las Chivas. The game between Cruz Azul and Pachuca ended in a draw. Read about *el idiota* the referee!'

As the newspaper boy jumped down, a man in a shabby blue blazer and burgundy nylon trousers climbed on. He said something quietly to the driver and then addressed the bus. 'Good morning, *señoras y señores.* I lost my job last year and am now living by the grace of God and the generosity of bus passengers.' He then pulled a bag of chocolate bars from a shoulder pack held together with safety pins and walked down the corridor, handing a bar out to each passenger. When he got back to the front he pulled a six-inch nail and a small hammer from his jacket pocket and tapped the nail against the metal handrail. Then, hitching up his sleeves, he started to hammer the nail up his nostril.

Most of the passengers stared out of the window or continued chatting, but I couldn't keep my eyes off him. His expression was impassive. He didn't seem to be in any pain; he just looked like he wanted to sneeze. He tapped until only the nail's head was visible and then walked up and down the bus collecting money from those who had eaten the chocolate and took back the bars from those who hadn't. He then pulled the nail out of his nose, thanked everyone and jumped off at the next junction.

WE EVENTUALLY cleared the urban sprawl of Veracruz and drove into the flat countryside. The bus passed mile after mile of grazing bony cattle, fields of sugar cane, corn and sunflower, tobacco and dry riverbeds. Three hours into the journey the old Greyhound began to climb. The landscape became more lush and fertile. I began to see banana, orange and avocado trees, giant ferns growing wild and orderly rows of coffee plants with red berries. Like Arturo, I saw *campesinos'* houses cut from the encroaching undergrowth. There were some huts with bamboo walls and palm-leaf roofs, but many more made from thin bricks and breeze blocks with brightly coloured water tanks glimmering in the sun.

As we drove, I read some old travellers' accounts of the train journey to Mexico City, the only useful thing I'd got from the Veracruz archive. A popular place to stop was Barranca del Infiernillo – the Gorge of Little Hell. It must be the ravine Arturo had been carried down in a sedan chair. I decided I would break my journey, stay a night in the nearest town of Maltrata, and visit the gorge the following morning.

The taxi driver who picked me up from Maltrata bus station was a big teddy bear of a man, dressed in denim dungarees. His hair was long and tightly curled, and his ear lobes stuck out at ninety degrees where they met his broad neck.

'Where are you heading?' he asked.

'Mexico City,' I said, not realising he was asking me which hotel I wanted to be taken to. I gave him the name of the hotel and we set off.

On our way into town a four-wheel drive Toyota sped towards us. The taxi driver flashed his lights and sounded his horn, then pulled over to the side of the road. '*Es Wilson, mi hermano,*' said the taxi driver. 'He's on his way to Mexico City.'

The Toyota braked, turned round and skidded to a halt in front of us. The man who walked out of the dust cloud mush-rooming around the car looked nothing like his brother. He was tall, with a V-shaped torso, wore light jeans, a vest and straw hat. He smacked the roof of the taxi and bent over to look in through the driver's window. '*Hola, hermano.*'

'*Mi amigo,*' the taxi driver said, jerking a thumb over his shoulder to where I was sitting, 'is going to Mexico City. Do you want to take him?'

I wanted to see this treacherous gorge, but I knew it wasn't going to help me find where Arturo had ended up. Tired from a day of bus travel, the possibility of a lift in a nice car seemed too good an opportunity to pass up.

Wilson looked at me. 'Thirty-five dollars okay?'

Though this was more than the bus would have been, a taxi all the way to Mexico City would have cost ten times as much. 'Sounds good, thanks.'

'I'm going anyway. It'll be good to have some company.'

I loaded my bag into the back of Wilson's car and got in the front, noticing with a pang of concern the writing on the sun strip at the top of the windscreen: THE FAST AND THE FURIOUS.

Wilson jumped in and gunned the engine. 'Hear that?' he said, nodding towards the roar under the bonnet. 'V-8, four-litre engine. Four hundred and fifty-two horsepower.' As he gripped his hand into a fist to emphasise his point, I saw a tattoo of the Tasmanian Devil cartoon character on his well-muscled bicep.

'*Vámonos!*' He beeped his horn and put his foot to the floor. The car fishtailed as the back wheels tore up gravel and then accelerated down the road.

After having travelled very slowly all day, I felt a momentary surge of excitement.

'Yahoooo!' he screamed, thumping the steering wheel and grinning at me, his gold teeth sparkling. 'It's my girlfriend's birthday. When we get to Mexico City, I'm going to take her clubbing.' He held the steering wheel with his knees and began to dance around in his seat, clicking his fingers above his head like Zorba the Greek. I was beginning to have a bad feeling about Wilson.

The road was good but narrow and very twisty. We accelerated towards a logging truck with a luminous *VEHICULO LARGO* plate hung from its back, thick green forest passing at a blur.

'*Rápido, rápido!*' Wilson screamed as he steered into a blind corner on the wrong side of the road.

'Wilson!' I screamed at him.

'Yahoooo!' he yelled again, as a pickup came round the bend, driving straight towards us.

'Watch out!' I shouted back.

Instead of braking, Wilson sounded his horn, flashed his lights and drove straight at the pickup.

I shut my eyes and heard the screech of tyres, then smelled burning rubber. Wilson laughed wildly and shouted, '*Pinche cabron!*' – fucking arsehole! – at the poor pickup driver, who had swerved onto the soft verge to avoid us.

The wind caught his hat and it flew into the back of the car, revealing his shaved head. I suddenly remembered Juanita's warning with horror: *Beware of a bald devil with a mouth full of gold.* I reached for the seat belt.

Despite public safety campaigns, many drivers in Latin America view passengers buckling up as a slight on their driving skills and an attack on their manliness. I was past caring.

'You don't like my driving?' he said, looking hurt.

'Too fast. Too dangerous. I would prefer to arrive an hour later than not at all.'

He slowed down marginally and turned up the stereo. He was stony-faced for a few moments, then he pulled out a silver pistol from his door pocket and started waving it about. *'No tengo miedo de nadie.'* I'm not scared of anyone. He slid an oversized magazine into the handle and cocked the pistol so a round flicked out of the top.

'Here,' he said, handing it to me as we careered round a corner, tyres screeching.

I had never held a gun before. It was cold to the touch and heavier than I expected. Just for a moment I thought about pointing it at him and telling him to stop the car, but it felt unnatural in my hands so I passed it back to him.

He kept the pistol on his lap as he slowed down. In front of us was a saloon car tailing a beer truck. 'Open your window!' he said suddenly, and put his foot down and pulled up next to the saloon car.

'Pinche cabron!' he shouted.

As we passed the car, I saw a man wearing a bulletproof vest in the back seat, cocking a pump-action shotgun and pointing it at us. I ducked down and Wilson pointed his pistol over me, out of the window.

Then I heard the man shout, *'Pinche pendejo!'* at Wilson and roar with laughter.

Wilson laughed too, sounded his horn and drove off. He slapped my leg. 'Don't worry. He's my friend. I was just making a joke.'

'Very fucking funny,' I said.

As soon as we reached the outskirts of Mexico City, I got out and hailed a taxi.

Not Lost, Just Not Sure Where to Go Next

THE CITY of Mexico had a population of just over 300,000 in 1898. Now there are said to be almost 30 million people living there. I would have liked to explore the city and see how much of the old city had survived, but as Arturo had spent just one night there on his way west I decided to follow suit. I would get some rest and then press on to Guadalajara, pick up Grandma's letter and begin my search for the Small Village outside a Small Town.

I found a cheap hotel in the centre in an alley off Paseo de la Reforma. The room was tiny and smelled strongly of disinfectant, but after the journey I'd had from Veracruz I didn't care. I slept for fourteen hours and would have slept longer if I hadn't been woken by an earth tremor. Dogs began to bark, then my window started to rattle and my bed to shake, as if the building was being driven over a giant cattle grid. There was something ghostly about the low groaning rumble from beneath the surface of the earth. I wondered if Juanita was sending me messages through the elements. Or if someone else was.

FIVE HOURS into the journey to Guadalajara, halfway up a mountainside, on a road in a clearing drilled out of red rock, the bus came to a standstill. The driver cut the engine and opened the door. 'The road's blocked,' he said, lighting a cigarette. 'I don't know who's done it, so don't wander too far.'

I walked through the stationary traffic: buses and pickups with families in the back, sheltering from the sun under oil-stained sheets and collapsed cardboard boxes. Truck drivers had already slung hammocks beneath their trailers and were swinging gently, seemingly happy to have a few extra hours' sleep. A shop that had clearly not expected the mountain road to become a car park had already sold out of everything apart from packets of deep-fried cheese pastry twists and a grapefruit drink called Squirt.

The pass remained gridlocked for most of the afternoon. Before we set off again, still several hours short of our destination, I went to talk to the driver. I didn't want to arrive in a huge city in the middle of the night, so I showed him my map and pointed to the last town before Guadalajara and asked to be let out there.

He raised his eyebrows. 'You want to go to Charcos?'

ONCE THE dust had cleared and the bus had ground and growled its way into the distance, I could see little sign of life in the town which I had just endured twelve hours' journey to reach. A man supping from a bottle of Modelo beer eyed me from where he was comfortably slouched outside the corner store, his vest pulled up over the top of his belly. Insects pinged into the naked bulb that lit the corrugated awning above his head. From the look on his face I guessed I was the first *gringo* he had seen for many years.

'You lost?'

'This is Charcos, right?'

He pursed his lips and pointed them, as if he were about to blow a kiss, towards an illuminated concrete arch over the road with huge lettering that said BIENVENIDOS A CHARCOS.

I smiled, acknowledging my foolish question. 'Any hotels here?'

He flicked his thumb behind him. 'They're down there.'

I asked for more specific directions, but he insisted I couldn't miss them despite the fact they had no signs and he didn't seem to remember exactly where they were. I picked up my bags and followed the direction he'd indicated.

'Hello, man!' called a boy as he passed me on a bicycle, his cigarette trailing a splintering glow behind him. Girls gathered round a bench giggled as I approached. I asked if they knew where a hotel might be. They giggled some more.

I was beginning to wonder if I should return to the main road, catch the next bus and try my luck in Guadalajara when I saw two women in short skirts sitting in a brightly lit doorway. I'm no expert, but I normally reckon that women who sit in doorways wearing short skirts around midnight will at least have a fair idea where the cheap local hotels are.

'Hey, where are you from?' said one of them. 'Argentina?'

'England.'

'But you speak Spanish.'

'I've just come from Colombia.'

'They speak Spanish in Colombia?'

I laughed, then realised that she really didn't know.

'Of course they do!' said the other. 'What language do you think they speak, Chinese?'

Not wanting to get caught in this linguistic dispute, I asked them where I might find a hotel.

'I don't think there are any, but you can stay with me if you like, I'm Ema.' She held out her hand.

I wasn't sure what kind of invitation this was, and my hesitancy must have showed because her friend, Cheli, immediately said, '*No te preocupes.* She's a respectable *señora,* from a good family.'

Ema said she'd call her son to help me with my bags. 'Come inside and wait.'

I felt embarrassed that my first impressions had been so wide of the mark. Inside I could see that Ema and Cheli ran a telecoms office. There were three *larga distancia* telephone cabins, three *locales* and two fax machines.

'It's pretty quiet now, so we can finish for the night, don't you think, Cheli?'

Ema's eldest son, Hugo – a good-looking boy, wearing a New York Knicks vest – arrived on his pushbike, picked up my bags and we walked the three blocks to their home.

Ema introduced me to her five other children and two restless Gordon setters, which dribbled everywhere. The family didn't seem in the least bit surprised to have a visitor arrive so late. They were squeezed onto a sofa in front of a television, watching the police chase a pickup with dragster wheels through Los Angeles evening rush hour. '*Qué barbaridad!*' How terrible! said Ema, handing me a plate of *quesadillas.*

'Is this near where you're from?' Hugo asked.

'I'm from England.'

He nodded. 'A long way away.'

Ema turned off the television and led me and the rest of the family upstairs to the half-built second storey. During the day it was a café. It had a jukebox, a couple of space invader machines and plastic tables still scattered with overflowing ashtrays and half-drunk bottles of Coke and Squirt. The family dragged tables and chairs out of the way, and swept the floor.

I pulled a hammock from my bag, slung it between two concrete pillars and gratefully settled down for the night.

In the morning I packed my bag, anxious to get out of the way before the first customers arrived.

'You can't go now,' said Ema, when I thanked her for her hospitality. 'You only just got here, and besides I received a call from Cheli this morning. Her husband wants you to address his youth club tonight.'

'About what?'

'"The wisdom you have gained from travelling the world."'

EVERY MORNING for six days someone would come up with a reason why I should stay. On the second day I had to meet Ema's beautiful young niece Yadira. On the third day there was the annual Señorita Charcos beauty pageant, and on the fourth day I had to meet all the contestants and give my own judgement. By the time the weekend came around, I had been invited to two weddings and a birthday party so my departure was delayed another couple of days.

Before I was allowed to leave, Ema wanted to take me with her family to visit *Los Santos* at a shrine by a lake called Boca del Rio. Two of her children were planning to go 'under the wire' to seek a better life in the States. Ema thought that their journey, and my own quest, required a special blessing. The idea was to get to the shrine as dawn broke, which meant we were to leave at 4.30 a.m. Ema sent Yadira to make sure that I got up.

I felt my hammock being rocked gently, then a light touch

on my shoulder. 'Hey, sleepy head,' she whispered in my ear, 'do you like my bikini?'

I opened one eye and then the other as she lifted up her T-shirt, peeled it over her head, dropped it onto my hammock and stood smiling at me.

'Are you awake now?'

'Most definitely,' I said, trying to look suave as I sat up in my hammock to face her.

'Good.' She put the T-shirt back on again and disappeared downstairs.

For an hour we drove on dust tracks through a deep forest in the half-light, arriving at a clearing at the edge of the lake just as the sun appeared on the horizon.

We climbed out of the car and walked towards where a small group of women were toasting tortillas on a hotplate above an open fire.

Yadira walked with me to a small pavilion-like shrine and peered through the bars, which were strewn with bouquets of flowers and Christmas fairy lights blinking blue, pink and green. Behind the bars was a glass cabinet protecting a gold-clad doll-like figure representing one of the saints to which the shrine was dedicated. At the foot of the cabinet were sticks of burning incense and toy birds which made electronic chirping noises.

Ema left us for a private *consulta* with the priest. When she returned, her eyes were shining and she had a smile on her face. 'We will both have luck,' she said.

'YOU LIKE music, eh?' asked the taxi driver as he left me at my hotel near the Mercado de Libertad in downtown Guadalajara that evening.

'*Sí.*' I shrugged.

He laughed. 'Then you've come to the right place.'

I didn't understand what he meant but took my change and carried my bags into the hotel.

My plan had been to pick up my post and go straight on to the small town next to Lake Chapala to see if any of the surrounding small villages had been where Arturo had lived and worked. But it was already 7.30 p.m., too late to pick up my post, so I walked through an *artesania* market to the tourist office, which was still open in the pedestrianised colonial quarter.

Guadalajara had been described as the 'Florence of the Americas' in one of the books I had read in Veracruz. Although that seemed to be overstating it, the centre was certainly attractive. In between the impressive colonial churches and government buildings were flower-filled courtyards and shaded cafés. Tourists rode in horse-drawn carriages along the cobbled streets around the central plaza. And ice cream and balloon salesmen did a brisk trade with families enjoying their evening stroll.

'A small village near a small town?' said the woman in the tourist office, her eyes widening.

'Possibly near Lake Chapala,' I said.

She reached into a cupboard and unrolled a large map on the desk and tapped a biro against her teeth as she studied the area around the lake. 'There's a small place called Ajijic near the town of Chapala,' she said, pointing at the strangely named village.

It sounded perfect. 'Was a cotton mill there a hundred years ago?'

She laughed and shook her head. 'No, *mi amor*. Definitely no cotton mills, not now, not a hundred years ago. *Nunca*.' Never. 'Sorry.'

I asked her if she knew of any small villages near a small town that might have had a cotton mill in them. She laughed again and shook her head.

'Any ideas where I might look?'

She stopped laughing. 'This is really important to you, isn't it?'

I nodded.

'Give me a moment.' She disappeared into a back room and returned with the telephone number for the chamber of commerce. 'It might be a bit late, but I'll try and speak to the press department if you like.'

'Thanks.'

She dialled the number and spoke to several departments, none of which was able to provide a list of cotton mills, past or present.

I thanked her for her trouble and walked back into the main square and let out a long sigh. I had banked on Chapala being the place where I would find whatever Arturo had left behind. I had come all this way only to find a dead end. Now I really wasn't sure where to look.

'I say, are you lost?' said a woman with a clipped English accent – something I hadn't heard in months. I turned round to see an elderly lady in a pink straw hat being pushed in a wheelchair.

'Not exactly,' I said. 'Just not sure where to go next.'

'Why not start with a beer? That's what I always say,' said the man pushing her in a thick South African drawl. 'We would join you but we're off to see some choral concert.'

'It's simply delightful to meet another Brit!' said the woman. 'I haven't been home for many years. I do miss the theatre, being at the centre of things. You know, I even miss the weather!'

I liked the way she spoke, like a theatrical Miss Marple. 'You must have been away a long time if you miss the weather,' I said.

'It's not that long, is it?' her husband asked.

'It's fourteen years since we moved to Durban.'

The man looked at his watch. 'We're going to have to scram, I'm afraid. Have a beer for me.'

The woman smiled, revealing a smudge of lipstick on her teeth, and gave me a regal wave as her husband pushed her through a group of pigeons scrapping for birdseed.

I DIDN'T take his advice but bought a grilled corn on the cob from a man at the edge of the square, went to bed and slept solidly until the early hours of the morning, when I was woken by the deafening screech of trumpets. After a few seconds of shock and disorientation I realised that the square below was la Plaza de Los Mariachis, one of the best places in Mexico to hear mariachi. And one of the worst to get any sleep. Now I understood why the taxi driver had asked me if I liked music.

I sighed, pulled on some clothes and went out into the plaza.

Mariachis were everywhere, their embroidered suits and silver buckles sparkling in the night lights. Five or six bands were playing, each one only a few feet from the next. They formed a circle around cowboy-hatted Mexicans, who sang along, their glasses raised in euphoric tequila toasts.

After each song, the band leader wrote its name in his notebook and called out suggestions for the next one.

' "La Flor"? "Hermoso Cariño"? How about "Amor de Mis Amores"?'

The mariachis who weren't playing sat on car bonnets smoking cigarettes, engaged in games of burro castigado. They threw each card down with a dramatic flourish, and when the game was won there'd be cries of 'Pinche cabron!'

I hadn't noticed the seediness of the area when I arrived in the early evening. In the small hours it was difficult to ignore. Mariachis weren't the only people whose services were for hire. Women with thick legs and short skirts gathered like moths around the brightly lit taco stands and by the swing-door entrances of late-night *cantinas*. Men with pockmarked faces and Brylcreemed hair hissed drug prices from the shadows of shop doorways.

'*Psst, gringo. Nieve pura?*' Pure snow?

I walked on without giving a response and sat at a plastic table outside a bar at the edge of the plaza. A waiter brought me a bottle of Bohemia beer and a bowl of chillied peanuts and shooed away a man selling lottery tickets and a woman selling hairclips and combs. In front of me a mariachi band played for a young couple, who were swaying, seared together by the music. When the piece finished the band leader asked what song they would like next, but he got no reply. He asked several times, and then put away his notebook and, together with his fellow mariachis, wandered off, instruments under their arms in search of their next client. Several minutes later I noticed the couple hadn't moved. Their arms were wrapped round each other, the girl's face wet with tears. Seeing her triggered the painful memory of my parting from Juanita.

'Young love, eh?' said a gravelly South African voice.

I looked up to see the man I'd met with his English wife a few hours before. I nodded sadly and offered him a bottle of Bohemia as he lowered his enormous frame into the seat beside me.

I asked after his wife and he sighed.

'It's very difficult for her. She was a magnificent ballet dancer. Danced all over the world, from Covent Garden to Sydney. Then she was a highly respected teacher. Now rheumatism has confined her to this blasted chair.'

I looked at him and I wondered for a second if he was going to cry, but he turned his attention to me.

'So tell me, what is it you're looking for in Mexico?'

I was about to tell him about Arturo and the small village, the mango orchard and the bags of silver, and was going to say I was on a treasure hunt, but the words got stuck in my throat. Something about the word treasure suddenly felt childish. 'Stones,' I said, 'I'm looking for precious stones.'

'Ya?' He told me he'd made his money trading diamonds and had only recently begun to slow down since his ninetieth birthday earlier in the year.

He could have passed for twenty-five years younger and I told him so but he swatted the compliment away.

'I have never made a purchase on the basis of price alone,' he said about his lifelong quest for diamonds. 'Quality, always quality. No matter what the cost.'

I felt similarly uncompromising about my own quest. I would follow it through to the end, no matter how long it took me. But keen to change the subject before he discovered that I wouldn't know a pink diamond from a tin of cat food, I asked where he had met his wife.

'In Germany before the war, 1937. I met two people on that trip: May, my wife, and Hitler.' He paused, swilling the remains of the beer. 'He was extraordinary. I saw him address a crowd of several thousand. Had them in the palm of his hand. I remember looking around at the other people in the crowd – priests, nuns, businessmen, young and old – all in absolute rapture. All under his spell. Whether or not they knew what he was saying, they believed every word.'

He was no great Hitler fan though. The Führer, he said, had let his people down.

I had never thought of Hitler as a mere disappointment.

'And he had no manners. Joseph Goebbels on the other hand, now he had class. He was a gentleman!'

'A gentleman?'

'He had manners, charm. Wasn't so obsessive as Hitler, who got a bit carried away.'

'Just a bit.'

He didn't seem to notice my sarcastic tone and launched into a rant about how America had shown a lack of respect to his people by appointing a black ambassador to South Africa. 'This is insulting to us . . .'

I called for the bill.

He thanked me for the beer. Looking solemnly into my eyes, he shook my hand with a vice-like grip and sauntered back towards his hotel.

I ordered another beer. And then another, and when I thought I'd drunk enough to sleep through the music, I went back to my room.

THE NEXT morning, my head fizzing from lack of sleep and my eyes stinging from the bright sunshine, I walked back out into the plaza. There were no mariachis, no prostitutes. The doorways that had seemed so sinister the night before were now just shop doorways: one sold mirrors, another postcards and T-shirts.

I dearly wanted to stay in bed, but couldn't rest. I wanted to pick up my post and see what the clue was that Grandma had told me about when I called her from Colombia.

I caught a bus to the Amex office, which was near the Arc de Triomphe-esque arch that, in Arturo's day, had been the entrance to the west of the city. The woman sitting next to me was wearing a floral print dress and fingering a rosary. During the twenty-minute journey she crossed herself and kissed the gold cross around her neck at each of the five or six churches we passed. Out of the colonial centre, Guadalajara seemed modern and affluent. The *avenidas* were wide and the trees that lined them were covered in pink and yellow blossom. We passed several cavernous glass-fronted shopping centres and expensive-looking restaurants with shaded terraces. At the entrance to most of the restaurants were hand-written signs – *VALET PARKING*. This in most cases meant a shabbily dressed man waving a red rag to guide restaurant customers into a parking space, watching their car, and maybe washing their windscreen if the tip was big enough.

The bus stopped at a rail crossing for a slow-moving goods train. It was the first train I had seen in Latin America. The rolling stock was grimy and rusty and it groaned and squeaked as it rumbled by. Men were perched on top of every carriage clinging to the tarpaulin covers, or holding on to the rails in between the wagons. Suddenly, a man carrying a small plastic bag ducked under the barrier and began running beside the train, trying to haul himself up. The men already riding the train cheered him on, but after three attempts he gave up and collapsed, exhausted, next to the tracks.

'*Ay pobrecito,*' said the woman with the rosary. Poor thing.

'Where is the train going?' I asked.

'Tijuana. It takes three or four days.'

'Why do they want to go to Tijuana?'

'They cross from there into the States to work. The ones that get there.' She nodded at the men holding on to the top of the wagons. 'Many fall asleep and fall off. You fall off, you die.'

It was the first post I had received since Guatemala. There was a postcard from Pablo in which he said he and his family were 'ready for the next mission' and the letter I had been waiting for from Grandma. I found a coffee house nearby and began to read.

Sheffield
March 2nd

Hello there, love.

It's extraordinary that by the time you read this you will be in Mexico. My father would be very proud you have gone so far in his honour.

After I sent the letter to you in Guatemala, I woke in the night wondering what other clues I could give you about how to find the place where my father lived. Don't tell your mother, but I pulled down the loft ladder and climbed up with my torch.

There was so much stuff up there it took me an hour to find anything, but then I found some of my father's photos that I haven't seen in years. I brought them downstairs and have been looking at them today. On one, I noticed something written in gold under 'F. E. Herrera, Fotografia Artistica' (the studio name, I assume). I can't make it out very clearly, but it looks like 'Tepic, Mexico'. It sounds familiar.

I looked at the map, and saw that Tepic is between Guadalajara and San Blas, which makes sense. The more I think about it, the surer I am that Tepic is the name of the town where your Great-Aunt Sophia was christened in the cathedral.

Anyway, as I said, don't waste too much time looking for something that probably isn't there, but let me know how you get on.

Lots of love,
Grandma

I stayed one more day in Guadalajara and in the evening called Juanita. 'Thank God you're okay,' she said. 'You met the bald *diablito* with the mouth full of gold, didn't you?'

'I survived.'

She was tearful. 'Remember what I said about it being harder for the one who's left behind?'

'I remember,' I said, feeling guiltier than ever for leaving.

'No one knows how much I've cried except me, my pillow and God.'

I returned to my hotel room and considered forgetting all about my Mexican treasure hunt. What did I really expect to find? Could it really be more important than a girl who loved me?

I wished that it wasn't.

But rather than going back south to console her, the next morning I climbed aboard a bus to Tepic.

MEXICO

San Blas · Tepic
· Guadalajara
Ceboruco
volcano
Lake Chapala

A Small Village Outside a Small Town Near Guadalajara

The day Arturo reached the Small Town was one of the most amazing of his life. His friend Don Domingo took him to a banquet at the house of a rich widow. As he entered he was greeted by waiters in black ties and tails who offered French champagne in Bohemian crystal glasses, and plates of caviar. This was a different world from the one Arturo knew. He decided he didn't much care for caviar and when he took a sip of champagne, he started to sneeze.

Every plate of food was unfamiliar. There was ham from Spain, pasta from Italy. The rice was flavoured with herbs from China and meats were infused with Indian spices.

A string quartet was playing under a chandelier and the seats they were sitting on shone brighter than daylight. When Arturo went closer he saw the chairs were made of solid silver.

The following morning, Arturo went to meet Don Domingo's uncle, Señor Egery, who was going to take him to work at the mill in the village nearby. Señor Egery wore a black cape and polished top hat and carried a small leather purse. They climbed into his carriage, pulled by six thoroughbred horses. The mansion gates opened and they rode out into the street, through a crowd of cheering people. Señor Egery threw gold coins out of the window to the men, women and children who were now running after the carriage. They drove around the plaza twice, until Señor Egery's purse was empty and then they went to the mill.

That was the beginning of your great-grandfather's first day at work.

Four hours after leaving Guadalajara, the road cut through a lava forest where the volcano Ceboruco famously blew its top – and itself – out of existence in the 1870s. It was a Dali-esque landscape of grey popcorn-shaped boulders and surreal ribbon-like formations with only the occasional shrub or prickly cactus poking through the rock to give a splash of colour. I envisaged Arturo covered with volcanic dust as he looked out from the seat of his stagecoach and wondered what impression this bleak scenery might have made on him.

The thought spurred me into thinking about what exactly I would do when I got to Tepic, which was only half an hour away. I took out my notebook and, riding the potholes in the road, jotted down a plan of action.

* *Find record of Great-Aunt Sophia's birth – convent*
* *Record of Great-Aunt Sophia's baptism – cathedral*
* *Place where Arturo lived (house with blue shutters and big oak door) – Tepic??*

* *Place where Arturo lived – Small Village?*
* *Look for place Arturo worked (Cotton mill, near water supply in Small Village)*
* *Look for records of imports of Arturo's shipments at San Blas*
* *Don Domingo?*
* *House of Egery?*
* *The village church Arturo helped to build*
* *Find record of Ecroyd ('Flash Harry from Oswaldtwistle'), his death and/or descendants*
* *History of bandits in the area*
* *The Mango Orchard*
* *A bag of silver??*

We passed a sign, BIENVENIDOS A TEPIC – 400,000 HABITANTES, a sign that confirmed the town was at least forty times larger than it had been in my great-grandfather's day. I looked at my list and wondered how much, if anything, I would find out. Or if I might be on a wild goose chase, as Grandma feared. I pressed my face to the window, convincing myself that if I looked hard enough I would see Avenida Arturo Greenhalgh or perhaps the town theatre named in his honour. I saw wide palm-tree-lined boulevards, two university campuses, shopping centres with hacienda-sized car parks, a Coca-Cola bottling plant and *barrios* that covered entire hillsides.

I found a hotel in the centre of town. My room was above a flower stall and a shop selling beans, nuts and fragrant spices. The pungent aromas drifting through my open window made me think of merchant ships arriving from the Orient at San Blas in the 1800s. If only in my imagination, I already felt Arturo's presence.

Coming from Guadalajara, I had crossed a time zone, and

the shops were just reopening after the siesta. I decided to start my search by looking for Great-Aunt Sophia's birth and baptism records. I'd only met her a few times, but clearly remembered her telling me about being baptised twice, once in the cathedral of the town where she was born, and again in the Methodist chapel when she got back to England. (Apparently my great-grandmother felt a Catholic baptism wouldn't count for much at the Pearly Gates.)

I asked the boy who worked in the hotel reception if he knew where birth and baptism certificates would be kept.

'*Qué chido!*' he said. How cool! He was playing with the gold crucifix he wore over the top of his white shirt. His name badge said JUAN. He was around seventeen and seemed unlikely to ever lose his job through a lack of enthusiasm. 'The whole town's there. There are certificates for everyone ever born here.'

'Where?'

'There are two places. Baptism records are in the office next to the cathedral on the Plaza de Armas. Birth records are in La Presidencia, on the opposite side of the square.'

Hanging in a wooden frame on the whitewashed wall of the cathedral records' office was a notice. I expected it to give opening times or a reminder that Jesus Christ had died for our sins. It simply said, 'We don't do loans.'

I pushed open the heavy door and came into a book-lined room. At the far end, behind a battered desk, was a woman in a green polyester dress with large yellow buttons. She looked at me over the top of her half-moon glasses as I explained that I was looking for a register of a baptism in 1902.

'That's a long time ago,' she said.

'Could you look for me?'

'I suppose so.'

She climbed a small set of wooden steps and pulled out four leather-bound volumes, each about two feet high and four inches thick. She dropped them one by one with a thud on the desk. 'You can take them to the table over there,' she said, indicating the corner. Her lip curled slightly. 'Be careful with these books. They're very old.'

I opened the first one. It was so big I had to stand up to turn the pages. Each entry was handwritten in black ink in the same neat hand. I wondered when this book had last been opened.

I turned one page, then another. I'd only looked at three pages when I flicked back to the second. Something looked familiar. Out of the thousands of entries I had been given to look through, Great-Aunt Sophia's was the second I came to. It was as if it had been waiting for me to find it.

She had been baptised by Father Luis Quintero on 16 August 1902. The entry gave Arturo and Mariah's names, as well as those of their parents. I couldn't believe I was seeing the names of my ancestors written on a page in a book in a town in western Mexico. I had to tell someone. I rushed over to the lady in the green polyester dress.

'I found it. I found it! Look!'

She removed her glasses and sighed. 'I suppose you want a copy?'

'*Sí, por favor.*'

She reluctantly pulled out a blank certificate, copied the details from the book onto it and stamped it with the cathedral seal. I smiled and thanked her for her trouble.

She called me back as I went towards the door. This time she smiled. 'That'll be ten *pesos*, please.'

La Presidencia, the municipal building, was just where Juan had said it would be. It was a grand colonial structure with a glass-domed roof. Inside, it was full of people registering complaints and paying bills. It had the feel of a train station in the middle of a rail strike.

I pushed open a door marked ARCHIVO, the only office not besieged by disgruntled citizens. Behind the counter were eight women, each wearing a white plastic badge with her name printed above the municipal crest. They were having an animated conversation about a hypnotist's show some of them had seen the night before.

'And he made him snort like a pig and lick his paws as if he were a cat. Then the hypnotist touched him on the head and said, 'You are Luis Miguel!'

'Luis Miguel?'

'Sí.'

'Did he sing?'

'And danced. He *became* Luis Miguel! The girls in the audience screamed. Then the hypnotist touched him on the head again and the poor boy woke up. He had no idea why he was standing on the stage with a theatre full of people laughing at him.'

'Was he good-looking?'

'Excuse me,' I said.

'*Ay perdona.* I didn't see you there,' said Ángela, blushing. 'How can I help?'

'I'm looking for a birth registered in 1902.'

They all stared at me in amazement. 'How old are you?'

'It's not my birth certificate.' I explained about my great-grandfather and how I was now following in his footsteps. All eight of them stared at me, open-mouthed.

'He came all this way?' asked Renata, who seemed to be in charge. 'And you have come after him?'

I shrugged. 'I always felt there would be something to find

here, so I thought I'd begin with his daughter's birth certificate and go from there.'

Renata shook her head in astonishment. '*Que increible, no?*'

Her colleagues all nodded. '*Señor,*' Renata said, 'what date exactly, so we can see what we can find for you?'

I pulled out the certificate I had just got from the cathedral. 'She was born on 1 August 1902, and christened on 16 August.'

Renata took the certificate and studied it closely. *'Ay mira.'*

They disappeared into a back room, returning with several maroon leather volumes about eighteen inches high.

'We were wondering,' Ángela said, playing with a loose strand of hair. 'Which of us do you think is the prettiest?'

Renata looked on with a disapproving smile while the others collapsed in fits of giggles.

'Only kidding,' Ángela said, winking, 'but it's me, right?'

'*Vamos, chicas,*' said Renata, opening the first huge book on a table behind the desk. The others gathered round.

'Do you want any help?' I offered, but they waved me away, gold bracelets tinkling.

'*No te preocupes.* We'll do it.' As they slowly turned the stiff parchment sheets, they gave me a running commentary: '*González. Otro González. Gómez. Otro Gonzáles. Muchas González, verdad?*'

They suddenly went quiet. Eight heads bobbed down to take a closer look. 'Ahh!' they shrieked in unison. 'Greenhal!'

They turned the register round for me to read. It smelt musty and there were spots of mould on the page. The entry was written in an elegant, ornate hand:

> *In the city of Tepic, at eleven thirty in the morning on the first day of August nineteen hundred and two, Sophia Greenhalgh, legitimate daughter, was born to Mariah Nuttall*

de Greenhalgh and was presented to el señor Don Arturo
Greenhalgh, married, cotton manufacturer, of 28 years of age,
at number seventy, Calle Veracruz, of this city.*

It was as if it had been written just for me, my very own clue
from nearly a hundred years before. Best of all, just as I had
hoped, it had an address. Could this be the house with the oak
door and the bright-blue shutters?

'Where is Calle Veracruz?' I asked.

'It's on the right, just off the plaza.'

Ángela made me an official copy and presented it to me.

'How much do I owe you?' I said.

She winked. 'No charge.'

FEELING I was on a roll, I set off to look for No. 70 Calle Veracruz
and found it almost immediately. At the beginning of the street
was a clothes shop. It was so full of racks of T-shirts and
mannequins that the shop assistant had to stand outside.

The first number I came to was 140, then 126, then 122,
then . . . 65? What had happened to the intervening numbers?
The house in front of me was a colonial-style building with
rotting wood shutters and trees growing where there should have
been furniture. Next door was 59.

I had read that in Japan buildings are numbered in the order
in which they are built, and in Colombia the houses were sometimes numbered according to the number of paces they were
from the street's beginning. On Calle Veracruz, however, I couldn't
discern any logic at all. I knocked on some doors but no one

* In Mexico, when a woman marries she takes her husband's surname and
keeps her father's.

could explain the numbering or where Arturo's house had gone. Number 70 had simply disappeared.

I thought of Grandma's warning: *I don't suppose you'll find anything after all this time. Things change.* I feared she might be right, but once I had found the address on Great-Aunt Sophia's birth certificate, I had felt sure Arturo's house would still be there. There was the saying 'safe as houses'. If something as safe as a house had been erased from the face of the earth, what hope was there for anything else?

But having come this far, I wasn't going to give up that easily. The scent hadn't completely gone cold. There was the convent where Great-Aunt Sophia had been born. Maybe there would be a register of all the people born there, and perhaps that register would give the address of Arturo's other house next to the factory.

I knew from the girls in the Presidencia there had only ever been one convent in Tepic. I walked south for two kilometres, following the instructions they had given, until I came to a church and the thick fortified walls of El Convento de la Cruz.

I walked along a cloister of worn flagstones, looking through the archways to a richly flowered courtyard with a dry fountain in the middle. At the end of the corridor was a small black and white plaque: *OFICINA DE TURISMO.* Sitting behind an L-shaped desk was a man with slicked-back hair. There was nothing on his desk apart from a small telephone switchboard, its tiny red lights blinking furiously. He looked up and smiled as if he had been waiting for me all day. *'A sus ordenes, señor.'*

'Is this a tourist office?'

'Nearly.'

'Nearly?'

'There are some plans to make this the main tourist office but, at the moment, I am only able to offer information on the convent itself.'

He told me it had been built in the 1600s as a shrine to the miracle of *la cruz* – the cross – although he couldn't say what the miracle had been. 'The convent has had many lives. It's been a prisoner-of-war camp, a refuge for travellers and a hospital. I suppose that was when your aunt was born.'

'Is there a register?'

'No.'

'Do you know of a small village near here with a cotton mill?'

'I'm sorry.'

He hadn't heard of the House of Egery, Don Domingo or Ecroyd either. He gave me a postcard of the convent and shook my hand.

The trail had gone cold.

By the time I got back to the plaza, it was dark and a three-piece band was playing to a small crowd on the steps of the Presidencia building. They wore the traditional dress of the Cora people, a bit like a short-sleeved judo suit with embroidered cuffs. The older man, who I guessed was the father, had thick grooved wrinkles etched into his face. He played the violin and sang as if his next meal depended on it. His son strummed a guitar, and his wife plucked a chipboard double bass. Both played with expressions of passive resignation.

I found a bench to reflect on my day. In just a couple of hours in Tepic I had found the first three things on my list. I was pleased to have discovered all I had about my aunt, who'd only been two years old when she had returned to England. But I'd found precious little about Arturo apart from an address of a house that no longer existed.

Where should I go from here?

Everything else on the list depended on my finding the Small Village. I pulled Grandma's letters from my pocket and considered what I knew about Arturo's life in Mexico. He had worked in a cotton mill in the Small Village, but I didn't know where it was. I knew he'd had a second house, probably near the cotton mill. I knew about the bandits, but I didn't know who they were. Maybe if I went to where Arturo had been there'd be a trace of him. Even if I didn't believe in the intergenerational memory that Joan had talked about, all travellers leave some kind of trail. Apart from Tepic, I knew he had definitely been to the port of San Blas, where he had sent and collected shipments. Perhaps there would be shipping records giving the mill's address, or his second house. I reread Grandma's words: *Perhaps there'll be a chance meeting.*

Juan was still sitting at reception, watching wrestling on a portable black-and-white TV. 'Look at this guy,' he said, pointing at a portly wrestler in a face mask stamping on his opponent's head. '*Es padre!*'

'He's your father?' I asked.

'No,' he laughed. '*Es chido!*'

I remembered that *padre*, as well as meaning father, was another Mexican equivalent of 'cool'.

I told Juan I had found the records of my great-aunt, but now needed to go to San Blas.

'*San Blas es padre!*'

I tried to get him to explain what was cool about the old port but got nowhere. I decided to take his word for it, taking into account that it might only be as *padre* as portly, masked wrestlers stamping on each other.

Back in my room I lay down, knowing that if I didn't get ready for bed immediately, I would wake up fully dressed with the TV still on. I reached for the remote to see what Mexican TV had to offer. Several hours later I woke up with all my clothes on, the remote on my chest and wrestling on the TV.

A ONE-LEGGED man in a frayed Panama hat was watering the plants hanging from the departure board in the local bus station, the hose threaded through his wooden crutch.

'Is this where the bus leaves for San Blas?' I asked him, trying not to stare as he squeezed the hose between his stump and the crutch, reducing the jet to a trickle.

He looked at his watch – '*Ahorita va*', anytime now – and pointed to one of the two platforms, where a woman sat knitting on a plastic chair next to a display of sweets, peanuts and individual Belmont cigarettes.

The bus pulled in and stopped next to the knitting woman, who never looked up.

Beyond the city limits, we climbed for twenty minutes through dusty arid terrain, then almost instantly, when we reached the mountain summit, the air became heavier, more humid, the roadside vegetation green and lush. The leaves of banana, mango and palm trees slapped the side of the bus as we drove by. In the villages children ran alongside us, holding up freshly cut coconuts and iced drinks. Others held string across the road in an attempt to exact a toll from passing traffic. I thought of Arturo's journeys to San Blas, and of the demands for a toll of a more sinister nature that he might have had to pay. In those days the journey from Tepic to San Blas usually took one day, the return at least two, and more in the rainy season when it was too muddy for the oxen to get a good foothold.

Crossing from the bus station into San Blas' central square felt like arriving at a theatre and walking straight onto the stage. The plaza was raised above street level, perhaps to protect it from high tides, and looked down on the market stalls below. The backdrop was another elegant Presidencia building, which was the length of one side of the square. It looked like the most natural place to start my search.

Eager to catch people before they disappeared for lunch, I walked in to look for their civic archives. On the door of the first office I came to was a box with COMPLAINTS AND SUGGESTIONS written in white painted letters.

At the counter a San Blas citizen was saying, 'You're a bunch of fucking arseholes. Why the fuck do I pay my taxes when you just sit playing with your dicks all day? Why don't you go and fuck your mother?'

The council official, his face dominated by a cigarette-stained walrus moustache, looked as if he was used to such complaints and suggestions, and wasn't going to take them lying down. 'I told you we would install a new drain in your street and we will. What part of that do you not understand? Have you not got anything better to do than come here and stop me getting on with my job?'

I considered whether this was the moment to break up their discussion with a request for information about the arrival of cargo ships from England in the 1890s. I thought better of it.

I decided to look for someone more disposed to help me. All the offices I came to were closed. The only person I could see to ask was a workman dressed in yellow overalls with a cordless drill resting on his shoulder. I asked him to whom I should talk about port and shipping records.

'There are no ship records here. Try the harbour master.'

I walked across the plaza and towards the waterfront. I soon saw that the Presidencia was one of a very few buildings in San Blas that didn't look as if it had been put together at a party after several bottles of tequila and with half the blueprints missing. The houses that lined the unpaved streets were cobbled together from naked breeze blocks and corrugated iron, their only concession to colonial design the iron bars embedded like cages around the windows. There were some old buildings but most were in a state of disrepair and had tufts of brown grass growing out of cracks in the walls. In amongst the houses were empty plots with horses and cows tied to palm trees.

The harbour itself was full of rusting fishing vessels, tethered to each other three deep along the quayside. Few looked as though they would ever leave port again. Masts leaned drunkenly across each other and pelicans rested undisturbed in their nests in the rigging. Seeing this decaying port, I tried to imagine what it would have been like for my great-grandfather to watch a cargo steamer nudge up against the quay and have its load of machinery or cotton bales winched onto waiting ox-drawn carts.

Next to the old customs office and *embarcadero* building I found a fisherman painting his upturned motorboat. The customs hall was just a shell and I wondered what had happened to it.

'It was wrecked by fire in the 20s,' the fisherman said.

I told him about my great grandfather being in San Blas in the 1890s.

'Ah, the boom years! That was before my time, but it was still a working port when I was young. When the boats came in they would sound their whistle and the whole town would come running to see the goods. It was here that I first saw a radio and first tasted ice cream.'

Anxious to find the harbour master, I asked for directions and he pointed me to a smoked-glass office a hundred yards away.

I walked into the modern building and was hit by a wall of cold air from a fiercely efficient air-conditioning system. The duty officer wore a crisp white uniform. Perhaps because of the air con, he looked better preserved than anyone I had yet seen in San Blas.

I told him I had come to speak to him about old port records.

He shook his head, 'I'm sorry. We only keep records for a month or two.'

Somehow, I wasn't surprised. San Blas didn't look like the kind of town to keep exhaustive records.

'Do you know anyone who knows about the history of the port?' I asked.

'My friend Raul,' he said. 'He knows everything about the history of San Blas. Give me a minute.' He flicked through his desk diary and went into a back office to make a call. When he came back, he gave me Raul's address and told me he would be waiting for me.

Raul's house was near the baseball stadium. He was sitting in an armchair, working on a collapsed ironing board laid across his lap.

When he saw me he said, 'You're the English guy chasing after his ancestor, *verdad*?'

I said I was.

'I don't know anything about shipping records, but there was an Englishman living here, who was on the run.'

'Really?' I felt my heart beating faster. Could this be Arturo running from the bandits?

'He had to be rescued by the British navy.'

'Do you know who it was?'

He drummed his fingers on the ironing board and shook his head.

'Do you know when?'

'1830s.'

Arturo's father hadn't even been born then. Another dead end. I was getting used to them. 'Do you know anything about textile factories around Tepic?' I asked him.

'There was a factory near Tepic that was run by some British people. A beautiful building. I think it was a copy of a factory in Belgium. They had a bit of trouble there too, I seem to remember.'

He couldn't recall where it was or the name of the factory, but at least it gave me another couple of clues to explore when I got back to Tepic.

I nosed around the harbour for a few more hours and unearthed another 'historian'. He turned out to be a drunk who knew four stories, none of which was relevant. He did tell me one thing that sounded very interesting: that the Viking Erik the Red landed in a small bay seventy kilometres south of San Blas in the twelfth century. But a quick check proved this to be utter rubbish.

'WHAT DID you find?' asked Juan when I returned to the hotel.

I told him I'd found out next to nothing, apart from the fact that San Blas doesn't keep port records and that Erik the Red landed nowhere near the town in the 1100s.

A shadow passed over his face. 'Most of the records are here in Tepic.'

'*No te preocupes*,' I told him. 'I wanted to go and see it anyway.'

When I got to my room, I dug out all the bits of paper I had on Arturo: his marriage certificate and shipping manifests from New York, the Baedeker guide, the letters from Grandma, Great-Aunt Sophia's birth and baptism certificates and notes I had made in Tepic and San Blas. I laid them all out on the bed, hoping to notice something I might have missed. I took out the list I'd made on the bus from Guadalajara.

* *Find record of Aunt Sophia's birth – convent (✓)*
* *Record of Aunt Sophia's baptism – cathedral (✓)*
* ~~*Place Where Auturo lived – Tepic??*~~
* *Place where Arturo lived – Small Village?*
* *Look for place Arturo worked (Cotton mill, near water supply in Small Village)*
* ~~*Look for records of imports of Arturo's shipments at San Blas*~~
* *Don Domingo?*
* *House of Egery?*
* *The village church Arturo helped to build*
* *Find record of Ecroyd ('Flash Harry from Oswaldtwistle'), his death and/or descendants*
* *History of bandits in the area*
* *The Mango Orchard*
* *A bag of silver??*

I fell asleep on top of my papers. I dreamt I was following a ball of wool through a maze. I caught a glimpse of Arturo's shoes and brown leather case disappearing round the corner. I pulled on the yarn, hoping it would bring me closer to him, but no matter how hard I pulled, he was always one step ahead, just out of reach.

In the morning I woke feeling deeply rested in a way I hadn't since I set out from England. Perhaps there had been more to the dream, bits I couldn't consciously remember. I felt close to something. It was an odd sensation, not knowing what I was close to or from where the feeling came.

Whatever it was, I had to find the Small Village near the mango orchard. That was where Arturo had worked, where he had had one of his houses, where he had helped to build the chapel. I felt certain that all I had to do was look at a map. I went down to reception and asked Juan where I could find one.

He rolled his eyes. 'The only place with good maps is the tourist office. Trouble is, you need a map to get there.' He scribbled detailed instructions of buses to catch, streets to look out for. 'It closes at midday.'

I soon gave up trying to follow his instructions and jumped into a taxi.

'What are you doing in Tepic?' the driver asked as we drove off.

I glanced at my watch. I only had twenty minutes before the tourist office closed. 'My great-grandfather lived in Tepic at the turn of the century.'

'I don't want to worry you,' he said, 'but I think he might be dead by now.'

'He is,' I said. 'He died in the 1950s.'

'I'm sorry.'

We drove the rest of the way in silence.

The tourist office was a modern two-storey building with parquet flooring. There were spotlit aerial photographs of Tepic on the walls. I could hear scampering and giggling. I followed the sound to a mezzanine floor where I found two boys wearing baseball caps, swivelling on office chairs and throwing coins at each other. They stood up, almost to attention, arms behind their backs. '*Buenos días,*' said one.

'Would you like a Diet Coke?' asked the other.

I told them I was after a map and had some questions about Tepic a hundred years ago.

'*Ay!*' said the first. 'I'll get help.'

Help arrived in the shape of María. She had bleached hair and pearls strung over the top of her olive-green trouser suit. She crossed the room with her hand extended and addressed me in impeccable American-accented English.

'I'm looking for the small village where my great-grandfather lived between 1898 and the outbreak of the Mexican Revolution,' I began, relieved to be speaking English. 'I know it had a river running through it and it was walking distance from Tepic. Can you think what village it might be?'

María laughed. 'There are many villages near here, and nearly all of them have rivers running through them.'

'He worked in a cotton mill.'

'Okay,' she said thoughtfully, 'but there were a fair number with cotton mills too.'

'I was afraid you might say that.'

'Do you know anything else about the mill?'

'I was told there was a mill near here where foreign people worked, and that the factory is a copy of one in Belgium.' I pulled out Grandma's letters. The first phrase I saw was, '*I don't want you to waste your time on a wild goose chase.*' The second was the name of the company that her father worked for. 'I think the factory was owned by the House of Egery.'

She sat bolt upright as if she'd just received an electric shock. 'You mean Casa Aguirre! Yeah, sure, they practically owned the state; they had factories and plants all over the place.'

I felt adrenalin coursing through my veins. 'You have information on them?'

'Yeah, sure.'

'Do you have a list of where their factories were?'

'Let me see what I can find.' She rummaged in a filing cabinet and brought a handful of folders back to the table.

She was paying particular attention to one black and white leaflet. I wanted to grab it, sure it would give me a name, a clue to where Arturo had worked, where he had lived, where he had left his bags of silver. Her lips moved very slightly as she read in silence. I held my breath. She opened her mouth to speak then thought better of it.

'Bellavista,' she said eventually, still reading the leaflet. 'Try Bellavista. It matches everything you said. There was a big cotton mill there, there's a river running through it, and it's a fifteen-minute bus ride away, so it would have been walking distance.' She carried on reading and then spotted something else. 'Hey! It says here the factory is a copy of one in Ghent.' She handed me the leaflet. The black and white photo of the factory's grand facade gave it a timeless quality. It looked like a place where the past might not be so distant from the present.

'Happy?' she asked.

I realised I must have had a broad grin on my face.

She looked pretty pleased with herself too. 'There's a museum there. It'll be closed by the time you get there so you should go tomorrow. Ask for Professor Roberto Monroy. He'll tell you all you need to know.'

FIFTEEN MINUTES after leaving Tepic, the bus slowed to cross a hump-back bridge over a fast-flowing river. By the bridge was a sign, *BIENVENIDOS A BELLAVISTA*. The road surface changed from asphalt to cobblestones. We went under an archway, past some stone terraced cottages. They looked old but unlike anything else I had seen in all of Latin America. They were colonial, but not Spanish in design. They looked *British*. The only houses I had seen like these were in textile and mining towns of northern England.

I climbed down from the bus and walked up the hill. At the top was a larger house with a balcony above the front door. It looked familiar. Where had I seen this before?

Next to the house gold and red railings stretched for fifty

yards. Another fifty yards beyond that was a building identical to the Wesleyan chapel Arturo's family had attended in Tottington.

The women who'd got off the bus with their wicker baskets at the same time as me had disappeared, leaving me with no visible evidence that I wasn't in an old part of Bury on an uncharacteristically hot day. From the shadows of the doorways I could even hear a football match on television. I wondered if I had accidentally wandered onto a film set for a period drama and half expected a production assistant to bustle me aside at any moment.

Then I saw the factory. The photo in the tourist office leaflet didn't do it justice. It looked more like an ambassador's residence than a cotton mill. It also didn't look particularly open. A heavy lock and chain hung round the iron gates.

'*Cerrado!*' came the voice of a crumple-faced old man. Closed. He hobbled from a side entrance with the look of someone roused from several days' sleep. Wheezing at his side was a pit bull terrier with no ears.

'*Buenos días*,' I said. 'I'm looking for Professor Roberto Monroy.'

'He's not here.'

'Is there someone else I could talk to?'

'I don't know where anyone is. We're closed.'

I dug into my pocket and produced a handful of *pesos*. He grumbled some more, kicked his dog out of the way, unlocked the gates and made a vague wave towards some stairs and said that was where I could find Fernando.

I didn't know who Fernando was, but climbed the stairs and found myself in a room like a classroom, one that hadn't taken down its open-day displays before breaking up for the holidays. It was stone-floored, and there was a faint smell of polish. There was no trace of Fernando so I looked at the display cabinets and the black and white photos on the wall. I was hoping to see a picture of my great-grandfather. There was a picture of a whiskery, dignified-looking man called Santiago Stephens but most of the photos were of angry crowds carrying banners, their fists raised. One was of *campesinos* hanging dead from a tree.

I heard shouts of 'Gooooooooooaaaaaaal!' and followed the noise upstairs. In Mexico the national play-offs register in importance somewhere between a presidential election and a papal visit. I came to a darkened room where two young men were watching the football on an enormous television. I cleared my throat.

'*Ay, disculpe, señor,*' said one as the other hastily switched off the television. 'I'm Fernando. How can I help?'

'Sorry to disturb you. I'm looking for Professor Roberto Monroy.'

'He's not here today. Is there anything I can help with?'

'I'm looking for evidence of my great-grandfather. He worked here with a Spaniard, Don Domingo, and an Englishman, Arturo Ecroyd, about a hundred years ago.'

'Was your great-grandfather called Stephens?' asked Fernando.

'No, why?'

Fernando looked disappointed. 'That's my name, Fernando Stephens. My great-great-grandfather was English. I just wondered if you might be a relative.'

I shook my head. 'Sorry.'

'What was your great-grandfather's name?'

'Greenhalgh,' I said.

'Could you write it down for me?'

I wrote in clear, capital letters: G-R-E-E-N-H-A-L-G-H.

'Greenhal?!'

I nodded.

'Greenhal?!' Fernando was shouting, his nostrils flared.

What had I said?

'*Casi todo el pueblo se llama Greenhal!*' Nearly the whole village is called Greenhal!

'It can't be,' I said. 'You're thinking of Arturo Ecroyd. He had a family with a woman from here. My great-grandfather was Arturo Greenhalgh. He was a Methodist.' I felt indignant he could have confused the two.

Fernando was laughing as he exchanged a high five with his friend. '*Ay caray! Un Greenhal! Un Greenhal!*'

'I think you've made a mistake. You must be thinking of Ecroyd, not Greenhalgh.'

'That's what I'm telling you. The whole village is called Greenhal!'

'It can't be.'

'It is!'

'The whole village?'

'Okay, not the whole village, but a good number.'

My lungs felt as though they had had all the air sucked out of them. I steadied myself against the back of a chair and breathed in slowly. So this was it.

'Do you want to meet your relatives?'

Fernando didn't wait for an answer. He led me out of the factory gates towards the row of workers' cottages and we walked into one of them. He introduced me to his mother and brother, who were sucking on chicken bones, their plates on their laps in front of the national play-offs on TV.

Before he'd explained who I was, Fernando disappeared. I watched the football over his family's shoulders but made no attempt at conversation; I didn't want to interrupt such an important game. My head was in such a state of confusion, I didn't know what to say anyway.

Ten minutes later Fernando bounced back in. Next to him, with a puzzled look on his face, was a good-looking, athletically built man, about five years younger than me. He was wearing a white T-shirt with BOY LONDON written on the front.

'This is Manuel, known as Güero,' Fernando said. '*Es tu primo!*' He's your cousin!

We shook hands awkwardly, like wedding guests forced to share a table.

'*Hola, primo,*' I said, finally finding my voice. I pointed to my sun-bleached hair. 'I'm *güero* too.' *Güero* is the Mexican word for blond. Mexicans consider anyone with hair lighter than black to be blond. Güero's hair was darkish brown, but his complexion was lighter than mine. 'You look English,' I told him.

He smiled. 'I have English ancestors, like you.' He hesitated, apparently reluctant to venture much further on the topic of family.

I seemed to be moving through the syrupy unreality of a dream. When he said, 'I have English ancestors, like you,' I felt a charge go through me, as if I was in a vortex and had travelled in time.

'Let's go and see Tío Arturo,' Güero said.

Another Arturo? I didn't know who this Uncle Arthur was, but nodded. After months of searching I was now being pulled along. My journey was no longer my own. This must be what it's like to die, I thought: to arrive at a point from where you surrender to forces beyond your comprehension and control. I felt no fear, no panic. I just observed all that was going on around me as though it was happening to someone else.

We walked back past the factory gates and followed a line of tall yellow-and-pink-blossoming trees. At the far corner of the factory was a cylindrical watchtower with slits just wide enough for a rifle. We turned into the plaza. Carved above the vast arched doorway of the Wesleyan-looking chapel was the Masonic symbol of an eye set within a triangle.

I couldn't fully tune in to what Güero and Fernando were saying, but registered something about Tío Arturo being my great-grandfather's grandson.

We arrived at an attractive house behind a well-kept hedge and crimson iron gate. Fernando took out a coin from his pocket and tapped it against the gatepost. My eyes were fixed on the front door.

No one came out.

He tapped the gatepost again, this time a little harder.

I heard a click and watched the door draw inwards, the gloss finish catching the sun. I held my breath. I saw a thickset man in his fifties. He reminded me of a picture I had once seen of Richard Burton's brother, who shared the actor's fine features and frame but whose face was a working man's. Then I heard my voice.

'*Buenas tardes,*' he said.

'*Buenas tardes.* My name is Robin. I am from England. I believe you're my uncle.'

He held my gaze a second longer and then smiled. 'You'd better come in then.'

Meet the Parientes

NOTHING CAN prepare you for what you hadn't imagined possible.

'*Pasa, pasa,*' said the man with the face of Richard Burton's brother. Come in, come in.

I followed him to a large room with a polished concrete floor. A ceiling fan rattled as it rotated slowly above us. Neither of us seemed to know what to say.

'I'll get a piece of paper,' he said, and started to rummage through a chest of drawers, his breathing a little laboured as he turned over its contents. He handed me a single sheet of lined paper and a chewed pencil. 'Show me.'

I wrote my name and the full names of my mother and grandmother. His brow furrowed. I then wrote my great-grandfather's name. I wrote it as he was known in Mexico: Arturo Greenhalgh.

He snatched the pencil from my hand and wrote his own name: Arturo Berecochea Greenhal.

We looked at each other.

He began writing again. The names of his parents, Manuel Berecochea and María Greenhal, and her father: Arturo Greenhal.

He spelt the surname the way Fernando in the factory had pronounced it, missing off the final G and H. Was this a Mexican simplification of the thousand-year-old English name? Or was he not related at all?

'I was named after my grandfather,' he said.

'Arturo Greenhalgh?'

'*Sí.*'

'Greenhalgh or Greenhal?'

'Greenhal, Greenhal,' he said, pointing at the way I had spelt my great-grandfather's surname.

Spanish-speaking people are notoriously lax in their spelling of non-Spanish names, even in the best newspapers. I didn't want to push the point as though I doubted his literacy.

'My great-grandfather managed a cotton mill about a hundred years ago,' I said.

'My grandfather managed the mill, that's true.'

'He had a big moustache.'

He smiled. 'It went like this.' And pretended to fashion the waxed tips of a handlebar moustache. 'It was wider than his face.'

That was just how I remembered it in the photos.

'He was here at the same time as Ecroyd –'

'*Ay, sí.* Ecroyd was here too. He was killed. I think it was about the time my grandfather left.'

'I knew Ecroyd had left a family, but I didn't know that Arturo Greenhalgh had left one too.'

He laughed. 'He did. One daughter, my mother, and she had eleven children.'

'Is your mother still alive?'

He looked down at his hands. 'She died in the 80s.'

A daughter? Eleven grandchildren? Could we really be talking about the same person?

'What was the name of the company your grandfather worked for?' I asked.

156

'Casa Aguirre.'

'And he lived here in the village?'

'He had two houses, one beside the factory, the other in town. Then he left to go back to England.'

'At the beginning of the revolution?' I asked.

He looked troubled. His hand trembled as he fumbled with the piece of paper. His breathing became laboured again. Was he angry?

Suddenly, he stood up. His chair fell backwards and clattered to the floor. He didn't attempt to pick it up, but rushed to the telephone at the far side of the room and dialled. *'Oye, Chela,'* he said in a fluster. *'Nuestro abuelo: ha regresado. Esta vivo. Esta aquí!'* – Our grandfather: he has returned. He's alive. He is here!

He has returned? Oh shit. They think I'm him. And now they're going to club me to death because he deserted them.

Arturo Berecochea Greenhal turned round and my fears of being clubbed to death evaporated. His face was creased into a wide smile. He waved his arms around wildly as he spoke. 'Yes, from England. He just arrived. No. A bus I think. I couldn't tell you. I didn't know he was coming. Yes, he speaks Spanish. No, he's on his own. He says he didn't know we were here . . .'

He was on his second or third phone call by now. After a few more he rejoined me at the table, still grinning.

'You were talking to your brothers and sisters?' I asked.

'Yes, and they want to meet you.'

'Are there really eleven of you?'

'*Sí,*' he said and proudly counted each of them off on his fingers. 'Lola, Petra, Virginia, Eva, Chela, Javier, Samuel, Pepe, Enrique and Margarita and me. That's eleven!' He held up six fingers to demonstrate his point.

'Eleven – that's a football team!'

'Ah, you like football, eh? My team is Las Chivas of Guadalajara.' He pointed at the Chivas memorabilia arranged like a shrine in one corner of the room. 'I saw England play Brazil in the 1970 World Cup. Bobby Charlton, Bobby Moore, Pelé –' He checked himself. 'How many children did my grandfather have in England?'

'Two. Great-Aunt Sophia, who was born here, and my grandma.'

'How many children did –' He hesitated and looked at the piece of paper with Grandma's name on it. 'Ruth, Arturo Greenhal's daughter, have?' He pronounced Grandma's name with difficulty, so it sounded like 'Root'.

'Just the one, my mother.'

His eyes widened. 'One? Wow, English television must be good!'

There was a knock at the door. It was Güero. He had left me alone to talk to my new *tío*, but had now come to take me to meet some of the other brothers and sisters, starting with Enrique, his father.

Tío Arturo looked troubled, as if he hadn't said all he wanted to say. 'Thank you for coming.' He shook my hand. His grip was warm, rough and strong. '*No te vayas, eh?*' he added. Don't you go anywhere, okay?

Güero led me to his father's home at the bottom of the square. Tío Enrique, Tío Arturo's youngest brother, was there to welcome me. He was taller and his features more refined.

'*Pasa, pasa,*' he said. He introduced me to his wife, a kind-faced, good-looking woman called Margarita, his very pretty daughters Ivonne and Margaret, and his younger son Luis, who was around nine. 'Margaret was named after Margaret Thatcher.'

He switched off the television and ushered me to a cluster of sofas and armchairs just inside the front door. He and his family then disappeared to the kitchen, from where I could hear whispered conversations. I was left to stare at a stuffed baby alligator on the coffee table. Its scaly skin was shiny, its teeth tiny but sharp, its tail arched above its body like a scorpion ready to strike.

They returned with drinks. Just as Tío Enrique was about to sit down, he suddenly remembered something and beckoned me to a framed photo on the wall at the far side of the room. It was of his mother with her children. They were all in stiff, studio poses and wearing solemn expressions.

'Does she look like your grandma?' he asked, pointing at his mother.

She didn't really, but she was almost identical to the way I remembered Great-Aunt Sophia – pretty and demure with a small chin.

I looked at the photo and pointed to one of the women. 'She looks like my mother.'

'That's Virginia. Güero will take you to see her *ahorita*.'

Judging from the haircuts, the photo had been taken in the 1970s. The men stood behind the women, who were sitting down, their mother in the centre. I followed his finger as he identified each one.

His wife interrupted him. 'The Berecochea sisters were known to be the best-looking girls in Tepic.'

'I can see why.'

'The brothers too!' Tío Enrique said in mock indignation.

That wasn't quite so obvious.

We sat down and I explained who I was and how I was related to their English ancestor. I asked what they knew about him.

'He was very *elegante*,' said Tío Enrique of his grandfather, adjusting an imaginary tie under his chin. 'Quitita, that's what we used to call my mother, always said how well dressed he was. He carried a cane with a silver head and the initials A.G. engraved on it. I had it until a few years ago. I don't have it now.' He looked thoughtful for a second, as if trying to think where he might have left it. 'And he had a gold watch too. *Muy inglés! Muy correcto!*'

Tío Enrique looked at me and I wondered how *elegante* I looked in my shorts and sandals, but nobody seemed to mind that I didn't have the sartorial grace of my great-grandfather.

'When did you leave home?' asked Ivonne. 'You've probably been away for many weeks, yes?'

'I set out nearly five months ago.'

Ivonne, Margaret and their mother gasped, holding their hands in front of their mouths. 'Five months! Who do you talk to?'

'Don't you get lonely?'

'Did your brother and sisters not want to come with you?'

'Who does your laundry?'

'Don't you get lost?'

I didn't get the chance to answer any of their questions, as Tío Enrique interrupted them. 'Europeans like to travel, *verdad?*' he said.

I nodded.

'Just like my grandfather. If he hadn't travelled, we wouldn't be here,' Tío Enrique continued.

I liked the way he cited my great-grandfather's extramarital activity as justification for my months of travel. 'How many members of the family are there?' I asked.

'About 300?' suggested Güero.

Tío Enrique nodded thoughtfully, then bunched his fingers together and said with a chuckle, '*Muchos, eh?*'

Muchos indeed. Not so much a football team as a football crowd.

The phone rang. It was Virginia asking when she was going to get to see *el pariente inglés,* the English relative.

As I made my way towards the door, Tío Enrique pulled me to one side and said furtively, '*Oye,* something I've always wanted to know. How do you pronounce our surname?'

Not only had they been abandoned, they had been abandoned with a surname they couldn't even say properly. Then again, the name Greenhalgh would probably be unpronounceable to anyone outside Lancashire, let alone to a people in whose language the letter H is always silent and the *sh* sound doesn't exist.

'Green, *como verde,*' I said, translating the first part of the name. He nodded – that much he knew. 'And then *halsh.*'

'Green*jalz?*'

'Not bad,' I said.

'Let me try,' said Margaret, trying not to giggle. '*Greenhunge?*'

'No, let me. It's Green*hulj,* right?' asked Ivonne.

Tío Enrique tried again, 'Green*jalce?*' It was as close as he would ever get.

Güero led me towards Tía Virginia's house, back towards the factory and then right, down a shady cobbled path by a stream. We crossed a bridge overlooking a sluice gate to an expansive concrete forecourt, fringed with purple flowers and mango and avocado trees. Walking towards us was a woman I had just seen in the photo. She could have been my mother's twin sister.

'*Bien-ven-ido,*' she said with slow emphasis and wrapped her arms around me. She kissed me on the cheek and then held me at arm's length to look at me.

'This must be the nephew from England,' called a voice from the entrance to the bungalow.

Güero introduced me to Virginia's husband, his Uncle Antonio.

He had deep blue eyes. I asked him if he had English blood too.

'I don't think so. My parents were both Spanish. I guess that's where the light eyes come from, but who knows?'

'We're a very cosmopolitan village,' said Tía Virginia. She disappeared into the kitchen and returned with a jug of lemonade, lumps of ice clinking.

Sitting opposite me, she fixed me with a determined look. 'So tell me what happened to my grandfather,' she said, as if trying to decide what she thought of me.

I told her how he had escaped from the revolution after being told to leave by bandits.

'Did he make it back to England?'

'Oh yes.'

'And what did he do when he got there?'

'He managed a cotton mill.'

'When did he die?'

'In the 1950s.'

'*Dios mío*. We thought he had died on the *Titanic*. Quitita – my mother – was convinced that was how he died, on his way back to see her.' She stared into the distance beyond me. 'The 1950s. Are you sure?'

I nodded.

'If only Mama María had known.'

'Mama María?' I asked.

'My mother's mother, Arturo Greenhal's *mujer*.'

I noted she used the Spanish word for both woman and wife.

'She must have died about the same time as him . . . If only she had known!' Tía Virginia swirled the ice in her glass pensively. 'Why did he never come back?'

'Well, there was the revolution . . .' I trailed off. *And his wife*. I was unsure how to broach this subject. I had already shattered the long-held belief about their English ancestor dying a glamorous and heroic death. I wondered how much more I should say, but could think of no substitute for the truth. 'You know that he . . . had a wife in England?'

'*O sí!*' said Tía Virginia – who I realised was known by the shortened version of her name, Virgin. 'She was here for a while, wasn't she?'

I nodded, relieved that I hadn't had to blow another myth out of the water.

'Then he was here for a long time on his own. Mama María was very good-looking . . .' She mimed the embrace of an intimate dance and started to laugh. With that one little mime she explained away the existence of 300 relatives.

The sun was beginning to fade and the mosquitoes to bite. I wanted to return to Tepic and send a fax to Grandma to tell her what I had found – I had to tell someone. But Tío Enrique had already asked me to return to his house so that he could drive me to visit his sister Chela. The fax would have to wait.

Tía Chela's house was a large two-storey building on one of the main thoroughfares in Tepic, not far from where I was staying. I ran back to the hotel to collect what photos I had of my family. By the time I returned, as well as Tío Enrique, his wife and four children, Tía Chela had assembled her husband, a quick-witted ex-boxer and baseball player, all eight of her children and a dozen or so grandchildren.

'I knew it!' Tía Chela said as she emerged from the crowd to give me a welcoming hug. 'I knew he'd come back.'

I liked Tía Chela immediately, despite the fact that, like everyone else, she seemed to think I was the reincarnation of their grandfather. Like Tía Virgin, she could have been my mother's sister. She was bigger-framed than either of them, but moved with grace, and her face shone from soft almond eyes and an ever-present smile.

My first impression of her was that she was the hub of the family. I mentioned this to one of her daughters later and she nodded, saying, 'She is very *comunicativa*.'

Tía Chela took me by the hand and introduced me to each of her children. I was beginning to feel a little overwhelmed. Just her family alone was bigger than my entire English family.

The introductions never stopped. Tía Chela's sons and daughters and their families arrived constantly. Tía Chela cleared a way through and shooed a couple of children out of a dark-wood rocking chair.

'*Esta mecedora*,' she said, resting her hand on the back of the chair, 'was my grandfather's.'

I sat in it and rocked to and fro.

'These were his too.' She walked over to two framed paintings on the wall. 'They tell the story of a relationship. This one is about courtship.' In the picture a young couple were kissing in a garden, a statue of cupid looking on.

Tía Chela moved on to the second painting. 'This one is about marriage,' she said. 'There were another two pictures, one about family, another about old age, but only the first two survived.'

I got up to get a better look. The man in the picture looked like Arturo. He had a big smile, round face, a waxed moustache. He was sitting at a small dining table with a woman in a blue pinafore dress. They were toasting each other with a glass of sherry. The caption under the painting read:

> *Más que el oro vale una buena esposa*
> *Y no hay otra tan deseable cosa*

A good wife is worth more than gold
And there is nothing else so desirable

Were these pictures intended as a reminder of what Arturo had
left behind in England or what he had in Mexico? Or did they
perhaps imply that a good wife is such a wonderful thing, it is
better to have two?

There was so much I wanted to ask, I didn't know where to
begin. Tía Chela seemed to sense the questions I was trying to
frame in my mind. Someone shouted to say Tío Arturo wanted
her on the telephone.

'We have much to talk about. Come back another day and
we'll talk *con calma*,' she said as she walked to the phone.

When she came back she passed on Tío Arturo's request that
I return to the factory the following day so that he could introduce me to his brother Javier. No time was given, but I was told
that he would be there waiting.

I took this as my cue to leave. As in all the other houses I
had visited that afternoon, I was asked to stay, but I wanted to
go back to my hotel, draw the curtains and lie down. The
telegrams office, where they had a fax machine, was already closed,
and it was too late to phone. It was probably a good job anyway.
I needed to sleep and see in the morning if it was all still true.

I STEPPED off the bus in front of the factory in Bellavista. There
was no sign of the grouchy caretaker or his earless dog from the
day before. The gates were open, so I walked in. As I reached
the factory steps, someone called my name. I turned round to
see Tío Arturo trying to keep up with another man, who was
walking briskly towards me.

'This is my brother Javier,' he said breathlessly.

Tío Javier had a silver pen and a miniature screwdriver sticking out from his shirt pocket. But the most noticeable thing about him was his eyes. They were as green as mine, the same colour my great-grandfather's had been. And they stared into mine as he gripped my hand firmly between his.

I assumed we were going to do a tour of the factory, but Tío Arturo disappeared and Tío Javier put an arm around my shoulder and guided me to his house, next door but one to Tío Enrique's.

As we walked through the front door, he whistled. Someone from deep within the house whistled back. His wife, Hermelinda, was waiting for us in the kitchen. She wore a pinafore with a dusting of flour down the front, and held a tortilla in one hand.

'Sit down,' said Tío Javier, pulling out a stool at the breakfast bar. He took two bottles of Modelo beer from the fridge and sat down with me. He had a more businesslike air than any of the other *tíos* I had met. His welcome was every bit as warm, but his questions were more rigorous. He really wanted to know everything.

I tried to answer all his questions about my family, what had caused me to retrace the steps of my great-grandfather, what had happened to him after his return to England, and about the precise pronunciation of the surname.

'What do your family in England think about your finding us?' he asked me, taking the small screwdriver out of his pocket and absent-mindedly twirling it round in his ear. I think he already knew that I hadn't had a chance to tell them.

'I need to send a fax.'

'*No problema*, I'll take you to my son's shop. He's got a fax machine.'

En route to his son's business in the centre of Tepic, Tío Javier drove me round the outskirts of the city to a patch of parched ground the size of a small football pitch. It was surrounded by a breeze-block wall.

'I learned the hard way that it doesn't pay to keep money in Mexican banks,' he said, and told me how his life's savings had been decimated several times, but most cruelly by the 'unplanned devaluation' of December 1994. That seemed a long time ago. It was no doubt a much fresher memory to him and millions of other Mexicans.

'It's better to invest in land and houses. *Esta tierra,*' he said, bending down, scooping up a handful of reddy-brown earth, 'this is something for me to leave my children. It's better than piles of worthless paper locked up in a bank.'

I looked at him and saw that he was speaking without rancour or self-pity. He just wanted me to know.

We got back into his pickup and drove on into town, but as we approached the centre, he had a better idea. 'Let's go and see Petra.'

Tía Petra, the second-oldest of the *tíos* and *tías,* lived in a house that was almost as big as Tía Chela's and filled with almost as many people. She greeted me with a hug, a quiet smile and the offer of almond biscuits her daughter had just made. We followed the sweet baking smell to the kitchen. It was noisy and chaotic, and I got the feeling that it would have been just the same any day of the week, with or without the arrival of a newly discovered relative from England.

A couple of grandchildren started to squabble over a Power Ranger toy. Tía Petra reached across the table, touched me on the forearm and beckoned for me to follow her. She led me to a room that looked as though it was rarely used, with two sofas crammed with lacy cushions. A bowl of papier-mâché watermelon slices and several crystal figurines adorned a glass-topped coffee table. On the wall was an oval mahogany frame about two feet high.

She lifted it from its hook and turned it to me. It was a photographic portrait of her grandfather, my great-grandfather, Arturo Greenhalgh. The only photos I had seen of him were small prints. Here he was practically life-sized. He looked very smart, as always, and wore a suit, starched collar and tie. His moustache, its tips stiffened with wax, extended across the width of his face.

'He looks like you,' she said. I couldn't see it but nodded. She added, '*Muy guapo.*' We both laughed and agreed that my great-grandfather and I were both *muy guapo*. Very handsome.

How would Grandma react to the news that I had discovered a village full of Greenhals? My new-found Mexican family were correct in assuming that she would get a surprise when my fax arrived, but they hadn't seemed to grasp, or hadn't wanted to grasp, that for Grandma the news was unlikely to be greeted with unalloyed joy. At the age of nearly eighty-nine how would she respond to the revelation that her hero, who was all a father should be, generous, kind and honourable, had been unfaithful to her mother?

There would have to be some realignment of old ideas with new realities on both sides. For Grandma it would mean coming to terms with Arturo's infidelity. For the Mexicans it meant accepting his abandonment of them.

Tío Javier left his pickup running outside a colonial courtyard a couple of blocks from Tepic's *parque central*. It was here that his son Javier, known as Javi, ran a dental equipment shop, and had his fax machine.

Tío Javier introduced us, told Javi I needed to send a fax and then disappeared.

'*Primo!*' said Javi, smiling. Cousin! 'It's good to see my great-grandfather's adventurer's spirit lives on.' Javi seemed to view my journey in much more practical terms than his father's generation: I had merely inherited our great-grandfather's appetite for adventure. The same inquisitiveness and restlessness that had driven him had driven me. And here I was.

He gave me some paper and found a table where I could write my messages – I had to tell Juanita too. He seemed to understand immediately how the news might be difficult for Grandma to accept.

'What are you going to say?' he asked.

'I don't know,' I said. 'I'll tell her she's going to have to write a few more Christmas cards this year.'

'Good luck.' He laughed and then left me alone to write.

'Dear Grandma,' I began, 'you might want to sit down . . .'

EVERY ONE of my new family had said to me, '*Mi casa es tu casa*' – that their home was my home – but it was Tío Javier who, immediately after I had sent the fax, collected my bags and carried them to a room he'd had made up for me in his house. It was his home that became mine for the next few weeks.

I quickly settled into Mexican village life. I enjoyed the quiet of the night, pierced only by the distant barking of dogs and the crowing of cockerels around dawn. I got used to the sound of the morning market, which had usually been packed away by the time I got up. I learned about the village's rhythms, and how unchanged it was from the time my great-grandfather was there. There were old certainties on which the villagers relied: the planting of the maize, the harvesting of the sugar cane. Wednesdays were generally windy, and so that was the day the village did its washing – although as every day was hot and dry I didn't see what difference it made.

'Doesn't it ever rain here?' I asked Tío Javier one day.

'Oh yes. The rainy season begins on 22 June.' He thought for a second and added, 'About midday.'

Most of all, it amazed me how quickly I became accustomed to being part of a family I hadn't even known existed a few days before. Tía Hermelinda would leave my breakfast of freshly squeezed orange juice and a plate of sliced watermelon, mango and papaya under a tea towel on the kitchen table. No matter what time I emerged from my room, she would always appear, as if by magic, spoon me some yogurt from a tub in the fridge and pour me a bowl of corn flakes from the packet she for some reason kept in the oven, along with the clean tea towels.

As often as not, Tío Javier joined me at the table, shaved and smelling of Old Spice, and would wait for his wife to bring him a coffee. He was always anxious to know if I had slept well and if my breakfast was to my liking. I always had, and it always was.

I was eating breakfast one morning, looking through the list I had drawn up on the bus ride from Guadalajara, when Tío Javier came into the kitchen carrying a giant VHS video camera on his shoulder. 'Tell me everything,' he said, pressing the record button. The camera was the size of a rocket launcher but made a timid squeaking noise as the cassette spools turned.

I looked up at him. 'What do you want me to tell you?' I asked. I've never been much of a talker first thing in the morning.

'Everything,' he said again, squinting into the eyepiece.

Lost for words I read aloud the list I had been looking through when Tío Javier had come in. When I got to 'Mango Orchard' I realised I hadn't even asked anyone about it.

'Tío, do you know where there was a mango orchard near here?'

Tío Javier didn't answer my question but put the camera on the breakfast bar and looked at the list over my shoulder. 'You found a bit more than you bargained for, eh?'

I grinned. '*Sí*.'

He pointed at Ecroyd's name. 'I can help you with that.'

After breakfast, he drove me into Tepic to meet Sara, the grand-daughter of the man Grandma had referred to as 'Flash Harry from Oswaldtwistle', the gambler, the drinker, the man who was murdered still owing my great-grandfather money. The man who had had the secret family in Mexico, although now, of course, I knew he was in good company.

In fact, Tío Javier told me as we drove along, Ecroyd had left not just one Mexican family but two, although all his grand-children, apart from Sara, had left Tepic.

'The Ecroyds,' said Tío Javier, 'are friends of the family. They are *buena gente*.' Good people. 'Despite what happened with Lupe.'

'Who's Lupe?' I asked.

Tío Javier laughed. 'Sara's mother, Ecroyd's daughter and my father's lover. Every time my mother saw her across the square in Bellavista, she would yell, "*Cabrona!*" and shoot at her with a rifle.'

'She sounds quite lively, your mother.'

'Ooph! You can say that again.'

Tío Javier pulled up outside the one-storey house where Sara lived with her daughter and grandson. Sara came to the door and embraced Tío Javier, and then, when he explained who I was, embraced me twice. She was probably no older than any of my *tíos* and *tías,* but seemed more frail and worn by life.

As she led me through to her living room, I thought how differently I would have felt about this meeting had it taken place before I had met my great-grandfather's family. It would have been the greatest discovery, but now all I really wanted to know from Sara was how her grandfather had been murdered.

She seemed happy to talk about it. 'His maid went to the market one Saturday morning,' Sara said, 'but she failed to close the front door properly. Eight men who were hanging around in the street saw the door was ajar, and entered the house to steal all they could. They didn't realise that the master of the house was still there, and when they came across my grandfather they stabbed him in the chest as he lay in bed.'

I'd always assumed Ecroyd had died in a fight, but, like my great-grandfather, it seemed he hadn't been granted a heroic death either.

'Eight men – no one could be really sure it was the same eight men – were rounded up by the Casa Aguirre security force and executed by firing squad in the town plaza.'

Like the Greenhal family, the Ecroyds were proud of their English heritage, although I noticed Sara was vague about her ancestor's legacy. Other than describing her grandfather's murder, she seemed happier to talk about her own family. She brought photo albums from her bedroom and showed me pictures of her daughter and granddaughters, who lived in California. 'You must visit them next time you're there,' she said, and wrote me their address.

Before we returned to Bellavista Tío Javier said he wanted to show me something. 'Those men who killed Ecroyd,' he said, as we walked across the plaza towards the cathedral, 'It had nothing to do with robbery. It was revenge.'

'Revenge?'

'Ecroyd was no angel. But his killers paid the price.'

He led me to the right-hand side of the cathedral tower and

pointed to some bullet holes in the wall, weather-worn to the size
of golf balls. 'This is where they were shot,' he said. '*La revolución
no fue para los niños.*' The revolution was not for little boys.

It wasn't until later that I learned about the conversations the
Greenhals had about my arrival. Not unreasonably, considering
that a defining chapter in their family's history had been abruptly
reopened after a hundred years, they wanted to be absolutely
sure who I was.

As soon as I had left Tía Virgin's house on the first afternoon,
she had been straight on the phone to Tío Arturo.

'What do you think?' she asked. 'Is he really a member of the
family?'

'I think so,' he replied. 'He looks like Magda, Petra's daughter.'

'I thought the same thing.'

'He seems to be *buena gente*, and he's polite,' said Tío Arturo.
'But I'll get Javier to check him out.'

During those first days I never really had the time to worry
about how the Greenhals were reacting to me; I spent every
waking hour meeting people, asking and answering questions.
I guess if I had been inventing the whole thing, I would have
been worried. However, although I wasn't aware of the conversations they were having between themselves, I sensed that they
were anxious to see some proof that I was who I said I was.

In the fax I sent from Javi's shop I asked Grandma for copies
of her father's photos, including the ones from above the fireplace, and answers to a few questions, including what part Arturo
had played in the First or Second World War. I only knew that
he hadn't died in either. If I could show that he had at least
taken part, it might in some small way compensate for the lack
of a heroic demise.

The following morning Javi called to say a fax had just arrived. Tío Javier was very excited, but I tried to manage his expectations. Javi had said the fax was short, so it sounded as if Grandma hadn't had time to dig out the photos or give me a very considered response.

I felt awful for Grandma. She would have been going about her day, probably expecting nothing more than a call from the milkman and perhaps for the greengrocer to deliver the vegetables. And then my fax arrived.

I thought about phoning, but the poor quality of the lines and the time difference – seven hours – made it difficult, and somehow I thought a fax would be better. That way she would have more time to absorb the news before she responded.

I went into Tepic and called in on Javi, who handed me the fax. He hadn't managed to decipher the English but correctly guessed that it didn't really tell us a great deal that we didn't already know. She had only just received the fax and, realising I needed a quick response, had written back immediately. Although she hadn't had time to copy the photos, she tried to answer some of the questions I had asked.

Did Arturo fight in either World War? No. In the first he was working in an essential industry, making bandages and officers' uniforms, and he was too old for the second.

Where did he die? In hospital in Manchester.

Also in her fax she asked how, if her father had left only one daughter behind, the Mexican family still had his name. In fact many of them didn't. Only the *tíos* still had the name; all the *tías* lost it when they married, but they and their families all considered themselves Greenhals.

She signed off by saying, 'I'll write more in a day or two.'

Catching the bus back to Bellavista, I bumped into Güero at

the bus station. A few minutes after we set off a smooth-looking man about the same age as Güero jumped on the bus. Güero beckoned him to come and join us. It was Tío Javier's youngest son, Manuel. He was the only one of Tío Javier's children still living at home, though our hours had not yet coincided, so this was the first time we had met. He greeted me courteously, though he seemed a bit put out that this new *pariente* from England was staying as a guest in his own house and no one had thought to tell him. I felt like the returning prodigal son, for whom the fatted calf is killed and who therefore upsets the brother who never left. It took him a few days to come round.

By the time I got back to Bellavista, Tío Javier had already phoned Javi and knew all about the contents of the fax. He seemed disappointed.

The next morning I was woken by the incessant snapping of firecrackers and the strains of mariachi music. I got up and made my way to the kitchen.

Tío Javier and Tía Hermelinda were sitting at the table, eating breakfast.

'Wow, look who it is,' said Tía Hermelinda, amazed at seeing me up so early.

'What's going on?' I asked sleepily.

'Did you not hear my *serenata*? Javi organised it for me.'

'Is it your birthday?'

'It's 10 May.'

I must have looked blank.

'*El día de la madre*,' said Tío Javier. Mother's Day.

Oh shit, I hadn't bought a present. '*Felicidades*.'

I caught a bus into Tepic to find the city centre awash with stalls selling every kind of Mother's Day trinket imaginable: mugs, glasses and cocktail stirrers that said, *Quiero a mi mamá*, ceramic love hearts, cakes with poems written on them and even packets with a grow-your-own husband for the single mothers. Men of all ages were scrambling to find something before everything closed for lunch. It reminded me of shopping for presents on Christmas Eve.

I managed to find some flowers that didn't look too much like a last-minute buy and then called in on Javi, who had said he would give me a lift back to Bellavista for the big family lunch. When he saw me, Javi held up a roll of fax paper almost a metre long. It had just come through. It included a letter from Grandma and several of the photographs I had asked her to send. Seeing them again was like being reunited with a long-lost toy or an old school report. Here they all were, just as I remembered them, if a little grainy after being copied and passed through a fax machine. In one Arturo stood several yards from the camera with Mariah and a nursemaid holding Great-Aunt Sophia somewhere in Bellavista. There was one of Arturo's Mexican house, which I now knew to be the director's house beside the factory in Bellavista. Another showed a stagecoach, like an image from a Western, being pulled by six horses driven by two Mexicans in pointy hats. Finally, I came to my favourite, of Arturo on horseback.

In the letter Grandma admitted that her first reaction had been to ask me to come home. She hadn't wanted me to find out any more. I was amazed by her generosity and courage. She sent the Greenhals her best regards, and said, 'This story of yours is both overwhelming and fascinating, but it doesn't sound like my father at all. He wasn't like that. Are you sure they didn't just move into his house and take his name? Please find the truth of it all.'

When I arrived back at Tío Javier's, Tío Arturo was there, sitting at the breakfast bar, looking over old photos with his brother. They leaned over my shoulder as I translated Grandma's letter – missing out the bits that questioned their right to the Greenhalgh name – and then showed them the photos that had come with the fax. The first few, in which Arturo couldn't be clearly seen, provoked little interest. But when they came to the photograph of him on horseback, they both yelled. *'Eso es, eso es!'* That's it, that's it!

Tío Javier passed me one of the photos which they had been looking at when I came in. It was exactly the same photograph as on the fax. On the reverse, along with a few telephone numbers written in biro, was a note in Arturo's hand. It said, in Spanish, 'This photo is dedicated as an affectionate memento to María Stephens.' It was signed, *'Con cariño, Arturo. 17 de noviembre 1908.'*

'Ya vez?' said Tío Javier, slapping me on the back joyfully. 'You see? You really are my nephew! You are family!'

The Horse

I WAS EATING breakfast when Tío Javier came into the kitchen with Grandma's fax in his hand. He looked very pleased with himself. He had spent much of the night studying the photos, and had just worked out where the one of Arturo on the horse had been taken: at the old electric plant, halfway to La Escondida sugar factory.

'Come with me,' he said.

I followed him outside. There was a horse tied to a post by the front door, saddled up and ready to go, chomping on a pile of dry grass.

Tío Javier pointed to the photo in the fax, pushed a Stetson onto my head and said, 'Your great-grandfather was dressed as a cowboy. Now it's your turn.' He gave me a leg up into the saddle before I had the presence of mind to object.

I had ridden a horse twice before. On neither occasion did I discover a latent equestrian talent. Both times the horses had seemed to sense my fear and enjoy exploiting it. Whatever I asked them to do, they did the exact opposite: when I wanted them to stay still they would break into a trot, when I wanted them to speed up, they would suddenly stop, ensuring that the front of the saddle struck me painfully between the legs. The last time I had been riding was in Australia a couple of years before, when, as well as riding the horse, I took it swimming in the sea. It was not a pleasant experience. The shock of the cold water loosened its bowels and after just a few minutes I found myself swimming in horse shit.

'Are you okay?' Tío Javier called.

I nodded, fiddling with the saddle, trying to maintain my pretence of calm confidence. Not only did I not want the horse to sense and take advantage of my trepidation, I also didn't want Tío Javier to think his new nephew was a namby-pamby *gringo*.

The horse, he assured me, was *muy mansito*, very tame, and would always obey my commands. As he ran through the instructions, my mind began to wander. I found myself thinking about Arturo on the back of his horse. Tío Javier's house was on the same street as the factory. The route to the old electric plant would also have been one he took almost daily. I had scarcely dared dream I would go there myself one day. 'Can we go via the mango orchard?' I asked.

'I'll follow you in the pickup,' he said. 'Any problems, just give me a shout.' He untied the horse and handed me the reins.

The horse continued to chew and twitch its ears. It didn't move.

'Pull on the reins!' Tío Javier called, unaware that I'd hardly taken in a word of his instructions.

I pulled and we began to *clip-clop* very slowly through the village, past the lookout tower at the corner of the factory and then out of town.

As we headed past the factory, a police car came down the hill towards us. It was as high as a tractor, loaded with weaponry, and equipped with a thick bank of blue and red lights and two searchlights mounted on the roll bar at the back of the driver's cab. The police do not have a good reputation in Mexico. I didn't want to get in their way.

The horse walked to the centre of the road and stopped. The police car came to a halt.

I tried to catch the driver's eye to make him understand that I was blocking his way out of equestrian incompetence rather than a deliberate attempt to sabotage police business, but the glare of the sun reflecting off the windscreen meant I couldn't see anything at all. A fan buzzed and whined from deep within the bonnet of the police car.

A policeman stuck his head out of the driver's window. 'Buenos días,' he said with a cheeriness that surprised me. 'Would you be so kind as to move to the side of the road so I can get past?'

Before I had the chance to reply, Tío Javier jumped out of his pickup, waved apologetically to the policeman and pulled the reins to the right. The horse moved to the side of the road, and the policeman carried on with his day.

We covered the two kilometres to the plant at the same leisurely pace, past the millpond and the narrow canals which Arturo had helped to build, fields of maize and sugar cane and occasional piles of smouldering rubbish: orange peel, sofa cushions, scraps of newspaper and porn magazines. There was no sound other than the distant hum of the pickup, the *clip-clop* of the horse and the rustling of the crops in the wind. I tried to imagine myself as Arturo, high on the back of my steed, and wondered what would have been on his mind as he made his way towards La Escondida or the electric plant. Would it be the business problems waiting for him? Would he be looking out for a bandit ambush? Or would he be focused on some secret assignation? As for me, I had the morning sun on my face and now that the horse seemed to be behaving, I was feeling that all was right with the world.

After fifteen minutes the path narrowed and came to an end. I stopped and Tío Javier walked ahead and opened the gate.

'This is it,' he said.

I tied up the horse and followed him into a clearing bordered by a curve in the river. There were two brick buildings, covered in graffiti.

Tío Javier pulled the faxed photo from his pocket and pointed to the left-hand building with a tiled forecourt now overgrown with weeds and tall yellow flowers. 'He was just there.'

The corrugated-iron awning on the photo was no longer there, but I could see where the beams that held it up had been, and where Arturo had sat on his horse and stared at the camera. He was here, and here I was, staring back at him. I felt a warm shiver pass over me, not so much as if someone had walked over my grave, more like I had walked over his.

I followed Tío Javier across the forecourt to the doorway. The door had gone and we looked in. Shafts of sunlight from holes in the roof pierced the dark. 'That's where the turbine was,' he said, pointing at a raised platform. It must have been enormous. There was enough room to inflate a hot-air balloon. The place had been stripped of everything. There was nothing left apart from several spent light bulbs, an empty tin of brown paint and an overpowering smell of urine.

We walked to the hacienda building next door. The door frames, floorboards, even the roof had gone. 'People here are like ants,' said Tío Javier. 'They find a use for everything.' He tutted at the way it had been spoiled by neglect and vandalism, but it was still beautiful. The tree-lined arc of the river and the sharp incline of the embankment behind the buildings created a natural amphitheatre. It felt like a cathedral to nature. The air was filled with the fragrance of wild flowers, the sound of songbirds and the gentle ripple of the water.

He told me that the plant had provided electricity for the Bellavista factory, the village and all the surrounding areas until well into the 1970s. The place meant a lot to him. When Tío Javier and his brothers and sisters were children, their mother, Quitita, used to take them there on Sundays. He showed me where she would barbecue their lunch, and the spots where he and his brothers would fish and swim.

'Something else,' he said. 'You were asking about the mango orchard.' His tone was of someone about to break bad news.

'Yes?'

'It was over here.'

He walked ahead of me along the riverbank, beating back the undergrowth with a cane. He suddenly stopped.

'What is it?' I asked.

'This is all that's left.'

There was a solitary mango tree, twenty feet higher than the surrounding scrub. Despite being just a few yards from the river, the long grass was hay-coloured and crunched underfoot. The tree was stooped and gnarled, its leaves yellow and what fruit it had was shrivelled and brown, and hung like conkers from slender stems. There was no obvious fork in the tree and no bag of silver.

'Do you see the colour of the water?' said Tío Javier, walking over to the river. It was light grey. 'There's a sugar factory upstream. The chemicals they use to whiten the sugar have killed the trees, and the fish too. They keep saying they're going to clean it up, but . . .' He shrugged and let out a sigh.

We walked back to the horse in silence. When we got there he said, 'You want to go on to La Escondida?'

I wondered if he was getting bored, trailing me in his pickup at such a slow pace. But having got this far, I was beginning to feel more confident and wanted to continue for the next few kilometres.

In the saddle once again, I decided to be more adventurous. I dug my heels into the horse's ribs and we started at a trot. Trotting, I realised, was more interesting than the plod we had been doing until then, but I was slightly out of position and shifted in the saddle to correct myself. As I moved, I accidentally yanked on the reins and dug the horse in the ribs again and was thrown to the back of the saddle as the trot turned into a fast canter. My foot slipped from its toehold in the left stirrup and I lost hold of the reins. I grabbed the front of the saddle to stop myself from falling and didn't dare let go for long enough to reach for the reins, which by now had got caught on the horse's ears.

I froze, holding on as tightly as I could. I tried to slow my breathing and think how I could get the animal to stop, but I was already winded and we were now moving so fast I was finding it difficult to breathe at all. My eyes began to stream as the warm air rushed past me.

I tried desperately to remember the command Tío Javier had given me to get the horse to slow down, as 'Stop, you bastard!' definitely wasn't working. I seemed to remember him making a '*Shhhh!*' noise. I had nothing to lose and the sound seemed appropriate.

'*Shhhh!*' I hissed as loudly as I could.

The horse broke into a full-blown gallop, its hooves thumping the ground.

Through my tear-brimmed eyes, I saw to my horror that we were galloping towards a tree whose branches extended across the path at a height perfect for decapitation. The animal was trying to kill me. I clenched my teeth, screwed my eyes shut and ducked down as best as I could.

I felt sharp, stubby branches scrape down the back of my head, neck and back. My hands were aching with the effort of gripping the saddle as the leather rubbed away at my skin. I began to wonder how much more I could take and whether it would be a less painful death to jump rather than fall from the horse's back. But just as these thoughts entered my mind, the horse slowed down, ambled to a snail's pace and stopped. I don't think I had happened on the correct command, just that the horse was too knackered to gallop any further. But not as knackered as me.

A minute later Tío Javier caught up with me. I was still breathing heavily, my shirt soaked with sweat and my arms draped around the horse's neck.

'*Que pasó?*' he called from the cab of the truck.

I just looked at him, still in shock.

'*Que pasó?*' he asked again, looking concerned. 'What happened? You look very pale.'

I slid from the saddle and leaned on the pickup. 'It ran,' I managed to say eventually.

'I thought something had happened. I found this on the path.' He handed me the cowboy hat. 'How fast were you going?'

'Fast enough to give me these,' I said, showing him the blisters.

He began to chuckle. '*Hijo de su madre!* I came round the corner and you were nowhere to be seen. You must have been going like you were in the Kentucky Derby!'

I explained what had happened, and the more I told him about the accidental yank of the reins and the dig in the horse's ribs, the more he laughed. Then I told him about the '*Shhhh!*' command and tears began to run down his cheeks.

'That makes it go faster!' he spluttered.

'*Sí*, so I found out.'

WITHIN THE hour, the whole family knew that riding skills were one thing I hadn't inherited from my great-grandfather. For days afterwards people, some of whom I had never met before, would pass me in the street and call, '*Oye, ssshhhh, ssshhh!*' and collapse in fits of laughter.

Why Did You Come?

THERE WAS one question Tío Javier had asked me several times, a question to which I had no ready answer. '*Oye*,' he would say, 'Why did you come and look for us if you didn't know we were here?'

I wanted to answer fully and truthfully but the truth is not always easy to explain, especially in a second language.

'It was because of the stories that Grandma told me about her father. It was obvious from what he had said that Mexico was a very important part of his life. He left suddenly, amid the drama of the revolution, and I wanted to see what he had loved so much about being here and what he had left behind.' This explanation, which I had given him several times, still required a leap of faith. It came down to my travelling for several months on the strength of a feeling, an intuition. To Tío Javier, who had made a career out of repairing precision medical instruments, it didn't seem logical.

It wasn't just my motivation he found difficult to understand; it was the sheer improbability that I had found them at all. How could I have tracked down a family I didn't know existed, living in a nameless small village, near a small town somewhere not too far from Guadalajara?

During the course of my travels, although I'd had fleeting

moments of doubt, I had felt the wind in my sails, as if I were being blown in a preordained direction. I had always believed that there was something to find and never really thought about the possibility that I wouldn't find it.

Tío Javier didn't think this was very logical either.

Every time I tried to make him understand what had inspired me to undertake my journey, and how I had managed to track the family down, Tío Javier would screw up his face in a grimace of incomprehension and ask again, 'Yes, but why did you come to look for us if you didn't know we were here?'

As I sat with Tío Javier in his backyard one afternoon, watching him repair a dentist's chair for one of Javi's clients, he asked me again. 'There's one thing I still can't understand. What made you come to the other side of the world to look for us if . . .' he paused and sucked on his teeth for a second '. . . if you didn't *know* we were here?'

Since the arrival of Grandma's fax with the photos that proved I was the great-grandson of their English ancestor, there had been a subtle change in the family's reaction to me. Tío Javier still didn't understand how I could have embarked on such a long journey on the basis of a hunch, but he now accepted it. And while he couldn't begin to comprehend why anyone would go and look for something they didn't know was there, the fact that I had became a source of great pride.

The horse incident proved another milestone in the family's acceptance of me. While they still found it funny, the runaway horse had nearly killed me and represented a sort of rite of passage. I was now truly one of them, albeit one who wasn't particularly adept at riding.

From the kitchen Tía Hermelinda pushed open the mesh

mosquito screen and called to ask Tío Javier if we wanted some *refrescos*. He didn't respond, but she brought some anyway, leaving a couple of cans of Bongo on the dentist's chair's tray which would normally have held dental instruments. Tío Javier didn't acknowledge the drinks' arrival. He was wiping his oily hands on a rag, his green eyes fixed on me as I tried one more time to explain how I had come to be with them.

'Mexico was always very real to me,' I began, my voice sounding strangely distant, as if the words were coming from someone else. 'I first heard the stories when I was four or five. My grandmother made Mexico so vivid, so exotic. Even though the stories related to another century, a forgotten time, there was something about what I was told that still seemed . . .' I couldn't quite find the right word. 'Relevant . . . still here.'

Tío Javier sat perfectly still.

'Arturo had told Grandma several times that he had "lost everything he had in Mexico". Grandma had taken that to be wealth – which he certainly did lose and never regained – but as a young boy I wondered what this "everything" could be.

'After he returned to England, there was no one to whom Arturo could confide his secret, so the telling of these stories about Mexico was probably the only way he could keep the memory of his lost family alive. They became a lament for what he had left behind. And somehow the sadness in his voice reached me as I sat on Grandma's knee, listening to her recount the same tales that she herself had been told as a little girl.

'I came because of the stories. Arturo told the stories. He told them because you were here. I didn't know you were here. But I came to look for you because you were.'

Tío Javier held my gaze for a moment or two and then nodded

slowly as he picked up a pair of pliers and began to tug at the inner workings of the dentist's chair. He cleared his throat and, turning away slightly, wiped his eyes with the back of his hand.

Trouble at 'Mill

JUST AS Tío Javier's attitude evolved after the arrival of the fax and the incident with the horse, so did that of the rest of the family. Whereas before they had accepted me kindly, they now welcomed me with open arms, moving heaven and earth to help me uncover – as Grandma had put it – 'the truth of it all'.

Tía Virgin arranged for me to meet the Bellavista-born writer Miguel García Rodríguez, Tío Enrique gave me several books, which I saw from their inside covers should have been returned to the city library several years before, and Tía Chela reminded me to come round and chat '*con calma*'.

I spent several days in the city and university libraries in Tepic, poring over decaying newspapers from the time Arturo was in Mexico. I had hoped they would paint a picture of what daily life was like, but under the dictator Díaz the Mexican press was a better vehicle for advertising than for quality journalism. I leafed through page after page of ads, most of which seemed to promise cures for gonorrhoea, syphilis or impotence. My favourite was for Bigotina Legitima – a tube of black paste which young men too young to grow their own moustaches could smear on their top lips to give them one 'in the style of the Kaiser'.

Arturo certainly had no need for a fake moustache, and impotence didn't seem to be a problem. Having looked through fifteen years of newspaper back copies, I realised that the only real evidence of Arturo's time in Mexico was the family. I remembered Tía Chela's invitation and gave her a call.

'*QUÉ MILAGRO*!' What a miracle! Tía Chela exclaimed when I arrived at her house. She said this every time she saw me. 'It's the family horseman! I'm glad to see you're still in one piece.' She gave me a big hug and ushered me through the house to the back door. On the shaded patio I initially saw only a silhouette of wicker chairs, hanging baskets and a caged parrot.

'I asked Virgin round to help me remember all the things I have to tell you,' Tía Chela said. Tía Virgin, whom I hadn't noticed, rose from one of the wicker chairs to embrace me.

'*Ay*, Robin, I have to come to town to see you now. Every day you're out gallivanting with Javi, Ivonne or Margaret, and you've been at the library too.'

In the post office that morning she had met a friend who happened to be the cousin of the person who'd found some old newspapers for me in the library. It was impossible to have any secrets in Tepic. As if reading my thoughts, she grinned and gave me a playful punch on the arm. 'And how's that *Guatemalteca* of yours, eh?'

I had given Javi's number to Juanita and she had sent me a couple of faxes. The contents of these were now known by several hundred of my Mexican family. Though Arturo's relationship with María had remained a well-kept secret in England, in Mexico it would have been anything but.

'So where would you like us to begin?' asked Tía Chela. 'You know about the strike, right?'

I didn't know a great deal about the strike. I knew that the museum in the Bellavista factory was dedicated to it, and many had referred to it, but no one had told me what had actually happened. The historians I had spoken to had said things like, 'And of course there was the strike . . .' but hadn't gone into any more detail, as if relating the truth of it could only be done when the wind blew in a particular direction and the planets were perfectly aligned.

While at the library, I had found nothing except a small piece in *El Imparcial*: 'The workers of the Bellavista factory, a hacienda situated seven kilometres from this city, declared themselves on strike. The motive for this action was the poor payment for their work.'

'It all began in the 1890s with the arrival of Don Arturo,' began Tía Chela.

I dug out my notebook.

'It was then that the regime of terror started.'

This is not what I had been expecting to hear.

'They said he walked around the factory with a horsewhip in his hand. He would beat the workers if they were even a few minutes late back from a break, if their machine broke or sometimes just if he felt like it.'

'The blows weren't just little taps,' said Tía Virgin. 'They were vicious, violent whippings that tore into the flesh and left permanent scars.'

I couldn't believe what I was hearing. How much more did my Mexican aunts have to tell me about my great-grandfather's past? Tía Chela's expression was quite at odds with the barbaric events she was relating.

'It was the period of the Díaz dictatorship. The bosses could do what they liked. The rural police were at Casa Aguirre's beck and call. Any time they wanted someone arrested . . .' Tía Virgin clicked her fingers. 'It was done.'

Tía Chela said, 'They used to say Casa Aguirre owned not

only factories but their workers' souls. They could fire a troublemaker's entire family and banish them from the region. Don Arturo had some cells built at the factory so he could lock up workers without having to wait for the *Rurales* to act. Worst of all, people used to say he killed people with his own hands.'

I was shaking my head as I listened in disbelief. According to all the accounts I had heard, Arturo had been a kind and gentle man. He never even raised his voice. I couldn't believe he had whipped anyone, much less killed people with his bare hands. Was everything I'd been told completely wrong? My mouth felt dry and my forehead beaded with sweat. Was the ancestor I had spent my life wishing to emulate nothing more than a vicious thug?

'*Disculpe*,' I said, interrupting Tía Chela, who was now describing Don Arturo pacing the factory floor, his hands dripping with blood. 'This is . . . This can't be true!' Tía Chela and Tía Virgin both looked at me, startled. 'Are you really saying that he actually murdered people?'

'So they say,' said Tía Virgin matter-of-factly.

'But this doesn't match up to anything I have heard about him. Everyone describes him as *un caballero*.'

'Don Arturo, a gentleman!'

'Yes. Arturo Greenhal, my great-grandfather.' For a split second Tía Chela's face froze in an expression of incomprehension, then she collapsed back into her chair and erupted in laughter.

'*Ay no, lo siento!* We're talking about Don Arturo *Ecroyd*! I don't think my grandfather would ever have killed anyone.'

I had been wondering what on earth I could say to Grandma. I could never have told her that her father was a killer, even if she had asked me to find out 'the truth of it all'.

'*Bien*,' said Tía Chela, getting back to her story. 'Let me tell you about the strike. Apart from Don Arturo *Ecroyd's* brutality,' she said with a smile, 'the conditions in the factory were very hard. Mama María, my grandmother, worked there. She told me how Ecroyd lengthened the mill hours to sixteen a day. She was either at work or asleep; there was no time for anything else. She never saw the sun. Her skin turned a grey-yellow colour. Everyone looked like a ghost.'

'This had been going on for years, but it got worse about a year before the strike,' said Tía Virgin. 'And that's when the Elías brothers started to get people together.'

I hadn't heard of these men.

'Pedro and Enrique Elías lived a few doors down from Mama María,' said Tía Chela. 'They were close with her brother Carlos. Don Pedro and Don Enrique were great readers, not formally educated but very clever. They read Engels and Marx and all the outlawed newspapers, like *Regeneración*. Whenever Don Pedro managed to get hold of an issue, he would copy it out in his neat handwriting three times to give to his friends in the neighbouring factories.

'Anyone caught with such a newspaper would be in all kinds of trouble, but Don Pedro was very careful. They were very careful with everything. Of course, workers' meetings were banned, but Don Enrique arranged meetings using a rock in the middle of a field – where they have the football pitch now. When they saw the *Rurales* approaching, they'd start talking about the weather. There was no rule against that.

'The Elías brothers insisted that everything had to be democratic. Every decision was discussed and then put to the vote, and one night in 1905 they voted to go on strike. Don Pedro had written a letter of protest about conditions in the mill to

the general in charge of the state. The plan was to march peacefully
to Tepic to deliver the letter.

'Mama María said the anticipation and excitement were unbear-
able – like waiting for Christmas – but she felt great anxiety too.
Finally, the day arrived, the day it all happened.

'The workers arrived outside the factory: men, women, old,
young, even children – every single worker, except one who was
inside to sound the whistle that normally marked the start of
the first shift but would now signal that the strike was to begin.
A cheer went up as the gates were padlocked, and the bosses
already inside the factory buildings came out to see why the
workers were not at their machines and what all the noise was
about. They shouted at the workers, "Get back to work, you
sons of whores!"

'"Go and fuck your mother!" the workers shouted back.' Tía
Chela laughed. 'Excuse the language.' She leaned forward conspir-
atorially. 'I shouldn't say *groserías* in front of the parrot,' she said,
nodding towards the bright green and red bird chewing clum-
sily at its perch.

'Our brothers taught it to say some dreadful things when she
first got it,' said Tía Virgin.

'And now I'm having to try and train it to be more polite. It's
dreadful to be embarrassed by one's pets!' Tía Chela smiled.
'*Bueno*, what was I saying?'

'Go and fuck your mother?' I prompted.

Tía Chela laughed again. 'That's right! Oh dear,' she said,
wiping her eyes. 'The insults continued as the procession made
its way past the front of the factory and towards the old road to
Tepic. The *jefes* were left rattling the iron gates and shouting at
the workers, who were now feeling confident and excited.

'As the procession passed through the village, they were joined by more protesters from other factories in the area. People silently saluted them with a raised fist as they marched by. They climbed the hill the other side of Bellavista and headed into the open country. The protesters were now silent, unsure what would be waiting for them in Tepic. Would the general meet them? Would he be sympathetic to their cause? What would the reprisals be from Ecroyd and Casa Aguirre?

'Mama María said her mouth was dry with fear. She wasn't very old. Her brother Carlos put his arm round her and told her not to worry. "We will win a great victory."

'Mama María had taken some tortilla with her. She broke a bit off and shared it with the women on either side of her.

'They were coming into Tepic and were near the Jauja factory, beside the river – crystal-clear water it was, not like it is now. As they were about to cross the bridge, Mama María looked up and there they were – the army, rifles pointed at them. Don Enrique made a simple gesture to the strikers to stay where they were. "I'll go and speak to them." He walked on alone to talk to the officer standing with his troops, in his hand the letter they had come to deliver to the general.

'Mama María saw the look in the eyes of the officer and his men, who were staring back at them with cold, unemotional faces. The two men spoke for a few minutes, then Don Enrique returned to Mama María and the other protesters. "I told the officer he has to let us pass as this is a peaceful and legitimate protest. The officer said he had orders to prevent us from entering the city. He said that if we try to cross the bridge, they will shoot. Comrades! We have three alternatives. We can go on, we can stay here, or we can return to Bellavista."

'A young man pointed out that there were only thirty soldiers and hundreds of protesters. Some of them would get through.

There were a few cries of *Vámonos!* Then Francisca Quintero, a woman who had worked in the factory longer than anyone, came forward to speak and everyone listened.

'"Of course some of us would get across the bridge into Tepic alive. But what then? Twenty, fifty, maybe a hundred would be dead, but the army wouldn't stop there. If they didn't kill us here, they'd kill us in front of the general's house, or if they didn't kill us they would throw us in jail and probably shoot us later. How will that help our struggle? If we are killed, we have lost our lives and won nothing."

'Some were looking restless, others nodded, she continued, "We have a duty to carry on this struggle. What we don't win today, we will win tomorrow. I vote we return to Bellavista. We must stay alive to continue our fight."

'Eventually Pedro Elías stepped forward. Mama María knew the vote could decide whether she lived or died.

'As Don Pedro spoke, there was absolute silence. "If we are to demand freedom from our government, we need to show that we're willing to exercise those freedoms ourselves. Therefore, I ask you all to vote by raising your hands."

'Don Pedro asked who wanted to advance on to Tepic. Mama María bent her head towards the ground and screwed her eyes shut. She didn't dare to look up. Don Pedro asked who voted to stay. Mama María kept looking to the ground. When he asked who voted to return to Bellavista, she lifted her hand.

'She only looked up when Don Pedro said, "Resolution number one: the comrades have expressed their belief that they have to preserve life. We don't want martyrs. Only the living can continue the struggle. Resolution number two: we have won what we didn't have: unity. If we remain united in our beliefs, we can win little by little. Resolution number three: the people and newspapers of

Tepic have not backed us. For this moment, they are stronger than us. We will keep our unity and keep fighting. Comrades, be proud of what we have done today. *Regresémos a Bellavista!*"

'Slowly, they turned round and started to make their way back to Bellavista. Some shouted, "*Viva!*" Others raised a fist to the soldiers. Suddenly, there was the crack of gunfire. Mama María looked back and saw the soldiers aiming towards them. As the bullets flew over their heads, Carlos grabbed Mama María's hand and pulled her through the panicking crowd. Some jumped into the river to avoid being hit. She saw arrow-like divots being torn from the grass on the banks of the river as bullets ripped through the turf and fizzed into the water. Others ran straight up the hill, everybody trying to hide behind everyone else. She ran and ran until she could taste blood in her mouth. When she turned round she saw that the soldiers had not pursued them. Even so, it was a miracle that no one was killed.'

Tía Chela sat back in her chair and smiled. 'So that was the strike. The Elías brothers of course were sacked, but within a week, Mama María and everyone else were back at their looms.'

'It was a failure,' said Tía Virgin, 'but it was a glorious failure. In Bellavista we are very proud because they say it was the first strike in the country and the first spark of the Revolution.'

There was a loud beeping noise and the sound of the gate scraping across concrete at the side of the house. A second later Tía Chela's husband, Tío Rafael, drove into the backyard in a maroon Oldsmobile. With a grunt he heaved himself out of the driver's seat.

'*Hola, campeón!*' he called as he walked towards me with a slight limp. We shook hands, his enormous palm dwarfing my own. 'I hear they're looking for some rodeo riders for the fair next month. Shall I put your name down?'

'I'd rather stand in the middle of the bullring dressed in red.'

'It can be arranged!'

All at once the children of the house began to appear. Our chat *con calma* was over. I was disappointed because I had wanted to ask to what extent Arturo had been complicit in the strike? How had the events at Bellavista influenced those that followed around the country? And how did Arturo's relationship with María flourish if they were on opposing sides of an enormous social divide?

Tía Chela again sensed that I was still full of unanswered questions.

'*No te preocupes,*' she said, patting my hand. 'Don't worry. We'll talk again in a few days. Javi is taking you to meet someone tomorrow who has something to show you. *Poco a poco* – little by little – we'll find you "the truth of it all".'

Then the Revolution

AFTER A week of trying, Tío Javier had finally managed to track down Tepic's most famous historian and had arranged for Javi and me to meet him in the city library. Pedro López González, known as Maestro Pedro, was the only Mexican historian who had seen the Casa Aguirre archive in Spain. If anyone could help me discover anything about the working life of my great-grandfather, it was him.

Javi and I arrived ahead of time and found a table in the corner. I leafed through my notebook nervously, rereading the questions that Javi had helped me prepare. I was anxious to make the most of the meeting, as Tío Javier had told me it would be brief and it was unlikely I'd be able to secure another.

The appointed time came and went. Javi walked up and down, jangling the change in his pocket. Before he sold dentures and dental equipment for a living, Javi had been a history teacher. Maestro Pedro was one of his heroes.

I got up and looked through a shelf given over entirely to books by Pedro López González, hoping he would come while I was doing so.

Another fifteen minutes passed. I sat down again.

I wondered if he had come in and, not realising we were there, got bored and left. The woman at the reception desk smiled at the very possibility Maestro Pedro could have come in without us noticing. I returned to the table and waited.

Despite the fact that I had no idea what he looked like, when a short wiry man with tidy thinning hair bustled in a few minutes later, I knew it was him. He too seemed instinctively to know who he had arranged to meet. He walked purposefully towards us, his polarised rimless glasses still darkened by the bright sunshine outside.

'You must be the investigator from England,' he said in his delicate, high-pitched voice.

I felt hopelessly flattered, but said I was.

He sat down and without any attempt at small talk opened the hardback book he was carrying and pointed to a blurred black and white photograph. 'Do you know who this is?'

I looked at it closely. The man in the photo had neatly parted hair, a wide moustache and the modest bearing of a civil servant. It could have been Arturo had it not been for the eyepatch and the baggy-trousered military uniform. I shook my head.

'This is Esteban Baca Calderón,' said Maestro Pedro. 'He began life as a teacher, but went on to be a soldier, union leader, politician and even helped draft the Mexican constitution, the most radical in the world.' He pointed to the eyepatch. 'He lost his eye in the Revolution, fighting alongside Obregón.'

Calderón had obviously lived an impressive life but I couldn't see what this had to do with me or my quest to find out about my great-grandfather. 'Maestro Pedro, could you –'

'Cananea,' he interrupted, his body taut with energy and purpose. 'Have you heard of Cananea?'

The name rang a bell. 'There was a strike there, wasn't there?' I said, trying to remember Javi's crash course on key historical events.

'*Exacto*,' said Maestro Pedro. He called out to the librarian on the reception desk to bring him a book. She brought it, open at the correct page, within seconds. 'In May 1906 Calderón made a speech to Mexican miners at the Cananea copper mine that changed Mexican history. They were getting a third of what the American miners were paid and he told them not to stand for it.' He read the book over the top of his glasses: '"Show them you are not beasts of burden! Show them you are not inferior to their legions of blond, blue-eyed men . . ."' He pushed his glasses further up his nose. 'The brilliance of Calderón's speech was to make poor working conditions an issue that provoked national anger.'

He called the librarian over again. When she arrived, he simply said, '*Agua*.'

'The strike began peacefully,' he continued. 'They marched through the town, waving banners and singing songs. They didn't see what was coming.'

The librarian brought the glass of water. Maestro Pedro took a few dainty sips and cleared his throat. 'But when they got to the timber yard, hoping to get the yard workers to join them, they were met by Mitchell, the American yard manager. He turned a fire hose on them, and when the demonstrators threw rocks at him, Mitchell started shooting. The strikers broke down the gates and killed him. That was the start of it all.'

The start of what? I was about to ask him, but he opened another book and turned it round to face me. The images on the page were grisly. One man with a bloodied shirt lay on a flat horse-drawn wagon, back arched and arms stretched stiffly over the edge. Another, with matted hair, eyes closed and bloody face, was being cradled by his fellow workers. There were four pages of photos. One that struck me as particularly sad was of a man face down on the dusty ground, his sombrero lying next to him. He was just a few feet away from some large boulders which might have brought him safety.

Maestro Pedro was silent for a moment as I looked at the photos. Then he said, 'Vigilantes were dispatched from across the border in Arizona. No one knows how many died. Some say it was ten to fifteen, others in the hundreds. The important thing is that it was in the newspapers, in the United States as well as in Mexico.'

His account of the strike was compelling but I still wanted to know what it had to do with Arturo. 'Maestro Pedro,' I began, 'can you tell me about my great-grand –'

'Once the army arrived, there was only going to be one outcome. Calderón didn't want any more miners to die and so he negotiated a ceasefire. The miners were ordered back to work. Anyone who refused was conscripted. Calderón was sentenced to fifteen years in prison.'

'*Bien*,' he said. He leaned forward on his chair, removed his glasses and rubbed the bridge of his nose. 'Cananea was so important because it made a labour dispute into a political crisis. It was the first time it had happened. It was the first step towards Revolution.'

'The way I understood it,' I said, thinking about what Tía Chela and Tía Virgin had told me, 'the Bellavista strike also had a political ideology. The Elías brothers were avid readers of Engels and Marx and the newspaper *Regeneración*.'

'But they were naive. They had no political organisation. The Bellavista strike didn't make any waves. Few newspapers even wrote about it. The Elías brothers failed because they had no real links with the opposition, whereas Calderón worked closely with them. You are right, though,' said Maestro Pedro smiling.

'The Elías brothers did read *Regeneración*. Do you know who sent it to them?'

I shook my head.

'Esteban Baca Calderón.'

'*Sí?*' said Javi.

'Calderón was from Tepic,' said Maestro Pedro. 'He saw what had happened in the Bellavista strike, saw the mistakes they made and learned from them.'

I smiled, thinking of Tía Virgin's description of the Bellavista strike as a 'glorious failure'. Even if it hadn't achieved any of its immediate aims, it had unknowingly helped inspire Cananea, the tipping point of the Mexican Revolution. But I still didn't know how this related to Arturo.

'Maestro Pedro,' I tried again, 'could you tell me what role my great-grandfather played in the factory?'

'Coffee!' he said, suddenly standing up. '*Vamos a tomar un café.*'

He walked out of the library. Javi and I followed, trying to keep up.

'I left some papers in my car,' he called over his shoulder as he disappeared into the depths of the car park under the plaza.

By the time Javi and I caught up with him, Maestro Pedro had a large brown envelope in his hand and was locking the boot.

'Got them.' He walked straight past us and back up the stairs.

Javi smiled and rolled his eyes.

When we got to the café, Maestro Pedro marched straight past the waitress and to a table by the window, under a print of Emiliano Zapata and Pancho Villa. 'The coffee here is *fabuloso*,' he said, digging into the envelope as the waitress came over. Maestro Pedro didn't even look up. 'We want coffee,' he said. Neither Javi nor I drank coffee, but neither of us thought quickly enough to say so. Then, when she had turned to go, he added, 'And cake.'

He pulled out a sheet of paper, but kept it on his lap so I couldn't see it. 'Your great-grandfather, what was his name?'

'Arturo Greenhalgh,' I said. He already knew this and I was beginning to lose my patience.

'Was he here for all of 1905?'

'He went back to England for a few months.' I looked through my file for the ship manifests from New York to check the dates. 'He took his wife and their daughter to England in September and returned to Mexico at Christmas time.'

'So he was in Mexico in March 1905?'

'Yes.'

'Just as I thought,' he said, nodding.

The waitress arrived with three cups of cappuccino. Maestro Pedro opened four sachets of sugar and emptied them into his cup, forming four mini-pyramids on top of the froth. He watched the granules turn dark and stirred them in. 'I wanted to show you this,' he said, finally passing me the sheet of paper.

The writing was neat and elegant, but a thick nib had been used, and it was almost indecipherable apart from two words at the top of the first page: 'Arturo Greenhalgh'.

I felt my skin prickle, stunned to have finally found Arturo's name on anything. 'It's him!'

'Hallelujah,' said Javi, leaning over my shoulder.

The letter was signed 'Los Operarios' – the workers – but I couldn't make head nor tail of the body of the text. 'Can you read it to us please?'

The waitress arrived with a plate of iced muffins.

Maestro Pedro took out a crisply ironed handkerchief and unfolded it on the table. He then opened his mouth wide and pulled out one of his front teeth, placed the tooth in the handkerchief and put it back in his pocket. 'Cake?' he said.

I shook my head. I didn't want cake or coffee. I just wanted to know what was in the letter.

He cut through a muffin with a fork and shovelled a piece into his mouth. He dabbed the corners of his mouth with his napkin and smiled a gap-toothed smile. 'It's a letter from the workers in Bellavista, written just before the strike, asking your great-grandfather to sort out the problems in the factory.'

Tía Chela had not mentioned him in her story, and I had assumed he was in England at the time.

He took the sheet from me and began to read. '"To Señor Arturo Greenhalgh. Our dear sir, this letter comes from all the workers, in view of the alarming increase in food prices, and the fact that we do not earn enough to eat. We have decided, by common agreement, to make this protest so that this wrong is remedied." They were very polite, these Bellavista workers, eh?' said Maestro Pedro. '"All the weavers who work on the sixteen-tooth pinion" – I suppose that was the name of a machine – "want to be paid twenty-five centavos per piece. The workers on the other pinion, an equitable increase. The carders want a pay increase, and not to be penalised when the machines fail. The workers *del pie y la tranza* [another department in the mill] want a pay increase and for the boys that work there not to be beaten."'

Maestro Pedro giggled. 'Who knows? Your ancestor might have been a real brute.'

Javi and I looked at each other. Javi opened his mouth to say something, but was interrupted by Maestro Pedro.

'The letter goes on to list other workers in the factory who also want an increase in salary. It finishes by saying, "These are the motives behind our demonstration. We're all in this together, we'll start and finish as one. We look forward to your answer, *Los Operarios.*"'

'That bit about the beating, it doesn't mean that my great-grandfather was the one doing it, does it?' I asked.

'I can only tell you what is written here,' Maestro Pedro replied.

Javi said, 'I always heard that Arturo Greenhal was the one who mediated between Ecroyd and the workers.'

'They were hoping your great-grandfather could help them. I assume he couldn't, so the strike went ahead.'

'Then Cananea happened, then the Revolution,' I said.

'*Sí*,' said Maestro Pedro, 'then the Revolution.'

Mama María

SIX MONTHS after the Bellavista strike Arturo took his wife and daughter back to England. He hadn't been in Tottington since he first left for America on the *Cephalonia* seven years before. He only remained in Lancashire a few weeks however, before returning to Mexico, where he stayed for five years without Mariah or Sophia.

I could imagine how difficult a time this must have been for Arturo. He arrived back in Tepic on 22 December and spent Christmas alone. Early in the New Year Mariah sent him a telegram telling him she was pregnant. While he was no doubt delighted, it must have been painful to realise this was a child he might not see for many years. This second child was Ruth, my grandma.

THERE SEEMED to be dozens of versions of the story about how Arturo and María, known to the Greenhals as Mama María, met. Tía Virgin said Mama María was Great-Aunt Sophia's nanny, and Arturo had taken his wife and daughter home not because Sophia was ill but because he wanted to get them out of the way before it became obvious that Mama María was pregnant. Tía Virgin told me this story with great relish and seemed disappointed when I pointed out that if it were true Mama María's pregnancy would have lasted over three years.

Tío Javier said that they had met when Mama María worked as a pastry chef at a Casa Aguirre banquet. Arturo, who was also a very good cook, went into the kitchen to help out, and fell in love instantly.

According to a cousin of Tía Chela, Arturo, being one of the bosses of the factory, took advantage of *el derecho de pernada,* the ancient feudal 'right' of *el patron* to have sex with whoever in his charge took his fancy. But this was hotly disputed by Tía Chela. 'They did meet in the factory, because Arturo was responsible for mending all the machinery and her loom wasn't working properly. He could have repaired it in a minute, but he wanted an excuse to get to know her and took three days to do it.' She laughed. 'And then he left a pink rose on her doorstep every morning.'

Whatever the truth, what was certain was that within a year of Arturo returning to Mexico Mama María was generally accepted as Arturo's *señora* and was settled in with him in the house with the blue shutters at No. 70, Calle Veracruz. Less certain was the future of the world around them.

INSPIRED BY Calderón's uprising at Cananea, the exiled Mexican opposition, based in the United States, called for a revolution in October 1906. They sent huge consignments of arms across the border to their underground militia, but Díaz's government got wind of the plans, intercepted the arms shipments and the uprising was crushed.

The following year there was another strike in which hundreds died, this time in Rio Blanco, near Veracruz. In his book *Barbarous Mexico* American writer John Kenneth Turner interviewed a witness to the Rio Blanco strike who said, 'I don't know how many were killed but on the first night after the soldiers came I saw two flat cars piled high with dead and mangled bodies, and there were a good many killed after the first night. Those flat cars were hauled away by a special train that night, hurried to Veracruz, where bodies were dumped in the harbour as food for the sharks.'

There were more strikes, more uprisings. Increasingly, foreigners were seen as supporters of the Díaz regime and oppressors of the Mexican masses. American- and European-owned businesses and haciendas were looted and set alight.

It became more difficult for Arturo to travel between Tepic, Bellavista and the other factories, and he was now accompanied by an armed guard every time he left the house. Tía Chela told me about the checkpoints on the mountain passes. 'The *Rurales* would wait under the shade of a tree, out of sight of those on the road. "*Quien vive?*" they would shout. Who goes there? And if the *Rurales* didn't recognise them, Arturo's guards would have to identify themselves quickly and clearly by their family and occupation. "I am Jorge, son of Fernando the carpenter, my brother Ricardo works in the spinning department of the Bellavista factory." If they didn't reply fast enough or to the satisfaction of the *Rurales*, the shooting would start. Sometimes, of course, it wasn't the police, it was bandits. Then the shooting would start straight away.'

In March 1908, eighteen months after María moved into Arturo's house on Calle Veracruz, their daughter, Quitita, was born. Because she was born out of wedlock, Arturo's name did not appear on the birth registry at the Presidencia. There was no baptism at the cathedral and she didn't have Don Domingo as her godfather. She was born at home, and, partly because of the difficulty Arturo was now having travelling around the country, he spent more time with her than he did with either of his other daughters when they were young. Quitita told her children that playing with her father as he sat in his rocking chair was one of her fondest memories. She loved his stories, the nursery rhymes he sang and the rattle he carved from a coconut shell.

I imagined myself playing with baby Quitita and my feeling of pleasure at making her smile and giggle. I imagined watching her sleep at night, and her voice being the first thing I heard in the morning. And I tried to imagine how I would feel when I realised I would never see Quitita and my other two daughters grow up together.

Around the time that Quitita was learning to walk, the Mexican opposition, which had been fragmented by the failed revolution, began to unite behind a new leader, a wealthy liberal landowner called Francisco Madero. He was nominated to run against President Díaz in the election of 1910. As campaigning started, even Madero was surprised by the enthusiasm of the crowds at his rallies. In Guadalajara he was welcomed by over 10,000 people and almost as many in Monterrey, despite the best efforts of the police and local authorities to make life difficult for his supporters.

Realising the extent of Madero's popularity, and keen to ensure that the national celebrations to mark the 100th anniversary of independence from Spain were not disrupted, President Díaz had Madero arrested and rigged the election. Madero escaped from jail and, disguised as a railway worker, fled across the border to San Antonio, Texas, where he met exiled supporters and began planning revolution.

Tía Petra had invited me to her golden wedding party. It was due to take place on my third weekend with Tío Javier, and I decided to leave the Monday after the celebrations. I felt I had learned as much as I was going to in Tepic, and although I was still tempted to go and see Juanita, I knew I first needed to return to England. My journey would not be complete until I had shared my findings with Grandma.

One morning a couple of days before Tía Petra's fiesta I was sitting with Tío Javier in the kitchen when there was a telephone call. It was Maestro Pedro. I had never seen Tío Javier remotely fazed by anything, but to Maestro Pedro he talked in short sentences, like a foot soldier speaking to a general, and even stammered a few times.

'*10.30? M-muy bien, M-maestro Pedro. A sus órdenes. Gracias, gracias. Adiós.*'

Maestro Pedro had found some more papers and requested my presence.

Tío Javier wanted to make sure I arrived on time and drove me to the city library.

'You asked what your great-grandfather's role was in the factory,' Maestro Pedro called across the library as he bustled towards me.

I had asked him three times and each time he'd ignored my question.

'Now I can tell you.' He fished inside an envelope with his thin, bony fingers and pulled out what looked like an accounts ledger. 'It's a list of bonus payments for all the Casa Aguirre management. It shows what I have long suspected, but couldn't prove.' He leafed through the papers and then placed a sheet in front of me.

Bellavista:

	1908	1909
Arturo Greenhalgh (Director)	*$4,500 pesos*	*$5,000 pesos*
Tomás Guevara (Escritorio)	*$1,000 pesos*	*$1,500 pesos*

'He was director?' I asked, stunned. He was a bigger fish in Casa Aguirre than I had imagined.

Maestro Pedro grinned and nodded.

'I thought Ecroyd was in charge of the factory.'

'He was, until the strike. Then your great-grandfather took over.'

Grandma had always referred to her father as a mill manager, never director. At last I had found out something about him to make her proud.

Maestro Pedro was absorbed in another file of papers. 'Your great-grandfather,' he said, without looking up. 'He was in Mexico until he went back to England in 1910?'

'He went back to visit his family.' I was thinking about what it would have been like for Grandma to meet her father for the first time. 'He returned to Mexico a few months later.'

Maestro Pedro nodded. 'But do you know what he did when he came back here?'

'He continued to work at Bellavista.'

Maestro Pedro shook his head. 'He had lost his job. He was no longer director of the mill.'

And yet he returned to Mexico anyway, for María.

Tepic Rising

ARTURO ARRIVED in New York from Liverpool on the *Lusitania* on 11 November 1910. He took the Richmond and Danville Railroad south to Jacksonville in Florida and another train to New Orleans, where he changed for San Antonio in Texas. There he rested for a night before continuing to the Mexican border. He had promised Mariah he would go back to England if things became too dangerous so he was certainly aware of the risks he faced in returning to Mexico. But he could not have known the Revolution was being planned a few minutes' walk from where he slept that night.

Following his escape from jail in Mexico, Madero, the Mexican liberal leader, had found lodgings at Hutchins' Boarding House. During the day he met other opposition leaders in a room above a bank in the centre of the city.

I wasn't able to find out where Arturo had stayed, but bearing in mind the size of the town at the time he couldn't have been far away. In one of the books Maestro Pedro lent me I found a photograph of Madero in San Antonio, cane in hand, walking past a tobacco shop. I studied the photo closely, hoping to see Arturo in the background, perhaps buying a box of cigars for the rest of his journey. He wasn't there, but it didn't stop me wondering how these two liberal-minded men might have got on had they met.

It was exactly at this time that Madero sent out his call for revolution. The three-point plan declared that land laws would be revised, that the presidential election was null and void and that Madero was to be the interim president. And then, sounding more like an invitation to a cheese and wine evening than a call to arms, the uprising was announced for Sunday, 20 November 1910 'from 6pm onwards'.

Arturo took the train from San Antonio, crossing the border at Eagle Pass and travelling on to Monterrey and Guadalajara. He was somewhere between Guadalajara and Tepic on the final five-day stagecoach journey when the Revolution began, although he probably didn't know anything about it until after he arrived in Tepic.

The first uprising in Puebla was crushed. Both the Mexican government and Madero believed the Revolution had been a failure, but in the following weeks spontaneous revolts erupted throughout the country. Among those who answered Madero's call were a rural worker called Pancho Villa in the north and a horse trainer, Emiliano Zapata, in the south.

By the spring of 1911, when Arturo had been back in Mexico five months, Madero's forces were in control of huge swathes of the country, but Tepic was yet to fall. General Espinosa, commanding Madero's western division, had swept down the coast towards Tepic, and by April had surrounded the city, with one platoon camped at La Escondida, the Casa Aguirre factory Arturo visited daily.

Even though Madero was widely supported, there was considerable anxiety in Tepic. I found an article in the Tepic newspaper *El Obrero* dated Wednesday 24 May 1911. '*They say that the rebels have already arrived; that they are already in the outskirts of the city . . . that they are well armed . . . and that they are looking*

forward to the final push, even though they know that we are well
defended and our main buildings are well fortified with machine
guns and rapid-fire weapons . . . and many volunteers anxious to
prove their bravery.'

The head of the army in Tepic was General Ruiz. Before
Espinosa's men cut the lines, he sent a telegram to the war office
in Mexico City, asking for help. The curt reply he received was
hardly encouraging. Referring to Ruiz's forces it said, 'Garrison
is minimal, and any resistance would be crushed by the revolutionaries.' Ruiz gathered his men in front of the cathedral and
marched them out of the city, leaving Espinosa to take the town
without a shot being fired. Months later, General Ruiz was
charged with abandoning the people he was supposed to protect.
At the hearing he produced the telegram and the matter was
quietly dropped.

On 7 June 1911 Madero made a triumphal entry into Mexico
City, where he was greeted by 100,000 well-wishers. People hung
out of windows and sat in trees for hours just to get a glimpse
of him. The giant statue of Christopher Columbus on Paseo de
la Reforma was completely obscured by a mass of humanity.
Their enthusiasm was not even dampened by a massive earth
tremor that shook the city a few hours before Madero arrived at
the train station. For a moment it looked as though Mexico had
found its saviour. President Díaz boarded a boat in Veracruz and
sailed for France, where he died in exile. The Revolution was
over. Or so it seemed.

But at the end of 1911 the federal army, which the now President
Madero had naively kept completely intact, revolted against him.
In Tepic, Espinosa, who had become governor, personally fought
off a group of soldiers who attacked his residence in the middle
of the night, just two blocks from Arturo's house. Early in 1912,

in the same week that Arturo took Quitita for her first day at kindergarten, a wave of strikes and army uprisings spread across the country. It was probably about this time that *El Jefe* first spoke to Arturo.

On the evening of 14 March 1912 Lieutenant Miguel Guerrero from the 8th Battalion reported for guard duty at Tepic city barracks with several large flagons of mescal. Guerrero had made sure he had enough liquor for all fifty-three men under his command, enough for them to be persuaded to start a counter-revolution. At 3 a.m., fearless with drink and roused by Guerrero's rhetoric, they grabbed their guns and ammunition and ran along Calle Veracruz, past Arturo's house, to the city jail, where they released the inmates from their cells. Each of the prisoners was handed a rifle and ordered to join the insurrection. Some of the prison guards managed to escape and warn other soldiers, so that when Guerrero's men arrived at the garrison they found it barricaded and ready for battle.

A fierce fight ensued, lasting for several hours, until Guerrero, realising that his former colleagues were better armed and less drunk than his band of revolutionaries, ordered his men to withdraw and turn their attention to an easier target. They marched back down Calle Veracruz, past Arturo's house, up to La Loma de la Cruz and the convent where my Great-Aunt Sophia had been born ten years before. The convent, now a military hospital, was under the command of Captain Roman Castro.

Castro was ensconced behind the fortified walls and had positioned snipers on the ramparts. As Guerrero's men approached, however, Castro saw that his small force was outnumbered almost ten to one and he ordered his men to hold their fire. Before handing over the rifles and ammunition that Guerrero demanded, Castro gave him a rollicking for his disloyalty to the army.

Guerrero replied that it was too late for regrets as he had already committed treason. His men took the arms and ammunition and marched out of town.

When Arturo left his house the following morning, the smell of gunpowder still hung in the air. The dead and dying were being taken to hospital, and spent cartridges, splintered glass and the debris of battle were being swept up. Within a few hours, the town was preparing to defend itself. The most important buildings – the army garrison, the Casa Aguirre building, banks, government offices and the municipal treasury buildings – were fortified and given a twenty-four-hour guard. Sharpshooters were sent to vantage points around the city, soldiers briefed, volunteers recruited and conscripts armed. A man was stationed at the top of the cathedral bell tower night and day to warn the population: 'Enemigo enfrente' – 'Enemy approaching.'

I imagined Arturo walking slowly round and round the central square with his bodyguards, smoking a cigar as he watched the town being readied for attack. How long would it be safe for him to remain in Tepic? How could he best protect María and Quitita? Was he, a wealthy gringo, actually further endangering them by remaining there? And if he left now, would he ever be able to return?

Even before his final meeting with El Jefe, Arturo must have known that the time was fast approaching when it would be too dangerous for him to stay. Tía Chela told me he tried to convince Mama María to leave with him and stay in the border town of Piedras Negras until he returned. She refused, fearful she might be stuck in a remote frontier settlement without friends or family. She would wait for him, but in Tepic.

For the next two weeks the atmosphere in the city became more tense as news spread of Guerrero's band terrorising the haciendas and settlements in the hills around Tepic. Looting and kidnapping, Guerrero also managed by one means or another to recruit a substantial number of men, and amass arms, ammunition and provisions for an extended campaign. He marched his men to the rocky peaks of the mountains to the north-east of the city, where they joined with two other sizeable rebel forces. Together they numbered 2,000, most well armed, the rest carrying knives and machetes. They fought and won a bloody battle near Tuxpan with government forces. Then they closed in on Tepic.

The battle for the city raged for several days, and by its end the stench of charred and rotting flesh filled the air. Dead and injured covered the streets around the hospital.

Thanks to *El Jefe*'s warning, Arturo got out just in time. As Guerrero's army reached the city limits, Arturo was riding out of town.

I thought of the day in Chimaltenango when I walked away from Juanita. I imagined Arturo riding away from Mama María and Quitita with the same hollow, deadened feeling of desolation.

I COULD understand why the family had believed the story about Arturo drowning on the *Titanic*. The dates corresponded. A few weeks after he had kissed María and their daughter Quitita goodbye, the 'unsinkable' liner collided with an iceberg and slid to the bottom of the Atlantic. They never saw Arturo again.

Leaving Again

'I WOULDN'T GET involved if I were you,' said Tío Javier, touching me gently on the forearm. 'This is women's business.' From the top of the church steps, we watched Tía Petra preparing to throw her fiftieth wedding anniversary bouquet into a melee of female guests jostling for position like footballers awaiting a corner kick.

'*Tía*, over here. My boyfriend's watching!' yelled one, waving wildly.

'*Oye*, Petra, this way!' screamed another in a turquoise dress.

'Don't throw it to Marcia, she's already got a husband.'

'Yes, but he's useless. I want another one!'

Tía Petra turned and tossed it, in time-honoured fashion, over her shoulder. There were gasps as the flowers arced slowly through the air. Everyone in the crowd watched as one as the bouquet looped over their outstretched arms and landed in the hands of a woman in a black lace dress, with short greying hair. She had been chatting on the bottom step and was the only person to have been looking the other way.

'Lola! *Felicidades!*' shouted Tío Javier, laughing at his sister's startled response to the bunch of flowers falling on her from the sky. She made a quick recovery and waved them aloft like a trophy.

Tía Lola, the eldest of Quitita's eleven children, lived in Guaymas in the north-west of the country. She had lost her husband the previous year and this was the first time that the family had seen her since his funeral. Within minutes of the bouquet falling into her hands Tía Lola found herself face to face with Cornelio, her childhood sweetheart, whom she hadn't seen for fifty years and who had also recently been widowed. Two months later they were married.

THE RECEPTION for Tía Petra's golden wedding was held in a country club on the outskirts of town. In the main hall there were place settings on peach and white linen tablecloths for about 200 people. On each table the necks of Modelo beer bottles stuck out from metal ice buckets next to the Jose Cuervo tequila. Two bands played simultaneously – a trio singing close harmonies on the stage in the hall and a *norteño* band playing under the shade of an awning in front of a dance floor in the garden.

It struck me how Mexican it was – or how unEnglish at least. I knew for a fact that a couple of weeks before, although there had been a plan to hold a party to celebrate Tía Petra and Tío Alejandro's fiftieth wedding anniversary, nothing had been organised and nothing booked. I thought about a golden wedding party I had been to for a great-aunt and -uncle in England. Months before it was due to take place I had received a gold-embossed invitation. It stipulated the time and place, whom I could take with me, what my attire should be, what there would be to eat, and what time I would be expected to leave. The party itself ran like clockwork: drinks and finger food, sit-down meal, speeches, more drinks, home.

Mexican parties, it seemed, were a great deal more spontaneous, more free-form. There was no timetable; no one knew who exactly would show up, who would eat what, if indeed there was to be any food (there wasn't, despite the place settings), or what time anyone would arrive. No consideration at all was given to what time anyone would leave. It just happened, like everything in Mexico.

I noticed Tío Rafael, Tía Chela's husband, nursing a drink. Normally when we met he seemed glad to see me. He would greet me with a slap on the back and a quip about something or other.

I called over to him. '*Hola, Tío. Como esta?*'

He seemed bemused and said '*Hola*' somewhat distantly. I was thrown. He had always been so friendly and suddenly he was acting as though he had never seen me before.

'Nice suit,' I said, at a loss for what to say and grabbing at the first thing that came to my mind. 'You look so smart I almost didn't recognise you.'

'*Gracias.* I bought it especially.' He held his jacket open for me to admire the silk lining. Suddenly he sparked into life. 'Really, you think I look better than the other day?'

'Yes, I think you do.'

'Do I look a little younger, thinner and perhaps more handsome than before, eh?' He was now playing to Tía Chela, who had joined us and seemed to find his coaxing compliments out of me very amusing.

Although I couldn't quite see what was so funny, I played along. 'Now you mention it, maybe you do look a bit younger, thinner and more handsome.'

He looked delighted. 'He's a clever fellow this English relative of yours.' He winked at Tía Chela and walked to the bar chuckling to himself.

Tía Eva, an aunt I was seeing for the first time, was helped up onto the stage with the aid of two walking sticks and a couple of grandsons, and was greeted with an almighty cheer. A large woman with frizzy hair and a raucous laugh, Tía Eva said something into the microphone which I didn't quite catch, but it had something to do with wedding-night activity. It made everybody laugh and Tío Alejandro look flustered. Then she launched into a song, and the band, although initially caught by surprise, soon followed her lead and the guests began to sing along.

Tío Javier appeared at my side, shaking his head and laughing. 'What do you think of that, eh? She can hardly walk but she can still sing and dance.' At the end of her song he applauded along with everyone else as she was lowered from the stage. He then said, 'Come with me. There's someone I'd like you to meet.' He stopped for a second, as if he had just remembered something important. 'When you get the chance, ask her about the letters.'

'What letters?'

'It's Lola's story. I'll leave it for her to tell you.'

Tía Lola still had the bouquet in her hand, but when Tío Javier introduced us, she put it down and flung her arms around me.

'*Ay!*' she said as she embraced me. 'It's so good to meet you finally.' She clasped my face between her hands. 'Seeing you I feel like I have another son, and I already have eight.' She hugged me again. 'Let's sit down.' She led me to a table in the corner of the hall, further away from the music.

Tía Lola had already heard everything I had told her brothers and sisters, but she wanted to hear it again from me. As I told her about my journey and my great-grandfather's life after he left Mexico, she watched me intently, never once taking her eyes from my face.

I asked her to tell me what her mother had told her about Arturo.

'She was four or five when her father left,' began Tía Lola. 'She was always mischievous, even then. Once when she was sitting on his knee, she demanded: "*Inflate.*" He did as she asked, puffing out his cheeks. She jumped up and down squealing with joy and suddenly, *wwhhuuumm!* She smacked her hands together, knocking the air out of his cheeks.' Tía Lola laughed, '*Ay*, poor Arturo, it wasn't what he was expecting at all, especially from such a sweet-looking four-year-old girl. There she was, sitting on his knee laughing at him, her face covered in his saliva.'

'That's just how she was, my *mama*,' added Tío Enrique, who had come over to join us. 'That's probably where Eva gets it from.' He nodded towards Tía Eva, now surrounded by a cheering crowd as she danced around with a bottle of tequila balanced on her head.

'And you know,' continued Tía Lola, 'the thing was that he was so particular. He even used to have a cup with a special lip on it so that he wouldn't dirty his moustache, but he hadn't bargained on his daughter knocking the spit out of him.'

'What else did she tell you about her father?' I asked.

'She adored him. She never forgot the times he read and played with her, and she longed for him to come back. She told me that for a year after he left she would save her puddings for him, because she knew how much he loved them.'

A group was chanting at the far corner of the hall, '*Qué bailen! Qué bailen!*' – Dance! Dance! First Tía Petra then Tío Alejandro were hoisted onto a table to do a turn to the accompaniment of the band and the hundreds of clapping guests.

'Look at Alejandro,' said Tío Enrique. 'He looks like he'd rather be at home watching television, doesn't he?'

'I can't imagine that they'd have done this for your great-grandfather's wedding anniversary, would they?' Tía Lola asked me.

'I doubt it somehow.' I nodded over to where Tío Alejandro was being helped down from the table. 'Though if Arturo'd been here, he wouldn't have had much choice.'

'Perhaps not.' Tía Lola laughed. 'I know I never did.'

'Tía,' I asked, intrigued by what Tío Javier had said, 'could you tell me about the letters?'

'The letters? Which letters do you mean, *mi hijo*?'

'I don't know. Tío Javier told me to ask you about them.'

'*Sí, sí,* okay. He means the ones my father told me about.' She stared into the middle distance for a second. 'Have you ever heard of Tomás Guevara?'

I remembered Guevara's name next to Arturo's on the ledger Maestro Pedro had shown me.

'He was a good friend of your great-grandfather. He worked at the mill as an administrator – did the accounts, I think. Guevara was from here. He came from a good family, was educated and spoke good English. Whenever Arturo went away, it was Guevara he trusted to take care of his affairs. He made sure Arturo was paid, looked after his horses, that type of thing. Most importantly of all, he knew Mama María and he would make sure she was all right.

'When Arturo left for the final time, Guevara was one of the last people he spoke to. As you know, that was the last any of us saw or heard of your great-grandfather.'

'And the letters were . . . his letters?'

Tía Lola was not going to be hurried. She took a sip of Coca-Cola, her rings clinking against the side of her glass. 'Arturo wrote a lot of letters, didn't he?' she said.

'Grandma told me that he wrote at the dining-room table

every Sunday afternoon. She knew he was writing to Mexico, but didn't know to whom. Now I know about Mama María, I imagine he must have been writing to her.'

'He was. In the 1940s, thirty years after Arturo left, Guevara died. When his son was going through his things he came across a big batch of letters, thicker than a pile of tortillas on a dinner table.' She held up her thumb and finger four inches apart. 'He looked at them and saw that they were all written to Mama María. Not one had been delivered. I suppose Arturo had been sending money, and Guevara had taken it for himself.'

'*Qué cabron,*' muttered Tío Enrique, shaking his head.

I tried to imagine my anger if all my letters had been stolen. Then I realised: Arturo had never known.

'But did his son not pass on the letters when he found them?' I asked.

'Guevara's son passed them on to my father, but after such a long time, he didn't see any point in stirring up the past. He threw them away.'

'No!' I felt sick. The letters would have shown Arturo at his most intimate and vulnerable. I was desperate to know how he had articulated his hurt, confusion and desperation. Throwing the letters away seemed such an act of vandalism.

'You have to understand that so much time had passed,' said Tía Lola. 'My father, along with everyone else, assumed that Arturo had long since died, and he thought nothing good would come of reading a bunch of letters from thirty years before.'

I nodded. I understood, but I still felt nauseous. It was hard to learn that these letters had existed, and then discover, in a matter of seconds, that they had been found and thrown away.

'My father told me about these letters years later, when my mother saw an article in a national magazine written by someone called Greenhal. By then fifty years had gone by. Mama María was dead, but Quitita, having spent most of her life believing that her father had died long ago, suddenly became convinced that the journalist had to be of the same family, that her father had survived and perhaps was still living. She wrote to the magazine, asking to be put in contact with the journalist. She got no reply. She wrote to the British embassy in Mexico City, but received no response, so she got the state governor to intervene. Eventually she received a short note from a consular official saying that there was no one of that name living in England.' Tía Lola shrugged. 'We didn't believe it, but what could we do? The trail had gone cold and we had no idea what had happened to our English grandfather.' Her face creased into a smile and she grabbed hold of my hand. 'Then you turned up!'

'*Hola, campeón*,' said Tío Rafael, limping over with Tía Chela to where we were sitting. He had the playful glint in his eye once again. 'How am I looking?'

'Very good,' I replied. 'Excellent.' He looked different, though. I couldn't quite put my finger on what it was.

'Do I look better than I did earlier this afternoon?'

What was with him today? His face was deadpan, but I could see I was walking into some kind of trap. Then I realised he was no longer wearing his smart new suit. 'You've changed.'

'*Muy bien*,' said Tía Chela. 'Very good, you noticed.'

'So I do look better than earlier this afternoon? I'm glad you think so.'

'Ah, Rafa,' said Tío Enrique, shaking his head and laughing, 'you're a bad man!'

I still couldn't see where this was heading.

'But, your suit . . .'

'Ah, that was just a cheap piece of tat.'

Tía Chela, Tía Lola and Tío Enrique were all now laughing so much people were beginning to look over from the dance floor.

'I gave it to my brother to wear.' Tío Rafael whistled to a man wearing a blue suit a few yards away. 'Have you met Pancho, my twin?'

UNLIKE MY great-grandfather, I didn't have a bandit telling me to leave town, but on the Monday after Tía Petra's party, as I packed my bag, I felt torn. From the moment I left Tepic I would be heading home, and the journey I had always dreamt of making would be coming to an end. Every mile I travelled north towards New York would be a mile further away from my Mexican family, and of course from Juanita.

Like Arturo, I had Grandma waiting for me, but waiting for me to tell her what he never had. For the first time I felt the true weight of his burden. Having spent so long chasing after Arturo, he would now be depending on me to mend the broken circle, to take 'the truth of it all' back home.

I went to see Tío Arturo to ask if he would drive me round Bellavista and Tepic to say my goodbyes. I hadn't seen a lot of him since I first arrived, but I sensed when I saw him at Tía Petra's party that he wanted to spend some time with me. He never actually said so, he wasn't the talkative type, but something told me we needed to talk.

The last house we visited was Tía Chela's. Tía Lola was also there. She made the sign of the cross on my forehead and muttered a blessing for my journey. 'Go well,' she said. 'I hope we don't have to wait another hundred years to see you again, *mi hijo*.' She tugged a handkerchief from her sleeve and dabbed the corners of her eyes.

As we drove away towards the bus station Tío Arturo pulled a wad of American money from the sun visor.

'*Toma*,' he said. Take it. It was sixty dollars, in two-dollar bills, issued to commemorate the 200th anniversary of American independence from Britain in 1976. I had never seen a two-dollar bill before and supposed he was showing them to me because of their rarity.

I looked at them. 'These will be worth something some day,' I said, handing them back.

He shook his head. 'No, no! They're for you.'

I knew Tío Arturo wasn't wealthy and that for him sixty dollars was a lot of money. I also knew that this was something he wanted me to have.

'Thank you, Tío,' I said.

He turned to look at me, his eyes brimming. 'Thank *you*. Thank you for looking for us. Thank you for finding us.'

When we arrived at the bus station, he parked his pickup in the taxi bay, lifted my bags out of the back and gave me a hug. '*Traela, traela, traela abuela.*' Bring her, bring your grandmother. 'We need to see her. Please bring your grandmother.'

'Tío, it's an awful long way, and she is eighty-nine.'

'Don't worry. We'll take care of her.' He gave me another bear hug and said again, '*Traela, traela. Por favor!*' He climbed inside the cab and drove away.

The Road Home

When your great-grandfather reached San Francisco he took the train across America. After escaping from the Mexican Revolution, Arturo thought that his moments of danger were behind him, but danger is often where you least expect it.

The rain hammered against the train windows and drummed the devil's own tattoo on the roof. The wind blew so hard Arturo thought the train might topple over.

They crossed the Great Plains. He always looked forward to seeing them stretching to the horizon, but the plains were now one endless lake. At every station the train driver and the guard discussed whether they should carry on, and when they reached New Orleans a policeman was waiting on the platform. He told them it was too dangerous to continue; the Mississippi was in danger of bursting its banks.

Arturo jumped on a horse-and-cart taxi outside the station, keen to get to a hotel before the river completely flooded the city. All the shops were boarded up and had sandbags stacked high around their entrances. Apart from the rain, the only sound was the horse and cart sloshing through the ankle-deep water.

They were a few hundred yards from the station when they heard a distant roar and the birds on the telegraph lines shrieked and took off. 'Oh my!' said the taxi driver. 'Here comes the river water.' He cracked his whip and tried to get the horse to turn into a side street, but the beast whinnied, pulling this way and that.

The roar became louder and louder and grew thunderous. Arturo turned round to see a wall of water coming towards them. 'Run!' shouted the taxi driver. They jumped down into an alley, and the horse followed them, but left the cart sticking behind it out into the street. Then there came a massive CRASH! and an explosion of water. The cart broke into pieces and the horse reared up and galloped through the water down the alley. Arturo was up to his waist, despite having climbed up some steps. He saw one of his cases being carried away by the current. The taxi driver told him to stay where he was, but Arturo dived in and began to swim after it. He swam as hard as he could and after a few minutes managed to hook his fingers round one of the handles. But then he had to swim back with the case, and the current was too strong. The water was choppy and Arturo swallowed several large gulps. He quickly became exhausted and gave up trying to swim. He floated for half an hour, his arm round his case, clinging on for dear life, until he drifted onto the lower branches of a tree, where he hung on until he was rescued, several hours later, still holding on to his case.

A few weeks later, he arrived back in England, his case still covered in mildew.

Three days after hugging Tío Arturo goodbye at Tepic bus station I was queuing at the border crossing between Piedras Negras in the Mexican State of Coahuila and Eagle Pass in Texas. It was a crossing my great-grandfather had used several times, but there was nothing I could see that he might have recognised. Beyond the concrete forecourt were high mesh fences topped with barbed wire. In front of me were a boy of around eight and a girl about two years older. They bickered in a mixture of English and Spanish.

'Shut up, man.'

'Shut up, *tu.*'

'Jerk.'

'*Idiota.*'

'*Tonto, bobo.*'

'*Dejame en paz!* I don't want you in my life!'

'I don't want you in *my* life, *pendejo!*'

'*Ay, ay, ay, niños, portense bien,*' their father intervened.

They began to imitate him, but in English so he couldn't understand. 'Behave! You're a very naughty boy!'

'You behave! You're a very naughty girl!'

I was at the back of a line that stretched thirty yards to the shade of the open-sided customs post, but I could see people being waved through with only the most cursory examination of their documents. It didn't look as though our delay at the border would last more than a few minutes.

The immigration official had a pencil-thin grey moustache, large gold-rimmed glasses and a kindly smile. He slipped effortlessly between languages. '*Buenos días,*' he said when I reached the front of the queue, and then, glancing at my passport, 'Good morning, sir.' He had a deep resonant voice enriched by a Southern drawl. Flicking through my passport, he raised his eyebrows. 'Quite a traveller, eh?'

The other passengers were all either wandering back towards the bus from the checkpoint or already in their seats. The bickering children were now racing round, trying to smear each other with melted ice cream, ignoring their father's attempts to shepherd them back onto the bus.

'Sir, do you have a visa to come into the States?' the immigration official asked me.

I hadn't been aware that I needed one.

'Do you have a ticket out of the States?'

'I was planning to buy one when I get to New York.'

'Hmmm.' He ran a finger along his moustache.

I looked over to the bus. The last passenger was climbing aboard. Smoke shot out of the exhaust as the driver revved the engine.

'I'm afraid you're going to have to step inside the office, sir.' He handed my passport to a colleague, who led me through a darkened-glass door to a reception room with chillingly efficient air conditioning.

'Take a ticket from the dispenser on the counter and they will call your number.'

The room was full of people sitting with bags at their feet, documents in hand. There was no conversation. Neither in America nor in Mexico, we were all in a state of limbo. Only a few minutes earlier I had been bathed in the Mexican morning sun. Now I was in a freezing prefabricated building of smoked glass and nylon carpet tiles, surrounded by people silent with fear and boredom.

When my number was called, I made my way to the desk,

dragging my bags behind me. The officer wore a black uniform with a silver name badge on the breast pocket which read AGENT COBB. He had a fleshy well-fed good-ole-boy face and a closely shaved head. When talking to his colleagues he wore a permanent grin. Addressing me, he was serious, polite and utterly humourless.

'Please do not lean on the counter, sir,' he said without looking up. He leafed through my passport and noted down the countries I had visited. When he got to Colombia he wheeled round to one of his colleagues and said excitedly, 'Hey buddy, I got one here! This guy's been all over. He's got no visa and he's just come from Colombia. Colombia, man!' They exchanged high fives.

'Way-da-go, man!' his colleague replied. 'This one's all yours.'

Agent Cobb punched the back of an office chair in his excitement. 'Man, Colombia. It's a slam dunk!'

I swallowed. *A slam dunk*. What exactly did that mean? My mind filled with images of Agent Cobb thrusting my head through a basketball hoop, earning more high fives and *Way-da-goes* from his colleagues.

'Is there some problem?' I asked, forcing myself to smile in a vain attempt to join in the fun, and not be the butt of it.

'Please do not lean on the counter, sir,' Agent Cobb repeated sternly, and went to show my passport to other colleagues and exchange more high fives and playful punches on the shoulder. When he came back, he handed me a form and told me to take another ticket and wait for my 'interview'.

'Interview?'

'Please sit down, sir, and we'll call you when we're ready.'

The bus driver came in and talked to Agent Cobb. I filled in the form. Then he came over to me. He said in English, 'Hey man, I'm real sorry, but we're going to have to go. Here's your ticket. You can take it to the bus station in San Antonio and they will refund your money.'

Was the bus driver just being impatient or did he know more than he was letting on? 'Hang on a minute, what did they say? How much longer will I be?' I asked.

'I don't know, but we can't wait any longer.'

'What am I supposed to do? When is the next bus?'

'Five hours. I gotta go. Good luck.' And he was gone.

AN HOUR later my interview began. I have always hated dealing with officialdom but I knew it was essential that I kept my composure. The questions came thick and fast.

'Why do you want to come to the States?' Agent Cobb asked me.

I tried to keep my answers as simple as possible. 'I'm on my way home.'

'When were you last there?'

'Six months ago.'

'Why have you been away so long?'

'I've been travelling.'

'Travelling?'

'I was following the route my great-grandfather took when he went to Mexico in the late 1800s.'

'Why?'

'Because I had a feeling he had left something behind.'

'Why?'

Agent Cobb was starting to really irritate me. 'I just did.'

'What were you doing in Guatemala?'

'Studying Spanish.'

'And Colombia?'

'I went to meet someone.'

'You were there for over a month.'

'He wasn't there.'

He arched one eyebrow. 'He wasn't there and you stayed for a month?'

'Yes.'

'Did you have any contact at all with any terrorist organisations?'

I decided not to tell him about the *Paramilitares*. 'No.'

'How about drugs? Brought any little mementos?'

I shook my head.

The questions went on for forty minutes or so. When he ran out of things to ask me, Agent Cobb tapped his pen against the desk and reread the notes he'd been making. He continued to tap his pen for several minutes. I tried to guess his thoughts, but his face was impassive.

'I'll give you one month,' he said eventually.

Was that my jail term? Wasn't I allowed some kind of representation? Was this the true definition of a slam dunk?

He dropped his pen on the desk, paused and picked up a heavy self-inking stamp, and brought it down with a *clunk* in the middle of an empty page on my passport. He handed it to me. 'You're free,' he said, smiling at me for the first time, 'to go and have your bags searched.'

The customs man was the antithesis of Agent Cobb. He wore black shades and was chewing on a toothpick. 'Park your bags on here for me will you, fella?' He pointed to a concrete slab between us. He opened one, but when he saw how tightly stuffed it was and how long it was going to take to unpack, he sighed, 'Jeez! On you go.'

* * *

HAVING MISSED my bus, I had no alternative but to haul my heavy bags to the nearby town of Eagle Pass. The expressions on the faces of the drivers who passed me confirmed what a rare sight pedestrians are on American roads. Cars swerved around me, their windows up, air con on, their drivers looking back at me with a mixture of fascination and bewilderment.

After half an hour I came to the outskirts of the town. It had a Mexican feel to it. *Piñatas* dried on a washing line, and a fruit stall by the road displayed plastic bags of pigs' fat alongside watermelons and papayas. In the middle of the field beyond was a Dodge station wagon with flowers growing out of rust holes.

As I got closer to the centre, things began to look more American. Sprinklers created tiny rainbows over the bright-green lawn of a marble-fronted bank. A revolving electronic display flashed the temperature: 101°F. I walked on, seeming to sweat even more now that I knew exactly how hot it was. I came to the car lot of EZ Pawn, empty apart from a supermarket trolley with a (presumably repossessed) hi-fi strapped into it, pumping out country and western music.

For the first time in months I felt invisible. I was just another person on the street – no longer the *gringo* outsider.

The Greyhound bus station was across the road from EZ Pawn. The waiting room had the feel of a down-at-heel betting shop. Shabbily dressed men smoked and dribbled spit onto the floor while watching horse racing on a flickering TV screen.

It was still several hours until the next Greyhound bus was due to leave for San Antonio, so I followed a sign outside the terminal to a travel agency a few blocks away called Eagle Tours. Their offering was limited to just one service: a minibus that promised to drop you at any address within the city limits of San Antonio. One was about to leave.

'Where you goin' in the city?' the girl behind the desk asked me. She stretched a piece of bubblegum from between her teeth, and then sucked it back in her mouth again.

I shrugged. I didn't think the hotels in Arturo's Baedeker guide would still be there, and I had no names of any others.

'You don't know, es okay, just tell de driver before you get there.' She handed me a Texas hotel guide.

The driver opened up the back of the minibus. 'San Antonio, San Antonio! We go now. *Nos vamos ya!*' He started loading bags. 'San Antonio, *la ciudad.* Come on, let's go.' He was a dark-skinned Mexican, short and muscular with long curly hair and veins sticking out from his muscles as he effortlessly lifted the luggage. He wore a green polo shirt patterned with golf clubs, its collar only partly obscuring a tattoo of a two-headed snake on the right-hand side of his neck.

He counted the passengers, made a note on his clipboard, handed a copy of the passenger list to the girl at the desk, jumped into his seat and threw the van into gear. Soon we were in open coun-tryside: pristine, manicured fields of wheat and corn stretching away to the horizon, every blade of identical height. Everything was so ordered, tidy, so American. In Mexico even the nicest houses often had steel rods sticking out of the top of them. Here, the neat roofs of farm buildings glistened in the late-afternoon sun.

I saw a road sign that seemed to say LITTERING IS AWFUL. When we got closer, I saw it said LITTERING IS UNLAWFUL.

In San Antonio, when all the other passengers had been dropped off, the driver glanced at his clipboard and said with a grin, 'The last, but not the least!'

I smiled.

'Speak Spanish?' he asked.

'*Sí,*' I replied.

'*Ay, muy bien! Fumas?*' Do you smoke?

I shook my head.

'Do you mind if I do?'

I shook my head again.

'*Muy bien*. It's polite to ask, but I hate it when I can't smoke. Rules, rules, rules.'

We arrived at the small chain hotel near the airport that I had found in the guidebook. Next to the entrance was a paved garden and a swimming pool little bigger than a bath. A family was splashing around, looking out through a perspex screen at the head and tail lights of fast-moving traffic on the freeway.

The driver and I walked into the reception area. A bald man in a business suit was talking to the receptionist. When they noticed us, both looked embarrassed, as though we had caught them doing something they shouldn't.

'It's Memorial Day. We're completely full, honey,' said the receptionist, an all-American girl with perfect teeth and long blonde hair.

I looked at the price card on the wall behind her. I couldn't have afforded it anyway.

She suggested a couple of other hotels nearby.

I knew that I was on my own now. Eagle Tours had delivered me to the address I had given them. 'Can I walk there?' I asked.

The receptionist laughed. 'It's a ride, honey. You don't want to be walking.'

I sighed. 'Is there a taxi rank near here?'

'*Es okay. Yo te llevo,*' said the driver, and then held up his hand in a leave-it-to-me gesture to the receptionist. He said to her in English, 'I find him hotel.'

'This is very kind of you,' I said as I joined the driver on the bench seat in the front of the minibus.

'No problem.' He spun the bus round in the car park. Before turning out into the road he held out his hand. 'Reynaldo, *mucho gusto.*'

His grip was fierce and his hand rough. He had a fresh cigarette in his mouth and squinted to keep the smoke from his eyes. There was a warmth to him, tempered by world-weariness. His face was leathery and the lines round his eyes were deep grooves. It was 9 p.m., and he had already been working fourteen hours but seemed happy to talk, perhaps even reluctant to go home. As he drove me from one fully booked hotel to another over the following hour and a half, he told me about his life.

Originally from Monterrey, Reynaldo had lived in the States for twenty-seven years.

'For the first fifteen years or so, I was involved in *la lucha libre.*'

I wondered whether this was some sort of insurgency movement, but when he mimed having his eyes pushed out I remembered that *la lucha libre* was Spanish for wrestling.

'I toured the States, the Dominican Republic and Central America. It was a great life. You get to know the other fighters, and they become your friends, your family. We fought in some pretty fancy places, especially down in Miami – real classy joints.' He chuckled. 'And then there were the uglier venues, the caged rings in backroom bars. There'd be nets up to protect us from flying glasses, and iron bars to separate us from the crowd. There was one place known as the bear pit . . .' He stopped. His expression suggested it wasn't a happy memory.

'Wasn't it difficult to be friends with people that you fought every night?' I asked.

'It was just a job. You tried to win, of course, but you didn't try to hurt each other. There were a couple of fighters on the circuit I really didn't like – real nasty pieces of work who would break your fingers for kicks.' He paused. 'Then it can get a little *feo*.' Ugly. He didn't elaborate, his silence hinting at something more sinister than the knockabout fights I used to watch on *World of Sport* as a child.

'Let's try this one,' he said, pointing the bus down the steep entrance of a hotel that looked almost identical to the first one.

It was similarly full.

'But, you know, it was a good life,' Reynaldo continued as we rejoined the freeway. 'In most towns I had a *chica*, if you know what I mean.' He chuckled again and took a long drag on his cigarette, exhaling a lungful of smoke out of the open window. 'To be a wrestler was to be, you know, a star. I stayed in some great places; I always had money in my pocket – they would pay me $500 in cash for every fight. Once, when I was top of the bill I got $3,000, but you can only have your arms broken and ribs busted so many times, so I gave it up. I didn't want to go back to Monterrey so I stayed here in San Antonio.'

'What did you do then?' I asked. 'It can't have been easy to give up that kind of lifestyle.'

'It wasn't. You know when you start *la lucha libre* that you can't carry on for ever. You enjoy it while you can and then you get out. Only trouble is, being a wrestler isn't good preparation for doing anything else.' He lit another cigarette from the stub of the previous one, which he then flicked out of the window. 'I just drifted about. I lived on the street, started to drink, take drugs . . . got married.'

I laughed. To me it seemed an unconventional and less than romantic progression towards matrimony but to him it was perfectly logical.

'I was never going to get married while I was on the road, so

I got hitched afterwards. She was a wonderful woman – very kind and patient. She tried to help me clean up and straighten out, but eventually she threw me out.'

'What happened?'

'I pulled a gun on her and she called the police. To be honest I can't remember it, but she said I did, and I didn't contest her claim in court. I just stood there with my head bowed. I said I was sorry, but it was too late. I spent three years in jail and she wouldn't see me after that.' He shrugged. 'Not that I blame her. I wasn't very nice back then.'

'This place is a bit cheaper,' he said, pulling into the parking bay of a motel right next to the highway. The front door was made of two-way glass and a notice on it said security cameras were in operation. A green fluorescent strip light above reception gave the place the unnatural feel of an underground bunker.

'Most of our guests stay for longer than one night,' said the angular young man behind the desk in a thick Eastern European accent. 'But anyway we have no rooms. Sorry.'

Before we set off again, Reynaldo pulled a wallet from his back pocket and showed me a photo of his youngest daughter, aged ten. 'I have two children,' he said, and then reeled off the names of five, by several different women. 'Now I smoke cigarettes, drive this bus and earn money for my children. My mother died of lung cancer last year, and since then I have started to smoke even more. Three packets of these a day.' He picked up a soft pack of Marlboro reds from the dashboard. 'I know they are killing me but –' he grinned and gave a wheezy laugh '– it's my only vice now, I may as well be good at it.'

Half an hour and two hotels later we arrived at the Motel San Pedro. Reception was a concrete booth in the middle of a parking lot with bulletproof glass covered in credit-card stickers.

I felt a cool air-conditioned draught coming from the vent in the window as I pressed the intercom button to speak to the receptionist.

Her Indian-accented voice came back tinny and disembodied through tiny speakers mounted on the wall. 'Yes, we have a room. It costs $58.12, including all taxes, payable in advance.'

It was substantially more than I had paid for any hotel in all my months of travel, but I wasn't about to argue. Even Reynaldo's patience would run out soon.

He refused to take a tip. 'No, no, no. It was good to talk. You save your money. My brother and I share a bed anyway, you see. I have to wait for him to go to work before I can get to sleep.' He shook my hand and drove off into the night, a trail of smoke rising from the driver's window.

It was almost midnight, so I dumped my bags and went out straight away to look for something to eat. The only place I found was a drive-in ice-cream parlour pulsing with disco music and neon lights. Waitresses in hot pants danced around on roller skates, serving chocolate sundaes, frozen yogurts and strawberry fudge whirls to teenagers leaning out of their car windows. Mexico seemed a long way away.

ARTURO'S SHIP from San Blas docked at San Francisco Harbour on 28 March 1912. From there he took the train to New York, stopping at New Orleans because of the storm, and when the floods subsided caught another train to Jacksonville, Florida, where he changed for New York. I wanted to travel the same way for at least some of the journey, so I reserved a seat on a train leaving Jacksonville for New York at 7 p.m. the following Saturday. That gave me five days to get to Florida.

* * *

ARTURO HAD been a constant presence for me in Bellavista – I was with the family to which we both belonged – but somehow, the moment I left, he seemed to disappear. The problems I had at the border were very much my own, and on the onward journey from San Antonio by hire car I felt lonely: isolated and separated not only from Arturo but from the country I was travelling through.

IT'S HOTTER IN HELL THAN HERE! said a sign outside a church in the outskirts of New Orleans. After two whole days of driving through sun-baked prairies without air conditioning, this was difficult to believe.

I found a hotel in an area between the French Quarter and a downtown business district. It was an uneasy neighbourhood where gleaming steel and glass office blocks rubbed shoulders with dime stores, never-closing bars and a derelict cinema where the homeless slept and men gathered round trestle tables in the doorway to watch games of chess.

As the light began to fade, I walked along Bourbon Street and into the Quarter, my finger wedged in the New Orleans section of Arturo's Baedeker guide. He had marked one section, presumably on his first visit to the town on his way out to Mexico in 1898: 'The tourist will do well to begin his exploration of New Orleans by taking his bearing from the roof of the St Charles Hotel.' I tried to do as the guide suggested, but soon discovered that the hotel no longer existed, and the office blocks would have made it impossible to see anyway.

Unlike anywhere I had been since crossing into the States, the noise and bustle came from people rather than cars. There were clowns, jugglers, hustlers and marching bands. Every few steps I was confronted with different aromas, some of which Arturo would have smelled too. Salty air from the Gulf, chicken roasting on street-side grills, pots of gumbo and Cajun jambalaya bubbling in open kitchens, cigar smoke, popcorn. But mostly the aromas were of the twenty-first century: joss sticks, incense and the warm beery smells pumped out from bar air-conditioning units. I tried to imagine the swing-door saloons that Arturo would have walked past and wondered what music he would have heard. The bars I passed had live bands playing jazz, blues, Dixieland and rock 'n' roll to near-empty lounges where a few tattooed and bandanna-clad bikers shot pool.

THAT NIGHT I went to bed early, wanting to set off towards Jacksonville first thing the next morning. At 3 a.m. I was jolted from a deep sleep by the deafening screech of the fire alarm. I stuck my head out of the door but could smell no smoke and see no panicking guests. I called reception. No answer. I had begun to get dressed when the alarm stopped. It was only then that I heard the storm. It droned, wailed and hammered at the windows as if the hotel were in a giant car wash. I stared out of the window, fascinated by its power and fury. I lay down and had just drifted off to sleep when the fire alarm went off again. It continued to sound every twenty minutes for the rest of the night.

I didn't set off for Jacksonville the next morning, or the next afternoon. A police advisory, broadcast every few minutes on the television, warned motorists to avoid making any journeys at all. I stayed in my room until the early afternoon, alternately watching the unnaturally grey-purple sky out of the window and the wind-buffeted weather reporters on the television, and at 5 p.m., realising how hungry I was, went out in search of something to eat.

I had taken just a few steps outside the hotel when a wooden pallet flew past me and bounced like a pinball off the buildings along the street. I stepped back inside, bought a pack of peanuts and a pecan pie from a vending machine in the hotel foyer and returned to my room.

The next morning the sky was a perfect blue. It was difficult to believe there had ever been a storm. I was now a day behind schedule, however. I had less than twenty-four hours to drive the 600 miles across Louisiana, Mississippi, Alabama, Georgia and into Florida, drop off the rental car and get to Jacksonville train station.

Before I left New Orleans I had to confirm my train reservation and pay for the ticket.

'I am obliged to warn you,' said the woman in the ticket office, 'that if the storm is too severe, the train might not run.'

'But the storm's passed; haven't you seen outside?'

She laughed. 'You haven't been here in the hurricane season before, have you? There's another storm, a big one, a category-five hurricane, blowing into Florida right now. They're getting pretty antsy down there.'

'But what do you mean, "the train might not run"?' I knew from watching television the day before that a category five is the most severe kind of storm there is. The idea of being in Jacksonville in the middle of a hurricane, without anywhere to stay or any means of getting out, was alarming.

'I mean,' she replied patiently, 'that if the storm makes it too dangerous for the train to run, it ain't gonna run. Now I only have three tickets left, so you're gonna have to decide if you want one.'

I didn't have much choice. I had to return the car to Jacksonville and get out again before the storm made travelling anywhere too dangerous. There would be no planes flying and the only train going north was this one. Even if it might not run, it was still my only hope. I handed over the money for the ticket and crossed my fingers.

THE FIRST few hours' drive up to Baton Rouge and on to the coastal plain passed quickly enough. The countryside was more varied than it had been through Texas. People dangled fishing lines over every available bridge into rivers, swamps and sea inlets. I began to notice armadillos – animals I had only previously seen in cartoons – occasionally tiptoeing next to the road, but more often flattened on it.

About ten hours into the journey, as I crossed into Georgia, I noticed that I had the run of the freeway. Heading in the opposite direction, however, were three lanes of solid slow-moving traffic. Vehicles of every description – Winnebagos, station wagons, saloons and sports cars – inched forward in a heat haze of exhaust fumes. Tables and chairs and mattresses were strapped to car roofs; caravans, trailers and boats were attached behind. As I drove on, the traffic on the other side of the freeway came to a standstill and cars were parked on the grass verge. Men stood on the roofs of their cars, straining to see the cause of the delay, and families ate from barbecues in the middle of the road. It wasn't until I had driven past thirty miles of gridlock that I began to make the association between the mass exodus and the hurricane I was driving towards, alone, at full speed. I slowed down as I thought it through. I wanted to travel to New York by train, like Arturo had, but so far following his route through the southern states of America had proved lonely and dangerous. I drove on, still unsure what to do. I could turn around, but if I did, I'd have to join the back of a very long line of traffic. I decided to carry on as I crossed a long bridge across a swamp. The Doors' 'Riders on the Storm' came on the radio as a bolt of lightning split the horizon and ricocheted around the darkening sky.

At 2.30 a.m., 500 miles from New Orleans, I caught myself swerving towards the central reservation. I fought tiredness for a few more miles and then stopped at a motel. In my dreams I was hunched over the wheel, surfing the car on tidal waves, desperately dodging levees and swerving round tornados like a skier on a slalom course. A television commentator was describing the action in a light Lancashire accent: 'That were grand, that were!'

'Arturo!' I said, as I worked out whose voice it was. And I woke up.

'WELCOME TO the world's largest city!' said Karen, the taxi driver taking me to Jacksonville train station after I had dropped off the car. 'Not the biggest population, you understand, but the *biggest*. Ain't that somethin'?'

'That's great,' I replied, unsure what else to say. Being the largest urban sprawl on the planet seemed a dubious honour, even if it were true.

'And I tell you somethin' else,' she said, seemingly intent on listing all of Jacksonville's proud boasts. 'St John's is one of only three rivers in the world that flow northwards.'

'Excellent.'

She had been talking as though on automatic pilot, but suddenly she looked at me studiously in the rear-view mirror. 'Say, what are you doing here, anyways? You just scootin' around or are you planning to stay? You know there's a hurricane about to hit town, don't you?'

'I'm catching a train out this evening, to New York.'

'New York? That train ain't due for a few hours yet, right?'

'Seven o'clock.'

She raised her eyebrows and whistled. 'That's going to be pretty tight. You'd better pray it ain't late.'

The skies had been getting progressively heavier throughout the afternoon. As we approached the station through an empty car park the size of several football pitches, the sticky humidity finally gave way to steady rain.

For what Karen had claimed was the world's largest city, Jacksonville's railway station was a distinctly modest structure. It had more in common with a bus shelter than a major rail hub. Inside it was no more impressive. The only seats were metal benches; there was no food other than the packets of sugar next to the coffee machine and the only form of entertainment was a badly tuned TV mounted on the ticket-office wall.

I went to check in. 'I'm on the seven o'clock to New York,' I said, placing my bags on the scales. The electronic display wavered between 48.3 and 48.4 lbs.

'Okay,' said the man in the blue Amtrak uniform, handing me a bag receipt. 'We're looking at an hour and a half delay on this service. It should be here before 9 p.m.'

'It's still definitely running, right?'

His answer hardly inspired confidence. 'It's running as we speak, but please listen out for further announcements.'

I found a bench close to the television. The images on the screen were sobering. Palm trees uprooted; waves exploding over sea walls; beach houses being ripped apart; yachts blown out of the water. One had buried itself in a surf shop, another had crushed a car.

'It's going to be quite a night,' said the man sitting on the seat next to me, the excitement in his eyes amplified by his bifocal glasses. 'We're in for a rough ride let me tell you, yes sir!' Bill, a retired tax accountant, was travelling back from Jacksonville with his wife Meryl. They had been visiting her sister in hospital.

'Don't be so dramatic, dear,' Meryl said, and then turning to me, 'Don't you worry, now. We'll be just fine, you'll see.'

Shortly after eight thirty it was announced that the train was running two hours late.

'Oh boy,' said Bill, 'The storm is going to overtake the train at this rate.'

Meryl looked up from her word-puzzle book to give him a disapproving glance.

There was another announcement. The delay was now three hours. There was a further announcement shortly afterwards, saying the train was still running late and they had stopped estimating when it might arrive.

At 11 p.m., with the train already four hours late, the outer edges of the hurricane reached us. Debris flew against the windows. The television and the waiting-room lights flickered and went out.

'Holy moly!' said Bill. 'Here she comes.'

We walked over to the window overlooking the car park, where the floodlights still shone and the rain danced on the tarmac.

'This reminds me of being in Korea,' he said quietly. 'For me the most terrifying part of being at war wasn't the fighting, it was the waiting around, often in the dark. When you're in battle you're full of adrenalin and you feel nothing can touch you. It's in the quiet . . .' He laughed. ''Scuse the pun! It's the quiet before the storm – that's when it gets you.'

The lights flickered on and off again; the windows began to rattle then bow in and out with the gusts of wind.

'Do you think the train will come?' I asked.

'Well, I'm hoping that if it doesn't they'll have to do something about getting us to safety. I mean, we're pretty exposed here, aren't we?'

When the electricity came on again twenty minutes or so later, the images on the television were of reporters in yellow waterproofs shouting into microphones, their fingers in their ears, trying in vain to hear the instructions from the studio.

'They always paint the worst picture on the television. It'll never be that bad,' said Meryl reassuringly.

'Baloney!' said Bill, who, back in the company of his wife, seemed to be relishing the prospect of being caught in the mother of all storms. 'In the worst places it's too bad for them to film. Imagine the power of this thing!'

Bill was behaving like a child seeing his first snow of the winter. He only lost his enthusiasm when the coffee machine ran out. 'Oh darn it! What are we supposed to do now?'

The train was now over four and a half hours late. According to the television reports, the eye of the storm was sixty miles south of the city and moving steadily north. The poplar trees at the far end of the car park were now at a forty-five-degree angle. Rain hammered against the windows. Bill turned up the volume on the television.

'Can't hear the darn thing with all this din.' He was no longer enjoying himself.

Meryl looked up from her puzzles and gave me a wink.

The train eventually arrived six hours late. I lost Bill and Meryl as we hurried through the driving rain, stepping over the tracks to the nearest carriage door. As the engine passed me I noticed its name. *The Silver Snail.*

* * *

WHEN I got to New York I had one last delve into the archives. I found the newspapers Arturo would have read as he sailed back to England. The major story was Scott's failed expedition to the Antarctic. I read Scott's final letter: 'Had we lived I should have had a tale to tell . . . which would have stirred the heart of every Englishman . . . It seems a pity, but I do not think I can write more. For God's sake, look after our people.' As I read this in the New York Public Library I was struck by the feeling that when I set out from England I'd left, like Arturo, with nothing but a bag full of hope. Now I was returning with responsibility. Responsibility for my English and Mexican families. Arturo was asking me to *look after our people*.

In the final hours before I caught the bus to JFK I found the manifest for Arturo's final voyage across the Atlantic. He had a second-class cabin on the *Caronia*, a ship once described by the American ambassador to Britain as 'the noblest and largest vessel that ever kissed British waters'. I was glad to see he had gone home in comfort. He set sail on 10 April 1912. Four days into the voyage the *Caronia* communications officer sent a wire to a ship coming in the opposite direction warning her of the presence of ice fields. The receiving ship does not appear to have taken the *Caronia*'s warning too seriously. The ship was called the *Titanic*.

I ARRIVED back at my parents' home and unpacked my bag. I looked through my photos of Juanita, and the postcards, letters and faxes she had sent me. I found a fragment of glass from Pablo's windscreen, one of the two-dollar bills given to me by Tío Arturo. I pulled my passport from a side pocket of my bag and laid it on the bed. It fell open at the American visa

Agent Cobb had given me so begrudgingly. Then I noticed some silver foil rolled into a long thin tube poking out of the pocket. I couldn't think what it could be. I picked at it, gently unrolling the tube until something fell on the floor. It was something I hadn't seen or thought about in months, and probably the only thing I wouldn't tell Grandma about. CB's Cartagena Carrot.

Vamos!

'NOW THEN,' said Grandma, as she greeted me on the front
step of her Sheffield bungalow. Taking hold of both my
hands she looked at me intently. 'This Mexican malarkey, is
it true?'

I looked back at her and nodded. 'Yes, Grandma, it's true.'

Despite all the letters and faxes we had exchanged, until she
actually saw me she had clung to the faint hope that the story
of her father's second family in Mexico might not be real. Only
when I stood in front of her did she finally accept it. She let go
of my hands and gave me a hug.

'You get to eighty-nine,' she said as she led me to the sitting
room that looked out on her well-tended rockery, 'and you think
you've seen it all. You don't imagine anything can surprise you.
And then you find this. It's remarkable. You don't know how
remarkable it is. My father wasn't like that. He was so . . .' she
paused, searching for the right word '. . . proper.'

I didn't mention Tío Arturo's plea when I left Tepic: *Bring
her! Bring your grandmother!* I knew if I told Grandma straight
away that hundreds of new relatives in Mexico were desperate
to see her she would dismiss the idea out of hand. I had to give her
time. In the meantime I showed her my photos.

'Oh, I say, what a lot of people. They all look very smart,' she said when I showed her the pictures of Tía Petra's golden wedding. 'What does she do?' Pointing to Javi's wife, Georgina.

'She's headmistress of an infants' school.'

Grandma nodded her approval. 'What about this bearded chap here?' indicating Tío Arturo's son.

'He's a doctor.'

Another nod, clearly impressed. 'And how about this girl?'

'That's Tío Javier's daughter Rebecca. She's a dentist.'

'Ooh, they're nice people then! They're just like us.'

I could have pointed out that we don't have any doctors or dentists on the English side of our family, but I let it go.

The one photo which really stilled her was the one of Quitita that I had photographed on the wall of Tío Enrique's house.

'Oh my goodness,' she said under her breath. 'She's just like Sophia. She's just the same. They could be . . .' And she stopped herself.

'Sisters?'

'Of course, of course. Well I never . . .'

For a long time she didn't say anything at all. She just looked at the picture, studying it closely, her head shaking very slightly.

'What did they say she was like?'

Quitita had died eleven years before, but her children – my *tíos* and *tías* – had told me a great deal about their mother. As I began to describe her, I realised how similar she and Grandma were, and how different their lives had been. They were both proud but kind, practical yet creative, lovers of nature – the sea especially – and of music. And they both idolised their father. When she left school Grandma won a scholarship to a ladies' college in London and became a music teacher. By the time Quitita was the same age she was married, had two children and was expecting a third. Grandma grew up during the First World War,

Quitita during the Mexican Revolution. Grandma had to live without her father for the first six years of her life, Quitita for the last seventy-one of hers.

We talked until the light began to fade. As I was leaving, she hesitated before opening the door. 'Now then, love.' She paused a little awkwardly. 'Are we, er . . . are we going to talk about this? Publicly, I mean? I do worry about what people might think.'

'Well, I was thinking of writing a book about it.'

'Fine!' she replied, as if suddenly liberated. 'We'll talk about it. I'll not be silly.'

In the weeks and months that followed Grandma and I talked constantly. She would write me letters and I'd phone. When I was in Sheffield I'd go and see her, and she'd feed me buttered scones and cake.

'It used to be me showing you photos and telling you stories when you were young,' she said on the phone one day. 'Now I'm at the end of my life it's the other way round. I rather like it like this.'

Despite being surrounded by friends, I felt more lonely than at any time on my travels. I missed Juanita sorely. Every now and then I caught a whiff of her perfume in a crowd or found my mind playing tricks with me: thinking I had just seen her or heard her voice or her laughter. The letters and postcards I received only increased my sense of loss. I scanned the pages of every missive quickly, my heart in my mouth, desperately hoping there would be no reference to a new man in her life. Only then could I relax and savour each word, enjoying every turn of her pen. Although she never mentioned anyone new, she didn't come up with any concrete plan for how we might meet again either. But there again neither did I.

As the long hot summer faded into autumn, life in London became bleak. In Latin America, where the sun was nearly always high in the sky, it had been my compass. If the sun was on my left in the afternoon I knew I was heading north. In autumnal London the sun hardly shone at all. I felt lost.

Just as Arturo had tried to keep his Mexican life alive by constantly writing letters, I too wrote frequently to the family in Mexico and of course to Juanita in Guatemala.

'When are you bringing your grandma?' asked my Mexican family.

Juanita wrote, 'When are you coming back to me?'

THEN, SHORTLY before Christmas, six months after returning from Mexico, I went to a party and met Ros.

'I've been told you drink tequila,' she said, handing me a shot, and disappeared into the crowd.

'I've been wanting to talk to you,' she said when I got her number from a mutual friend and phoned her a few days later. She invited me to a fancy-dress party the following weekend in the house she and some friends rented from an ambassador in Oxford. Ros was dressed as Wonder Woman, a costume that included thigh-length leather boots. She wore her outfit with an alluring lack of self-consciousness, turning heads wherever she went. She looked stunning.

I KNEW I should write to Juanita about Ros. When I left Guatemala Juanita and I had promised we would tell each other if we found someone else. I had to be honest with her, but although I knew I wasn't actually being unfaithful, as we had agreed to split up until we could find a way to be together, I did feel guilty.

It was the most difficult letter I had ever had to write. How could I tell Juanita that I had found someone new? Writing seemed callous and cold, but her mother no longer had a phone in the house.

The regular stream of postcards and letters dried up. She didn't respond to my letter at all, which made me feel all the worse.

I WENT home to spend Christmas with my family in Sheffield. It was the first time since I'd been back in the country that all my family were in one place. Together we pored over the photographs and I recounted the story of how I had found our Mexican cousins and the weeks I had spent with them. Grandma could now name all Quitita's eleven children and a good number of the younger generation too.

'This has given me a whole new lease of life,' she said when I showed her a fax from Mexico wishing us all a happy Christmas.

The morning I was due to return to London for New Year, Grandma took me to one side and said, 'I've been thinking a lot about Mexico.'

'Yes?'

'Let's go! *Vamos!*'

THE WEEKS leading up to our departure were frenetic. First there was a party, Grandma's ninetieth-birthday party. She was in great spirits. After years of careful living the discovery of the Mexican Greenhals seemed to have liberated her from previous constraints. She now didn't feel she had anything to lose. 'I've got to ninety, I may as well live a little,' she said. 'And anyway, if I do keel over when I'm in Mexico, at least there'll be enough people to carry the coffin!'

Ten days before our flight Grandma realised that her passport had expired some ten years previously. 'I never thought I'd go

abroad again,' she said. 'The last holiday I went on was a coach
trip with the lip-reading class to Bridlington.'

I WAS too busy with preparations to pay much heed, but I began
to feel the tectonic plates of my life again shifting beneath my
feet. I was excited beyond measure about returning to Mexico and
taking Grandma with me. Likewise, the Mexicans were beside
themselves. Javi was now faxing me on an almost daily basis. There
was something else, though. Something I couldn't quite pin down.

Ros and I had been spending more and more time together.
Although she didn't plan to travel with me to Mexico, she was
excited on my behalf as she understood how important it was
to me. But I had a nagging feeling of disquiet. Something wasn't
quite right.

Since returning to London the sense of intuition that had guided
me during my travelling had grown flabby through lack of use.
City life protects us from the elements and nature. We have heating
when it gets cold, light when it gets dark, television when we need
entertainment. Somehow, instinct gets stripped away.

Suddenly it was back. It hummed like a guilty conscience.

Although I couldn't believe I was walking away from another
wonderful woman, I finished my relationship with Ros. I was
running on instinct. I felt I had to cut all my ties before I returned
to Mexico.

Fiesta

I HEAR THE shouts before I see the crowd.

'*Ya llegan!*' They're here!

'*Tía! Tía Ruth!*'

Cameras flash.

We are in front of the Salon de Baile, a large, functional building used for school dances, weddings and parties. The front is bedecked with Union Jacks, Mexican flags and clusters of balloons.

'I'm not used to all this attention,' Grandma says. 'I hope they won't be disappointed in me.'

I take her hand and give it a squeeze. 'You are everything they could possibly want you to be.'

Javi comes out of the crowd to help Grandma out of the car.

She smiles. I am gripped by emotions: fear, excitement, pride, love. It is as though all my life has been leading to this moment. Javi opens Grandma's door.

'This is it then.' Grandma takes his arm.

Mariachi trumpets strike up a fanfare and applause ripples, rises and grows thunderous.

'*Viva Tía Ruth! Viva!*'

A small girl with ribbons in her hair comes forward and hands Grandma a bunch of pink roses. Before she darts back into the crowd, she gives a little curtsy. A TV cameraman with an assistant holding an arc light walks backwards as Grandma moves towards them. The bank of photographers continues to snap and flash away.

'*Tía, aquí!* Over here, over here!'

All eleven of Quitita's children have arranged themselves in order of seniority. Tío Arturo stands patiently behind Tía Lola, Tía Petra and Tía Eva, his face wet with tears.

Because of the sheer number of people, they spill out onto the stairs and Grandma is lost in a sea of hugs and kisses. I push my way through to be by her side. Everyone's talking. I'm trying to translate, but they're all too excited to listen. They stroke her hair, touch her cheek, hold her arms, look into her eyes. Grandma is laughing. Everyone is laughing.

'*Hola!*' says Grandma during a brief moment when she isn't being held by anyone.

'You said, "*Hola!*"' says Tía Lola excitedly. She turns to her sisters. 'She's speaking Spanish!'

A hand on my shoulder. It's Tío Arturo. His eyes still glisten with emotion, but he has a broad smile on his face. '*Mi hijo!* You did it! You came back with your grandmother. She's here! You're here! You brought her!'

I find I can't speak, but my tears soak into his shoulder. I then lose sight of Grandma as I am held in one embrace after another.

I catch up with her as she reaches Tío Javier.

'You have the eyes of my father,' I hear her say. I translate and he beams with pride. More kisses, more hugs.

'*Su família!*' says Tío Pepe. He gestures around him. '*Família Mexicana!*'

Grandma laughs and says, 'My Mexican family' as if trying the phrase for size. And then repeats, 'My Mexican family. A very handsome family!' Tío Pepe laughs and envelops her in yet another hug.

'*Hola, Tía Ruth!*' says Tía Virgin, tired of waiting and pushing past Tío Pepe.

'She looks just like your mother,' Grandma says to me, and then to Tía Virgin, 'Hola, Tía Ruth!'

Tía Virgin looks momentarily confused and then laughs. 'No, you!' she says, pointing at Grandma. 'You are Tía Ruth!'

'Oh yes, so I am. I'm used to just being Grandma.'

'She's just like Quitita,' I hear Tía Chela say to Tío Pepe.

'If only she could have been here today,' he replies. 'They're so alike – same skin, same voice, same laugh.' Tears start to roll down his cheeks.

There are another 200 people inside the hall, who give Grandma an even bigger ovation as she enters. On stage, in front of two giant fans the size of aeroplane propellers, is an eleven-piece mariachi band in silver-embroidered wide-rimmed sombreros, tight-fitting black suits and cowboy boots. The band keeps playing through the welcome, and as soon as it finishes the dance floor transforms into a mass of rhythmic shuffling, shimmying and twirling, accompanied by whoops and whistles for each new arrival on the floor.

'I don't think I'll dance,' says Grandma, and she makes for a seat.

Tío Arturo walks over, his hand outstretched towards her.

'Oh no, it's been too long. I'm too old to dance,' says Grandma.

He drops dramatically to one knee. '*Tía, por favour!*'

She acts flustered, but I can tell she loves the attention. 'Just one dance then.' She dances with him, and then Tío Javier, then Tío Samuel, then Tío Pepe, then Tío Enrique and then Tío Arturo again.

Through the windows I see a series of flashes. I wonder what the photographers are doing outside. Then there's an almighty crash of thunder and rain begins to drill on the metal roof, almost drowning out the mariachis. I remember it's the rainy season, which began on 22 June, 'about midday'.

There's a cheer and Tía Eva climbs onto the stage. She shouts to the bandleader, who nods, and she launches into a song, '*Cruz de Olvido*'. She sings with real emotion. The lyrics seem like Arturo's lament.

> *La barca en que me iré*
> *lleva una cruz de olvido*
> *lleva una cruz de amor*

> The boat in which I will leave
> Carries a cross of oblivion,
> Carries a cross of love

Her sisters, always her greatest fans, sing along. Between verse and chorus, the trumpets soar over the other instruments, and a grandson brings her a Cuba libre which she knocks back in one.

Next, Tía Chela's daughter Lizzy gets up to sing. Like Eva, Lizzy is 'good at a party'. She's joined by her sister Blanca, who keeps on mouthing 'I don't know the words!' between fits of giggles. Then Tío Javier's grandson Jorgito, wearing baggy shorts and standing on a stool to reach the microphone, sings another.

Javi makes his way to the stage. He calls for me to translate his speech to Grandma.

'Today is a day that we never thought would happen. That we never thought possible. Then, last year, like Christopher Columbus who discovered the continent of America, Robin set out, to discover . . . us!

'And now, having come from the other side of the world to be with us, from the land of our English ancestor, we have Aunt Ruth, Quitita's sister. Aunt, we thank you from the bottom of our hearts for travelling so far to be with us. Quitita would have loved to be here.' Javi looks across at Grandma. 'Thanks to your visit, the whole family has come together. A united family is a strong family. Let's make sure this party isn't the last.'

The packed hall roars its approval.

I make my way to the stage. There are so many things I want to say. I feel so humble and yet so proud. I see myself as a tiny part of something so wonderfully vast it is beyond my comprehension. I see this as just one second in time that connects the past with the future, linking generations with generations.

Pictures, sounds and smells from my journey fill my head, memories from my childhood of sitting on Grandma's knee. I see images of Grandma and Quitita sitting on their father's knee, sense the family over the ages with their sorrow and their joy.

I'm at the microphone and several hundred people are looking at me. I don't want to cry, not now. I feel Arturo's presence there with me, looking out at the family – my family, his family.

'Thank you,' I say, abandoning all hope that eloquence will come. 'Thank you for everything.'

Mariachi makes way for disco. The dance floor fills instantly. Tía Lola's new husband, waving a bottle of tequila, catches the mood. 'Everybody happy. I'm happy. You happy. Everybody happy!'

I am talking to Tío Enrique. His shirt front is damp with beer.

'You know,' I say, my arm round his shoulder, 'the fantastic thing about being here is not only that you are all family, but that you're all such great people too.'

'Yes, but *somos familia.*' We're family.

'I know that, but what I'm trying to say is that as well as that, you're *buena gente.*' Good people.

He shakes his head in incomprehension. '*Somos familia.*'

Finally I see his point. We are family, *punto.* Nothing else matters.

There's another great cheer and I look over to where the noise is coming from. Through the mass of clapping, dancing and cheering people – now three or four deep at the edge of the dance floor – I see Grandma dancing with a triumphant smile on her face. This ninety-year-old, who little over a year ago felt that she had seen all that life could possibly throw at her, is soaking up the love and adoration of her new family, dancing to 'Staying Alive' by the Bee Gees.

THE FOLLOWING morning, still abuzz from the day before, Javi takes us to Bellavista.

'Oh my!' says Grandma as the cottages and the factory come into view. 'It's just as I imagined it, just as my father described it to me. And it's so peaceful.'

The peace doesn't last. Waiting for us on the steps in front of the factory are 150 or so members of the family. They cheer when they see Grandma. A professional photographer, who has been hired for the occasion, has to stand further and further away, as more and more people move into the shot, until he's standing in the fountain near the main gate. There are endless calls of 'Whisky!' – the Mexican equivalent of 'Say cheese!' – but eventually we begin our factory tour.

The looms are lying exactly as they were abandoned when,

after 140 years of continuous production, the factory closed in 1979. Even the threads and bobbins are still in place. The factory floor is quiet, but it's easy to imagine the deafening clatter, grind and churn of the endless rows of machinery.

'I remember this smell,' says Grandma, as she walks up and down. 'This takes me back to when I used to visit my father at the mill in Astley on my way home from school. He'd be sitting at his sloping desk, which was always stained with cotton oil, sucking on his pipe. "Let me just finish up Ruthie," he'd say, "and we'll go home." And someone would come in and give me a glass of milk and some biscuits while I waited. This smell takes me right back. Makes me feel at home.'

She walks back to the entrance, where Tío Enrique is waiting for her. He is to be Grandma's chief guide.

'Shall I tell you about the ghost?' he asks her as we come out of the factory and go through the side entrance of the director's house, where Arturo had lived.

'There are many people who have seen it, my father for one. Some people say it's the ghost of a Frenchman who used to work here, others say it's the factory founder, and I've even heard some claim it's your father, keeping an eye on his grandchildren!'

'Oh my goodness,' says Grandma, after I translate for her. 'What does he look like?'

'He's dressed in winged collar, waistcoat and bowler hat. On the stroke of midnight he comes out of the director's house, and when he gets to the clock he always checks his pocket watch, then walks round to the other side of the factory and back again.'

'Oh my goodness,' says Grandma again. And then, when Tío Enrique is out of earshot, she says to me, 'I don't think it could be my father, do you? He didn't die anywhere near here, after all.'

We catch up with Tío Enrique at the side entrance to the

house. I'd not been allowed into it before, but Grandma's visit has made all things possible. The first room we pass through has a pile of old school desks in one corner, but otherwise the house is empty. The bare floorboards are carpeted in a thick layer of dust, but I am glad it is still intact so that Grandma can see her father's residence was once as grand as she had been led to believe.

We return to the factory and walk through the main room where the looms are.

'Here,' says Tío Enrique, taking a handful of bobbins and stuffing them into Grandma's handbag. 'A memento of your visit.'

We are led past the giant turbine that sits in an enormous hole perhaps forty feet deep in the factory floor.

'This will have been driven by the waterwheel,' says Grandma. 'The carders and tenters, as we used to call them, would have worked through there; the spinning would have been done just here, and the weaving where we just came from. Oh yes, it all looks very familiar.'

Tío Enrique, who had obviously thought that he would be providing the technical explanations, looks seriously impressed.

We end the tour in the museum, where I met Fernando the year before and learned that '*nearly the whole village*' was called Greenhal. I didn't realise at the time that it was dedicated to the plight of the workers, the strike of 1905 and the lead-up to the revolution.

'Crikey!' says Grandma, looking at a black and white photo of twelve *campesinos* hanging from a tree with ropes around their necks. 'What did these poor chaps do to deserve this?'

Tío Enrique nods to the bobbins he had put in Grandma's bag. 'They stole from the factory.'

When we leave the museum Tío Enrique invites us to his house for a drink. Grandma sits by the coffee table looking at the stuffed baby alligator, just as I had that first Sunday afternoon the previous year. Tío Enrique pours out glasses of Squirt and empties a packet of tortilla chips into a bowl.

There is a knock at the door.

'*Olivia! Pasa, pasa,*' Tío Enrique calls out. Come in! Olivia is Mama María's granddaughter. Her mother was from Mama María's marriage after she gave up hope of Arturo ever returning from England.

'It's a great honour to meet Don Arturo's daughter,' she says. 'I knew Quitita very well. We were very close. I'm just sorry that she couldn't be here to welcome you.'

'Thank you,' replies Grandma. 'I wish I could have met her too.'

Tío Enrique hands Olivia the bowl of tortilla chips.

She takes a handful and digs me in the ribs. 'This is what women were like to your great-grandfather: have one, then another, then another.' She and Tío Enrique laugh heartily.

'What did she say?' asks Grandma. 'Something about tortilla chips?'

I don't believe what Olivia says about Arturo, but even if she believes it herself, it certainly doesn't come across as an insult. If anything, it's a compliment, as if to say, 'What a boy your great-grandfather was!' Either way, I have to answer Grandma, who's looking at me expectantly.

'She was just saying how Arturo really loved tortilla chips: he'd have one, and then another . . .'

Grandma takes another handful and nods enthusiastically. 'Me too! They're very moreish, aren't they?'

When I translate for Olivia and Tío Enrique, they look at each other mystified.

A foghorn-like klaxon sounds outside the front door. The family has hired an old bone-shaker bus – complete with extended bonnet and thunderous engine – to take us to Santa Maria del Oro, a volcanic lake about an hour away.

'Oh I say,' says Grandma as we climb aboard. She has been saved a seat behind the driver. 'A family outing!' Only on a bigger scale.

We play games and sing songs. The men sit at the back and drink beer. Tía Lola starts a singing game in which people are called by name to dance. If they don't stand up and dance immediately, everybody smacks them on the head. Grandma is spared. I am not.

We have to stop several times for Tío Arturo to have a pee. 'Weak bladder,' says Grandma. 'Just like my father.'

After we arrive by the lake and are sitting under the shade of a *fresno* tree with plates of barbecued fish inside us, the manic exuberance of the previous twenty-four hours begins to fade into a relaxed contentedness. The adults are at six long tables. Twenty to thirty children play by the shore, swinging from a rope into the water. Grandma and I sit with Tía Lola, Tía Chela, Tía Virgin and Tío Javier. Without the noise and crush of the fiesta, they talk properly with Grandma for the first time and ask questions about the things they have always wanted to know. What was Arturo like? How did he talk about Mexico? What did he like about Mexico? What sort of life did he have when he returned to England? How was he as a father? Has Grandma ever met the Queen?

They in turn teach Grandma how to eat from a flute of rolled-up tortilla without emptying it into her lap, how to spot a good tequila and how to make a margarita.

Tía Lola is in the middle of telling Grandma about Arturo's cake recipes, which her mother passed on to her, when Grandma notices a cat stalking the remaining fish roasting on the barbecue.

'*Quítase!*' she hisses, picking up a paper plate and shooing the cat away.

'What did you say?' asks Tía Lola, astounded.

'I said, *"quitase",*' says Grandma, a little bashfully. 'My father always used to say it. I'm not entirely sure what it means. "Get out," I presume.'

'Yes, that's right. What other Spanish did your father teach you?'

Conversation stops on the other tables and all heads turn to Grandma, who has now sat down again and is thinking. 'Well, he used to sing me a lullaby. Let me see if I can remember it: *Duermete mi niña.*' She begins tentatively and looks at me for reassurance. 'Does that sound right?'

'It means, "Go to sleep, my little girl."'

She looks relieved. 'I wasn't sure I had pronounced it right.' She clears her throat and carries on singing. *'Que tengo que hacer / Lavar los pañales / Y sentarme a coser.'*

I translate for her. 'For I have something to do / Wash out the napkins / And sit down to sew.'

The *tías* are looking at Grandma open-mouthed, but soon begin to sing along.

> *Palomita blanca, pico de coral*
> *Cuando yo me muera*
> *Quien me va a llorar?*

> *Little white coral-beaked dove,*
> *When I die*
> *Who is going to cry for me?*

Here is a song that Arturo sang to both Quitita and Grandma. Quitita sang it to her children. And now they are singing it back to him. After he went back to England Arturo was told he could no longer be in the chapel choir because he sang in the 'Mexican way'. He was a musical man who had his voice taken away. Here, in a lakeside garden filled with his Mexican grandchildren, Arturo's voice has returned.

ON OUR last morning before returning to England Tío Javier drives Grandma and me to the cemetery on the valley side overlooking Bellavista. But en route he has a better idea. 'There's something else I want to show you first,' he says.

He turns by the factory watchtower and drives past the millpond and through the fields of maize and sugar cane and past occasional piles of smouldering rubbish. I understand where we are going but don't say anything to Grandma, who is looking out of the car window contentedly. When Tío Javier parks by the gate to the old electric plant, Grandma climbs down and breathes in deeply.

'It smells wonderful,' she says, and looks around her at the hundreds of butterflies that fill the air. 'My father told me about this place.'

Neither Tío Javier nor I had told her where we were.

'He told me about the flowers, the river and the butterflies.' She takes my arm and starts walking, ignoring the building in front of which her father had been photographed on horseback, straight towards where the mango orchard was. It's like she's in some kind of trance, lured on by the butterflies dancing around us. She stops in front of the one remaining mango tree and looks up. It is covered in blossom and several large ripe mangos are hanging from the lower branches.

Grandma picks one and walks alone to the riverbank.

'This is what I wanted to show you,' Tío Javier says. '*Es un milagro.*' It's a miracle.

'It is,' I say, smiling.

We're both silent for a minute and then he clears his throat and says, 'You know, Javi is opening a new shop soon and needs someone to run it. I've built a house on the land I took you to last year. It's yours if you want it.'

Not for the first time I feel overwhelmed by his generosity. I look across at Grandma; she is smiling and smelling the flowers. I know I no longer have to return to England for her. But I know, for some unseen reason, I must return. I still want to find my place but the sense of intuition that has led me to the mango orchard is now telling me to go home.

Tío Javier drives us to the cemetery. Many of the tombs are enormously elaborate, giving the place the look of a miniature city of gothic skyscrapers.

Tío Javier and I go ahead to beat down the long grass and return to escort Grandma slowly over the uneven ground. As we approach the family plot, I can feel Grandma's hand gripping my arm more tightly.

Behind orange-painted railings, the plot is sizeable but modest in design. There are two graves. Mama María is on her own in one. A tin can wrapped in foil which presumably once held flowers rests on top of her grave. The hand-painted plaque says in simple Spanish:

Mama María
12 July 1954, aged 65 years,
Remembered by her children,
Rest in peace.

Next to that is the marble double grave that Quitita shares with her husband, Manuel.

'María Eva Greenhal de Berecochea,' Grandma reads aloud. 'Died 19 March 1984, aged 76.' Grandma's voice cracks a little as she reads the date of her sister's death. She removes her glasses and rubs her eyes. 'It brings it home. Seeing it there written in stone.'

She links her arm with mine again and we walk away in silence. Just before we reach the car, she takes my hand. 'Thank you, love. Thank you for everything. This is what my father would have wanted. And I wouldn't have missed it for the world.'

Epilogue

THE NIGHT after I returned to London from Mexico, the telephone rang, jolting me from a deep sleep. I looked at my watch. It was just after 2.30 a.m. Cursing whoever would call at such a time and the fact that the telephone was at the other end of the room, I got out of bed to answer it.

'Hello,' I said crossly. There was a momentary pause on the end of the line. I could hear hesitant breathing and then a familiar giggle.

'Did I wake you?' My tiredness and anger fell away. It was Juanita. 'I just called to tell you that I'm in London.'

Acknowledgements

While, as Grandma said, there are three versions to every story, *The Mango Orchard* is unashamedly my version. That said, I am conscious that this story isn't just mine, but also Arturo's, Grandma's and my Mexican family's. I have been as faithful to the facts as possible and have altered very little other than the order of some events, in the interest of readability, and a couple of character names, in the interest of privacy.

My original journey was in the mid 1990s but when I returned to England, the story was still too fresh and I wasn't ready to write a book. Ten years later, the moment felt right. I set off to retrace my steps, noting what I had missed the first time round. On each journey, there were hundreds of people whose generosity and kindness made it what it was, and made the book possible. Here are just some of the people who helped me along the way.

I did very well out of the Hughes family, staying with Robin, Eva, Peter, Erik, Nina and Liv in several countries. Particular thanks to Janeth Ortiz, Olga, Lili, Pati, Eduardo and Luís Marroquín, the Guarin Torres family: Pedro, Hilda, Sergio, Daniel, Diana and Marina. Also to Cynthia in Guadalajara, Ema in San Marcos, Claudia and Rob for the flat in Hampstead, Dr Gastón Julian Enríquez Fuentes for keeping me sane in Salamanca, and

of course Javier Berecochea Greenhalgh and Hermelinda García
de Berecochea for taking care of me in Bellavista.

I am indebted to the staff at the National Archives at Kew, the
British Museum, the Caird library at the National Maritime
Museum and the Merseyside Maritime Museum. In the US, to
staff at Ellis Island and NYC Records office. In Mexico, to Jorge
Vidal at Museo Historico Naval in Veracruz, the staff at la
Biblioteca Nacional, and Archivo General de la Nación in Mexico
City and in Tepic, to the staff at la Biblioteca Magna and the
library at Universidad Autónoma de Nayarit. There, with help
from Oscar, the university librarian, and especially the historian
Pedro López González, I managed to piece together what happened
in Tepic during the first years of the Mexican Revolution. Special
thanks also to Fuensanta de Icaza de La Sota and Pedro de Icaza
Zabálburu in Bilbao, to Rosaura Sandoval Arroyo and Manuel
Stephens for their stories, and to my cousin, Javier Berecochea
García, for his dedication in helping me make sense of it all.

During the writing process, I benefited greatly from the patience
and wisdom of a great number of people. Gordon Glick, James
Rutter, Amy Lawrence, Yasmeen Cappuccini and Jon Webster all
helped with the early drafts. I received invaluable help and guidance from Ann Lewin and Hilary Dennison, who read the manu-
script almost as many times as me. Anne Aylor helped me make
the story into a book, and Rory MacLean helped me pull the book
into shape. I would like to thank all of those at the various writers'
groups who have made insightful comments on my book. In particular, those who attended Anne Aylor's courses and workshops and
all the members of Jojo Thomas' Housemans group, but especially
Justin Carroll, Alistair Anderson, Caroline Swain (also for the proof-
reading), Charlotte Stretch, Safeena Chaudhry Jennie Pitman and
Jojo herself.

I'd like to thank Sir Lance Hodgson for introducing me to Annie Quigley, Annie for introducing me to Ernest Hecht, Ernest for suggesting Oli Munson as an agent, Oli for introducing me to Trevor Dolby, and getting him to sign me to Preface. Thanks to Trevor and all those at Preface and Random House for their tireless work, especially Nicola Taplin. Thanks to Mark Blank for keeping my notes safe during my original journey, to Fiona Hale and Clare Gill for typing them up, and Maciek Bral for the Dictaphone. Thanks to John and Sue Kelly for taking care of my flat, until I had to sell it, Ampita for help with translations, Dot Cooper for her genealogical search guidance, to Tanya White for the website, Giles Cooke for the cover design and my brother Andrew for the photos and occasional literary suggestions, Empem for her critique of the photos and the Cutts family for looking after me. A special thanks to my parents for their belief, unstinting support and grammar master classes. I'd better also mention Javi, my Godson, as he'll be most annoyed if I don't.

Heartfelt thanks to all my great grandfather's Mexican grand-children: Lola, Petra, Virgin, Arturo, Eva, Chela, Javier, Samuel, Pepe, Enrique and Margarita, and their families. And finally to Grandma and Quitita, the sister she never knew. Without your stories, mine wouldn't exist.

UNITED STATES

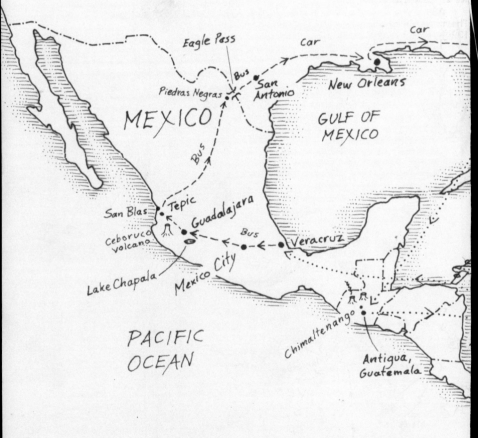

Eagle Pass

Car

Car

Bus
Piedras Negras

San
Antonio

New Orleans

MEXICO

GULF OF
MEXICO

Bus

San Blas

Tepic

Ceboruco
volcano

Guadalajara

Bus

Veracruz

Lake Chapala

Mexico City

Chimaltenango

PACIFIC
OCEAN

Antigua,
Guatemala